SEARCHING FOR
GOD
IN CHRISTIANITY

SEAN A. NOLAN

Published by Deep River Books
Sisters, Oregon
www.deepriverbooks.com

Cover design by Jason Enterline

ISBN—13: 9781632695680
Library of Congress Control Number: 2022900857

Printed in the USA
2023—First Edition
30 29 28 27 26 25 24 23   10 9 8 7 6 5 4 3 2 1

To those who stood, stand,
and will stand.

Thy Nature and Thy name is love.

Charles Wesley[1]

TABLE OF CONTENTS

PREFACE

The truth is in Jesus.

Paul (Eph. 4:21)

We live in a world which has lost its sense of truth. A generation is being taught that truth is relative. True has become personalized, truth is what you think and feel, in this vast unquantified universe you are the center of understanding. Truth under this worldview is determined by your experiences, emotions, and thoughts.

Billions of people live under the idea that they are their own truth. The departure from a jointly held set of values, rules, and moral standards—to a mindset that you can do as you please and that this self-determined morality is entirely ethical—is playing out all across the globe. The ability to accept a shared external truth, such as Jesus Christ, has been degraded in our time.

When I think of truth, I think of credibility. I will spare you a long essay here about the various philosophers who have made bold claims about faith being illogical—and then the inevitable demise of their position. Instead, I want to focus on the Christian claim to an absolute truth, found in the person of Jesus Christ.

In Philippians 4:11 (NIV) the apostle Paul says, "I have learned to be content whatever the circumstances." Before Paul wrote these words, he had been imprisoned for two years in Caesarea; this led to him being under house arrest in Rome, where he wrote this famous statement. A few years later we see Paul back in Rome and in prison again. During this second imprisonment Paul was held in the Mamertine Prison which was built on top of the city's sewer system; when the sewer backed up it would overflow into the lower cell where Paul was imprisoned. Paul was chained to the wall in a standing position, and due to his short stature would have found himself knee-deep in feces. Historians believe that the smell was so bad that prisoners asphyxiated from the deathly toxins.[2]

During his time in this jail-sewer, Paul wrote 2 Timothy and through it affirmed that literally being cast into a living hell had not dislodged the contentment he spoke of years earlier. Paul's truth was true in debate (Acts 17:22–31) and debasement.

I ask you, what makes a man give up a life of absolute wealth, honor, and status to stand knee-deep in human waste? Paul was either insane or right; his circumstances remove the possibility of a middle ground. No credible scholar, Christian or secular, has ever said that Paul was insane; his writings are too coherent for that accusation to have weight. Paul had seen something; he had seen the great absolute truth and he was dedicated to passing it on. None of the philosophical streams that have supposedly killed God came from such a place; they came from insane thinkers, agenda-driven leaders, or highly privileged philosophers writing from well-appointed offices.

Paul encountered a truth so powerful that it conquered a literal living hell. Paul's claim to truth wasn't relative; it was an external truth found in Jesus Christ that took hold of Him. On the surface it looks like any truth professed by a man in a jail-sewer would never take hold in humanity at large, but this man in a sewer encountered truth so strong that it pulled in his opposition (Phil. 1:13). The force of its truthfulness is seen in the level of allegiance Paul displayed to it, the peace it delivered, and the engagement his captors displayed with its message. Paul's demonstration of the truth that is in Jesus asphyxiated the unbelief of all who heard about it—and by the thousands people embraced a truth that did not have the benefit of institutional support, well-heeled thinkers, and popularism, rather, it had the benefit of being true.

As you read this book, truth will ask something of you: it will ask to become your truth.

> Jesus said . . . "You will know the truth, and the truth will set you free." (John 8:31–32)

INTRODUCTION

Bill Cunningham, who was the long-time fashion photographer for *The New York Times*—and *was* New York fashion photography—recalled in an interview at the 92Y in Manhattan what he called the most exciting fashion show he had ever seen. He recalled being at the Palace of Versailles in France while American and French designers showcased their respective collections. With moments of deep emotion, Bill shared how an American designer had African American models come out in stunning display—and how this night happened against the backdrop of riots in major cities across the United States. To Bill, the real America came forward that night. In a single show, a revolution was produced: "the end of the Couture and the beginning of the ready to wear."[3] A nation whose culture was in turmoil stood on foreign shores and birthed a renaissance of personal expression—one that is still a defining influence in society to this day. The young, brash, and underrated United States delegation ended the cultural leadership of the wealthy elite and opened the way for the everyday citizen to showcase personal artistic expression. This night was of the people, by the people, and for the people.

There is a scene in a documentary chronicling Bill Cunningham's life[4] where this unassuming eighty-year-old man tries to convince a young lady to allow him to enter Paris Fashion Week. Cunningham humbly and softly tried to present his credentials; the young lady, somewhat understandably, ignored him to talk to another guest. At this moment another man came over, grabbed Bill, and quickly brought him in, saying these words: "Please, he's the most important person on Earth." To have Bill Cunningham publish a photo of your garment was the definition of success; and it was said that to have Bill Cunningham put his camera down on your garment was death.

Bill had been in the game for so long that he knew originality. A designer might have found a garment in a magazine from decades ago and recreated it, thinking it would go unnoticed. This was largely true, but not with Bill. Bill knew imitation when he saw it, and he knew when a so-called new outfit is actually a modern-day copy of a classic. Bill raised his camera for authenticity and innovation, and to have Bill raise his camera was life, opportunity, and oxygen itself for the budding designer. If Bill published it, everyone wore it. As Anna Wintour, the long-time editor of *Vogue* magazine, once said, "We all get dressed for Bill."[5]

This book is a journey into why the cameras are down on the church in this generation, and how we get them up again. It is easy to blame society for turning away from the church. In some cases this is true—sin is sin, and there are those who have chosen a path of rebellion over the one Jesus offers. But I don't feel this is the norm. I truly believe that if Christians were to evacuate all other concerns and share the how and why of the core Christian message in a way our culture can digest, if this was to happen at large, I firmly believe the cameras would go up. Let's have faith for a church so true and strong that the culture would "get dressed" for its message.

We cannot give up on our generation and condemn them to the "mockers" basket. As God's people, we must fight to capture again who and what we are, and then help our generation understand the truth of Jesus and His church. In this I give my goal: to speak into who Jesus is and what His Church is. To foster a conversation—one centered on our culture, understanding the true heart and message of both Jesus Christ and His followers. A "reformation" within our culture of what Christianity is meant to be—namely that Jesus's message is one of love and not division, the church an institution that protects and doesn't harm, the Gospel a truth that is essential to daily life and spirituality, not irrelevant. Reformation always precedes revival. The 'beating heart' of reformation is a corrected understanding of Christ, which results in the enthronement of Jesus in Christians hearts. Once Christ is revived in His church and Christians alike, He *will* be revived in the culture.

This book has not been written to further Christian academia. It is written to give a framework for cultural engagement and to help the church appropriate the power of heaven—to enable all to find hope and wholeness in and through Jesus Christ and His glorious church.

My heart is to translate theology into English, into the everyday and hopefully in the process bring clarity and confidence to your journey with God. Theology close to life or theology for the people, is the guiding principle of this book.

PART ONE

HOPE HAS A NAME

If we would find God amid all the religious externals, we must first determine to find Him, and then proceed in the way of simplicity. Now as always God discovers Himself to "babes" and hides Himself in thick darkness from the wise and the prudent. We must simply approach to Him.

A. W. Tozer[6]

This book is an attempt to proceed in the way of simplicity, in the sense that it seeks to uncomplicate two thousand years of theological thought and insert these truths into the modern day. "It may be too much for some, too little for others. Of both these groups I ask forgiveness."[7] But to those for whom it is enough, I pray you find Jesus, find peace, and in doing so lead the wise.

Sean A. Nolan, Western Sydney, Australia.

1

······•◆•······

WHO DO YOU SAY
I AM?

Who do you say that Jesus is? If you were to ask fifty Christians this question you would probably get fifty different words back. He is: Lord, Savior, friend, comforter, kind, gracious, harsh, scary, optional, Abba Father . . . the list is almost endless. These varying responses drive us to ask: Who is Jesus, and how should we present Him to a generation that is becoming increasingly uninterested and confused about the church and its Lord?

This is where theology comes in. *Theo* is Greek for God, and *ology* basically means to study something, so theology means God-study. Theology is the process of studying God, and doctrine the outcome of that study. If you researched every time the Bible mentioned the word "love" and then did an overview of all the key thinkers in the church who wrote about love, this would be theology.

Doctrine is the statements or conclusions that come from this research, such as a church deciding to love a community that is persecuting it. Why do they show kindness in the face of hostility? They do this because they have read the Bible, prayed, listened to Christian leaders, and come to this conclusion (doctrine). Right thinking leads to right living, and right thinking comes from understanding something properly. If you think that God is disappointed with you even one percent, you can't settle in His arms; you can't accept that you belong in Him. This is where theology and doctrine come in. If you have the right thinking about God you will be able to rest peacefully in the Christian life.

God in Baby Form

In Luke chapter 2 Jesus is brought as a baby to the temple, this is the first presentation of Jesus to humanity and it is the beginning of humanities faith and doubt in God's redemptive plan. To be completely honest, I don't blame the people of the day for doubting. I mean, if you think about it, here is the God of the Old Testament, the God of Mount Carmel and the Red Sea, going up the temple steps in baby form.

In the Old Testament, once a year on the Day of Atonement, the high priest would enter into the third and most sacred part of the temple in Jerusalem, the Holy of Holies. To enter this section of the temple, the high priest had to go through a thorough cleansing ritual. Jewish tradition says he would then have bells attached to his clothes and a rope around his leg. When the high priest entered on this Day of Atonement, he would visibly see what the Jewish rabbis called the Shekinah glory of God, a cloud that manifested just above the mercy seat which was the space where the cherubims' wings on top of the ark of the covenant met.[8] The high priest would sprinkle the blood of a goat on the mercy seat and thus the people's sins were atoned for (Lev. 16:15–16). This is where the bells and rope come in: if the high priest was not pure and had either lied about his sins or not completed the cleansing ritual accurately, he would drop dead. The others would hear the bells make a sound as he fell down dead, and they would use the rope to drag him out—not daring to enter themselves.

Given all this, can you begin to realize just how amazing (or ludicrous) it was for this Shekinah glory to take the form of a baby and come up the steps in the hands of Mary? I have to honestly say I would have been struggling to connect the dots and believe. But this really happened, and it was how God the Father, Son, and Holy Spirit chose to break out of eternity and reveal themselves in our space-time.

The people of the day had to accept the seemingly ludicrous as fact. God stripped Himself of all Jewish religious and political traditions and came in baby form. I wonder what it is that we need to strip off Jesus in our time? Religious traditions, political affiliations, cultural preconceptions? I wonder, would our eyes recognize Jesus if He came to us free of the added extras of the past two thousand years? Would we find the pure sight of our Savior ludicrous, just as the people did two thousand years ago?

The God Man

Everything in the Bible and Christianity is centered in Jesus Christ, so we must understand who Jesus is, why He came to Earth, and what He represents. Jesus is the second member of the Trinity in human form, He is one person with two natures.[9] He has a fully divine nature; John calls this the *Logos* or Word. He also has a fully human nature.[10] In the beginning of Romans Paul speaks about this:

> concerning His Son, Jesus Christ our Lord, who was a descendant of David according to the flesh and who has been declared to be the powerful Son of God by the resurrection from the dead according to the Spirit of holiness. (Rom. 1:3–4)

So, what do both of these natures say to us about God? We must remember that Jesus is not only the Son of God, the second member of the Trinity, but also the perfect revelation of all the members of the Trinity to humanity. If we want to know what God the Father or God the Holy Spirit is like, we look at Jesus. If we want to know what God was like in eternity past (before the Genesis creation), we look at Jesus. And if we desire to know what God the Father, Son, and Spirit will be like in the future eternity that we will spend with them in heaven, we look at Jesus. Just as an ambassador comes to tell a leader the will, mind, and desire of his nation's president, Jesus has come to reveal the will, mind and desire of the eternal God to humanity. Jesus is the exact representation of God to humankind (Heb. 1:3).

If Jesus is the *fullness of God* (Col. 1:19) and God fills *all in all* (Eph. 1:23), then Jesus is the true and proper theory of everything, in human form.[11] The conflict that science and the Bible have is that in science the theory of everything is sought through human intellectual pursuit; in the Bible the highest way of obtaining knowledge is not intellectual reasoning but love. When you truly know love, you truly know God; it is this knowing of love that is the highest level of understanding.[12]

> I pray that you, being rooted and established in love, may have power, together with all the Lord's holy people, to grasp how wide and long and high and deep is the love of Christ, and to know this love that surpasses knowledge—that you may be filled to the measure of all the fullness of God. (Eph. 3:17–19, NIV)

The God of Love

God is love. This is a statement about God's eternal essence, being, and nature. This is a powerfully simple thought, but it is also a deeply complex one. To try to break this down, I will list some key points:[13]

1. *God is.* God just is. God doesn't "exist;" to say something "exists" is to limit it. If something exists, it has a start and finish, and is subject to the world it exists in. God doesn't simply "exist"— He has no beginning and no end. He just is.

2. *God is love.* Love is the substance of God. Just like you and I are composed of flesh and blood, God is literally composed of love.[16]

3. *"God is" means God is love.* God's love is not stagnant; it is active.[17] The statements "God is" and "God loves" are synonymous; they are like saying a person inhales and exhales; they confirm and explain each other.[18] For me to breathe I must inhale and exhale, for God to be He must love.[19]

4. *Love is personal.* Jesus is God standing on earth engaging relationally with humanity. God is made clear and known through the loving actions of His Son.

What I want to establish at this early stage is that love is who God is; it is His very nature. In 1 John 4:8 and 4:16 the apostle John gives us the statement "God is love." We can use this for understanding God's essence, being, and nature. In verse 8 John tells us that if we do not have love, we do not know God; from this, we can confidently reverse the statement of verses 8 and 16—"God is love"—and say that love is God.[20] God and love are one and the same.[21] For John, love is the substance of God's being; to know love is to know God's eternal nature.[22] (1 John 4:16, ESV)

Karl Barth affirmed the above idea that God is love and love is God—but he did so with a worthwhile caution: when we understand God as love and love as God, we must lock this understanding in the Father's sending of His Son.[23] Barth said, "God's act is His loving"; this means that love is defined by God's actions, specifically the action of sending His Son.[24] As I write this, my wife is packing up our house, as we are moving out while some building work is being done. If I say "I love you" as my heavily pregnant wife moves boxes, but just sit at my desk and write, I am not loving her. Love is an action, so properly: God is not love, He is loving.

The main point here is to understand that God's active love is seen in Jesus's activity on Earth.[25] Jesus's activity on Earth began at creation, continued through the Old Testament, culminated in the New Testament, and continues today through the Holy Spirit and the activity of His church. Christian love can never be divorced from Jesus and His church.

Karl Barth, the father of modern theology, wrote that God's loving is the being, essence, and the nature of God.[26] He saw 2 Corinthians 5:19 as the center of theology: "in Christ, God was reconciling the world to Himself."[27] This reconciliation is the clearest revelation of God's divine nature of love.

2

HOPE HAS A NAME

As we have already often said, and are not ashamed of often repeating—the love in the Father, is nothing else than His very nature and substance itself.

Augustine, c. 415[28]

The Name of Love

My parents named me Sean because it is a derivative of the name John; "John" means "God is gracious." My parents wanted me to have a name that identified me with God's grace. This is nice and kind of sweet, but it doesn't mean that I, as a person, am automatically gracious. My name doesn't give insight into my identity, character, or nature. It is at best a sentiment my parents wanted to convey to me, or at worst just a descriptive word. The same is not true of Jesus.

Jesus is the only baby in the history of the world to name Himself. In the first few chapters of Luke's Gospel we see the archangel Gabriel appearing to Mary and Joseph. Gabriel instructs them to name the baby Jesus. Gabriel also confirms Jesus's deity as the Son of God and attributes the role of the Messiah to Mary's baby. After the fall of the archangel

Lucifer, Gabriel became the highest-ranking angel in heaven. Gabriel is God's proclaimer, and in this instance he is proclaiming the desire of God to name this baby: Jesus, Son of God and Messiah. Gabriel communicates God's name for this child, and this child is the God who sent Gabriel.[29] Jesus is literally naming himself.

Gabriel tells Mary to call her baby Jesus, and that this child will be attributed the titles of Son of God, Son of the Most High, which infers the title of Messiah (the Hebrew version of the Greek word "Christ"; see Matt. 16:16; Mark 14:61-62; Luke 1:32, 35). In the New Testament, the Apostles condensed all this down into the Lord Jesus Christ. So, what do these three words mean?

- Jesus: "Yahweh Saves" or "Yahweh is salvation."[30] Yahweh is the proper or high name for God.

- Christ: "Anointed One." The Jewish people believed this Anointed One would come, like a powerful prophet or king of old, and vanquish all their enemies; think King David or Elijah.

- Lord: master with absolute authority and ownership rights.[31]

The name Jesus means "Yahweh saves" or "the God of Israel saves." "Christ" and "Lord" are more titles than names. Christ is a redemptive title referring to Jesus being the prophesied Anointed One from God who will redeem, and Lord means that this Jesus is one with absolute authority. Our Savior's name means: "Yahweh saves"; "Master and Lord"; and "Anointed redeemer of God."

So why did Jesus (as God) give Himself these names and titles through His archangel Gabriel? And when we say that there is no higher name than Jesus, what exactly are we inferring?

Just like you and I are composed of flesh and blood, God is literally composed of love. Love is the nature of God and Yahweh is the high covenant name for God that reveals His nature. Putting these together, we come to understand that love is the substance of Yahweh.[32] Understanding this, we can comfortably adopt love as a descriptive name for God. Jesus knows God is love, as He is God. We can add to this that Jesus knows God's love is active and that this activity will manifest in our existence as salvation or reconciliation.[33] Knowing this, Jesus gives Himself a name that is descriptive of this truth: He names Himself Jesus, which means "Yahweh saves," or paraphrased, "the God of love saves." If we follow our theological process and combine our understanding of God's essence, being, and nature with our finding on what Jesus's name means, we end up with a doctrine. We are putting together the idea that Yahweh is love and that Jesus is saying that He, as the Son of Yahweh's love, is about reconciliation. Thus, we end up with the truth that Jesus's name means "loving reconciliation."[34] Jesus's name is extracted from His identity. Jesus set this whole thing up; through Gabriel He gave Himself a name that is absolutely linked to His being of love, a love outworked as reconciliation.[35]

I feel very strongly that if Jesus were to walk in the cities of this modern world, He would live and talk with the everyday people who desperately need Him. In doing this, Jesus would tell them who He is in a way that is true to who He is and clearly understandable to His listeners. Jesus would just say it straight out, in a way our modern world could understand: My name means loving reconciliation. And in My name the identity of God is revealed, and the purpose of the church made known: to love and reconcile humanity to God.

We are living in a time where the secular world is increasingly convinced that Jesus's message is one of hate and not love, and that the church is an institution that harms society rather than helps communities. Defining the identity of our Lord and the function of His church from this raw definition of Jesus's name—loving reconciliation—is very helpful. Jesus's identity is love, and the function of this love that the church carries forth in the world is reconciliation. Imagine a Jesus and a church defined by love and reconciliation, a Jesus and church defined by God's core identity as revealed through the name: the Lord Jesus Christ.[36]

God's name is synonymous with His identity. In Old and New Testament times a name was not only identification, it was an identity. Philip Comfort outlines that the term "name" in Hebrew most probably meant "sign," and that in the Greek "name" is derived from a verb that means "to know." The Scriptures make it clear that the name and person of God are inseparable.

In Bible times names were given to express something about a person or to express something through a person.[37] This is seen in 1 Samuel 25:25 with Abigail's explanation to David of Nabal, whose name literally means "fool": "For as his name is, so is he: Nabal is his name, and folly is with him!" (NKJV). If we desire to know and understand God, we can gaze at his creation and look to His acts in our lives. These reveal His creativity and faithfulness, but these can be subjective and open to interpretation. To understand with certainty the nature, being, and essence of God, we must look with fixed gaze to the name given to the one and only Son of God, for he is "the exact expression of His nature" (Heb. 1:3). No other name carries direct meaning of someone's identity, because no one else has ever looked into their own being and then extrapolated a name that perfectly describes their essence, being, and nature. Further, no other person has ever had an essence, being, and nature of love—a love which is active and vibrant, seeking out broken people to save and redeem. The Lord Jesus Christ truly is the name above all names.[38] Hope has a name.

It is also interesting to note the wider activities of Gabriel. Gabriel comes to the priest Zechariah in Luke 1, tells him that he is the one who stands in the presence of God, and commands that Zechariah name his son John. Gabriel's comment to Zechariah about standing in the presence of God is a direct instruction to Zechariah as a priest to do as he says; Gabriel's command is not his own but God's. This may not be as straightforward as the command Gabriel gives to Mary, but we must be mindful of the contexts of the conversations. Mary was going about her daily business, but Zechariah was the priest chosen to enter the temple and burn incense. Zechariah knew this instruction was from God in response to his prayers and that it was not optional.

So why this name? Why John? It is most interesting to combined three things here: John's name, the origin of John's name, and John's function. John's name was given directly from God, and means "the Lord has been gracious."[39] John's function is to usher in the new covenant of grace. I want to add to this the meaning of Mary's name: "rebellion." Mary was just like us in the sense that she got her name from the regular old way of parents picking it—no angels involved! But while Mary's name was not hand-picked by God, *she* was. (To fill the story out, we might as well add in the meanings of Zechariah and Elizabeth's names: "God has remembered" and "God is an oath." Lastly there is Joseph; he is not Jesus's father, but his name appears in Luke 1 and means "he increases.")

When we put these together, mindful of the function of each person in the story, we get the Gospel message loud and clear: God implants loving reconciliation in the heart of humanity's rebellion and this process is forerun by grace. If you want, you can add in the idea that God remembers, and He is an oath—total integrity. God graciously remembers our futile situation as those born into rebellion, and He brings about loving reconciliation for us. God's integrity when it comes to grace-based salvation is absolute.[40]

Love, Reconciliation, and Reformation

John Wycliffe, Jan Hus, Martin Luther, John Calvin, John Knox, and Ulrich Zwingli were key leaders of what is called the Reformation, where Protestant Christianity comes from. Protestant Christianity is the super broad term for all Christianity except for our Orthodox and Catholic friends. The term "Protestant" comes from the fact that these brothers all protested the idea that salvation comes from a combination of faith and works. They said nope—it just comes through faith.

The Reformation was a critical time in the two-thousand-year life of the church. The Gospel had become mixed with human effort, law, religion, nationalism, and business. The Reformers labored to prove that salvation was a matter of receiving Jesus Christ's righteousness by faith and about building the kingdom of God. This seemingly simple change in the way Christians understood salvation evolved into the Protestant denominations we know today.

In many ways a reformation is needed in our world today. However, the reformation of today needs to look different than that of the 1500s. In the days of the Reformers the church had become toxically interlocked with the government. The message of Christ needed to be pulled out of the overgrown religious system—a system that gained great financial profit by telling people that they have to earn salvation by their actions.

We have a very different problem today. In the modern Western world, the church is not intimately intermingled with society, Christianity in our generation is being removed from secular society. We need a reformation that helps to inject Christian faith back into the hearts and minds of people. We actually have the complete 180-degree opposite problem that the reformers of the 1500s had. Martin Luther, John Calvin, and others who came a few centuries later on like Soren Kierkegaard, were all trying to rescue the Gospel by surgically removing it from the religious institutions of their day. We on the other hand are seeking to inject the Gospel back into the dialogue and overall life of our societies. With this in mind, we need a doctrine that can help achieve this goal: a goal of evangelistic injection.

Love, Reconciliation, and Mission

The primary doctrine of the reformation of the 1500s was salvation by faith. This doctrine was constructed by many thinkers over many years and is recorded in many volumes. An easy-to-digest form of this is known as the "five *sola*s" (*sola* being a Latin word meaning "alone" or "only"). These five points are doctrinal statements that emerged to help communicate the deeper ideas behind salvation by faith:

Sola fide: by faith alone

Sola Scriptura: by Scripture alone

Solus Christus: through Christ alone

Sola gratia: by grace alone

Soli Deo gloria: glory to God alone

Christianity is not a religion; it is participation in the life of God through Christ.[41] The church is not to offer another religion, rather the gift of life in Christ. The foundation of this gift is the identity of God, as revealed in the name of Jesus Christ.

We need to develop doctrines that will allow Christianity to be injected into the cultural landscape of today's world—or if you will, incarnated into our world's consciousness. The five *sola*s represent strong doctrines developed to stop the Protestant church from falling over in the storms that encompassed its birth. Likewise, a doctrinal framework is needed to ensure that a move of incarnational Christianity can emerge, one marked by being in the world but not of the world. We need an incarnational Christianity that truly follows in the method of God the Father, coming into the very heart of the culture to inject hope into the lives of the people—a hope that challenges wrong living by loving and sacrificing with such dedication that it moves many to leave all they have to follow.

"Incarnation" is a big word with a simple meaning. To incarnate something means to put meat on it (e.g., carnate, carnal, carnivore). This is why theologians call the entry of Jesus into the world through Mary the incarnation. In Mary's womb, the Logos of God had flesh put on Him; thus Jesus was incarnated. We need to take the Gospel and see it incarnated in people, our communities, and our culture.

Love, Reconciliation, and Proclamation

When I was at Bible college, I worked a job in a major department store in the center of Sydney. I remember one particular Saturday when a number of my colleagues told me about some men who had assembled in the mall outside the store we worked in and were loudly shouting at people to repent and convert. The words "sin" and "wicked" was constant, and the word "love" barely mentioned. I remember a number of staff members coming to me, quite shaken, and asking me if God hated them. After a whole day of this "preaching" going on, I decided to go down to the mall to talk to these guys. My plan was to tell them I was a Bible college student from a *conservative* college and ask them to stop, as they were ruining the fruit-bearing witness I and other Christians had established in this store over many years. I went down in the afternoon followed by a bunch of very inquisitive colleagues—colleagues who thought this was the nerdy Christian equivalent of a major title fight. To my surprise, I knew the group; some were even from my college. I managed to get them to stop, for the day.

I tell this story to make the point that the name of Christ reveals two things: 1) the essence, being and nature of God: love; and 2) the purpose of God bringing His essence, being, and nature to humanity in Christ: reconciliation. Love and reconciliation need to be the framework for our evangelistic practice.

These brothers were genuine, but they were only giving half the story. They were passionately conveying the idea of reconciliation, but there was no love in it. As a result it wasn't a representation of God, Jesus, or the true church. Likewise, kind acts that offer social help or physical aid but neglect to communicate the idea of reconciliation through the cross of Christ are in themselves lovely, but they are not a representation of God, Jesus, or the true church; they are simply humanitarianism. For something to be sharing the Gospel it must be bringing the ideas of love and reconciliation together in unison. Love leading to reconciliation, reconciliation happening through love. Only when you see love and reconciliation together do you see God, Jesus, and His true church. Only then are we operating under the beautiful name of the Lord Jesus Christ. The name of Jesus Christ is the identity of the church; it is the standard by which something is Christian. Jesus's revelation of loving reconciliation is not an optional element of Christianity—it *is* Christianity.

Loving reconciliation is our considered definition of mission, and the framework for engaging our community and culture. To fail in love means our mission has no soul, no beating heart—essentially, no identity. To fail in articulating the message of reconciliation through the cross means our mission has no purpose and that it will fail in its most precious task: delivering people eternally home.

> Never encourage any degrees of heat without light.
>
> David Brainerd, 1747[42]

Love, Reconciliation, and the Church

> The Church is when God allows certain people to live as His servants, His Friends, His Children, the witnesses of the reconciliation of the world with Himself as it is taken place in Jesus Christ, the preachers of the victory which has been won in Him and over sin and suffering and death, the heralds of His future revelation in which the glory of the Creator will be declared to all creation as that of His love and faithfulness and mercy.
>
> Karl Barth, 1953[43]

The church is the functional embassy of heaven on earth, taking its direction from the decrees issued from the temple eternal, a temple that is not part of this created order (Heb. 9:11). The church began in Acts 1 with Christ's ascension, and was empowered in Acts 2 with the coming of the Holy Spirit. From the very start the church has struggled with identity.

> So when they had come together, they asked Him, "Lord, are You restoring the kingdom to Israel at this time?" (Acts 1:6)

In this verse, the Apostles are asking Jesus if He is going to restore the power, might, and splendor of former Israelite kingdoms, such as those of David and Solomon. The Apostles were wanting to see the church begin with earthly might. Instead, Jesus sent the Holy Spirit to endow them with heaven's authority.

While on holidays with my wife I bought two framed prints. My wife lovingly protested as she felt the horrible, somewhat scary, gothic frame that they were in would ruin the esthetic appeal of the home that we as newlyweds were setting up. I did what all good husbands do and lovingly ignored her. In my defense, I bought the pictures as they reminded me about the above verse. The pictures are a set, by Margaret Dovaston, called the *Conference* and *Setting the Boundary*. They depict some Victorian-era businessmen presenting legal plans to a cardinal for approval and consultation, and the same businessmen presenting a model ship they intend to build and use commercially to the same cardinal. These pictures depict the exact opposite of Jesus's desire in Acts 1:6–8; instead, they depict a church that has decided to build a worldly kingdom for itself on earth.[44] The cardinal here is not representing loving reconciliation; he is representing a Christianized government focused on the gain of both money and status.[45]

When I looked at these paintings, and when I look at current attempts to Christianize the world through means outside of the command to make disciples of all nations, I feel God's heart melt. Where did Jesus go? Where did the Gospel of loving reconciliation go? Religion is the result of unbelief. If we cannot believe God by faith, we construct a complex system of manmade spiritual stairs, designed to climb up to gain the very thing God brought down in Christ: Himself and His power (Phil. 3:10). When religion fails to convince the community to follow Jesus, it resorts to quarrelling with the culture (2 Tim. 2:23-25). This quarrelsome spirituality often involves a 'rear–view' mentality, one that becomes argumentative as it is frustrated by people not conforming to past cultural norms. I am not seeking to be mean–spirited here, especially as I empathise with this frustration. What I am seeking is a way forward, which is not found in arguing with the culture, or withdrawal from the culture. The solution here is to "assert the strength of our Master," which happens when we present ourselves as available clean vessels that He can use to make more disciples (2 Tim. 2:20-21).[46] This is what built the Christian generations of the past and it is the only way that such a thing can return. We must be mindful here that when an argument is won, as opposed to a person, the conflict is simply pushed into the future because a repentant change of heart has not taken place. Friends, it may be that like Joseph and Mary we have lost Jesus? In seeking Him again we should know that He will be found in His Father's house—"Did you not know that I must be about My Father's business?" (Luke 2:49, NKJV).[47] We cannot rely on the spiritual infrastructure from past revivals to uphold Christ in this generation. As the church of Jesus Christ, we must be shaped by Jesus Christ, gaining His power to reach the world anew.

> It is the one task of the Church to proclaim this Name aloud to the world. The Church exists, through Christ, for this end. Whenever she forgets this, and forgets it to such an extent that instead of summoning men to decision (through this Name) she simply argues about Him, then she has ceased to be the Church.
>
> Emil Brunner, 1927[48]

I am a grateful Australian who grew up with moving stories of my paternal great–grandparents and grandparents: Australian Army,

Airforce WW2. And maternal grandparents, great–uncles and aunties: British Army India, POWs Burma Railway WW2. The point here is not about attacking patriotism, being proud constructive members of our respective nations is a biblical command and deeply worthy of admiration. The issue I am highlighting is what occurs when Christians start thinking that the Gospel is synonymous with a particular manmade ideology.[49] Scariest of all is when Christians begin trying to Christianize their environment through means other than building the Church by prayer, faith, surrender, and mission.[50]

This is tantamount to idolatry as it bypasses the Gospel, local church, and Great Commission, presenting an alternative way of saving individuals and society. In such a situation we must "audit the definition of what it is to be a Christian."[51] The Gospel is heaven's message of salvation and must be quarantined from manmade agendas.[52]

My agenda here is not to attack, but rather to build.[53] Evil begets evil. Attacking an issue like this one doesn't build anything; it just creates deeper division. Rather than turn this point into an attack, I desire to offer the idea of loving reconciliation as a framework for both personal evangelism and cultural engagement.

The church has a dark history of using the respect given to it by genuine followers as a catalyst for earthly gain. In stark contrast to this, a doctrine of loving reconciliation based on the name of the Lord Jesus Christ gives rise to a cause that is not about earthly gain but rather the establishment of Christ in men—eternity in temporality, a generation participating in the life of God through Christ.

Jesus came and made God understandable to humanity, we as the church need to do the same. We need to express the good news of Jesus in art, sport, music, entertainment, and as many areas of society as possible. Producing an alternative form of the world's art, sport, music, and entertainment. In doing this we show society that Christ and His message is not here to save them and then lock them away. Rather, Jesus came to enable them to live out their gifts and skills in a much healthier and eternally fulfilling way. The job of the church is to reconcile humanity to God, by getting people to participate in the life of God through Christ. Religion seeks sterility through isolation, God seeks relationship through engagement. The church must engage with society in ways society can comprehend, carrying with it the name and identity of God, heaven's offer of loving reconciliation.

Love, Reconciliation, and Provision

In John 14:12–14, Jesus says these words:

> I assure you: The one who believes in Me will also do the works that I do. And he will do even greater works than these, because I am going to the Father. Whatever you ask in My name, I will do it so that the Father may be glorified in the Son. If you ask Me anything in My name, I will do it.

What does it mean to ask in the name of God? I think this is a rather genuine and constant question for many Christians. There are two key ideas in answering this question:

1. God's identity—which His name reveals
2. The meaning of Jesus's full name—specifically the titles of Lord and Christ that the Apostles attribute to Him in the Bible

We have covered that the identity of God is revealed through the name of the Lord Jesus Christ. We have arrived at the idea that love and reconciliation are the definitions of this name. So to ask in the name of Jesus we must be asking in the context of love and from a desire to reconcile. Alongside this are the titles of Jesus, previously outlined:

- Christ: Anointed One
- Lord: master with absolute authority and ownership rights

When we add in these titles to the definition of Jesus's name, we get the idea of love and reconciliation wrapped in absolute authority and fully appointed by God to help humanity.

The hallmark of a servant's devotion to a master that has absolute authority is obedience motivated by love. In 2 Kings 2:2 Elisha modeled this heart loyalty to his lord and master, one appointed by God.

> Elijah said to Elisha, "Stay here; the LORD is sending me on to Bethel." But Elisha replied, "As the LORD lives and as you yourself live, I will not leave you." So they went down to Bethel.

Another beautiful example of this is Ruth:

> At this they wept aloud again. Then Orpah kissed her mother-in-law goodbye, but Ruth clung to her. "Look," said Naomi, "your sister-in-law is going back to her people and her gods. Go back with her." But Ruth replied, "Don't urge me to leave you or to turn back from you. Where you go I will go, and where you stay I will stay. Your people will be my people and your God my God. Where you die I will die, and there I will be buried. May the Lord deal with me, be it ever so severely, if even death separates you and me." (Ruth 1:14–17, NIV).

To ask in the name of Jesus, we must be asking in the context of love and from a desire to reconcile. But we also must be asking from a place of obedience. The reason why obedience is needed is that Jesus works through us. If we are living in obedience, then we are people of stability.

Have you ever seen a fire hose when it is first turned on? A lot of water comes thundering through, and the ability of the fireman to hold it steady is key to it fulfilling its function. If the firefighter can't stabilize the hose because too much power is thundering through, then the water will end up unfocused and do damage. The same is true of God working through us. An obedient life is a life filled with God's will, a life through which God's answers to our prayers can flow. If we are not living in obedience, then God fulfilling our requests will become disastrous. Great power that is not controlled causes chaos. Obedience is best thought of as blessing infrastructure. It is never about legalism; it is about provision.

Love + reconciliation + obedience = asking in the Name. Removing one of these makes the equation incomplete. It would only be fair for us to acknowledge that requests operating outside of this formula are not in God's name. When a request is motivated by love, seeks reconciliation, and comes through a person who is living in obedience, these requests are always answered. They fit the will of God and there approval will not harm the life that through obedience is stable. To ask in the name of God is to ask from His identity, with His motivation and with a walk that is capable of withstanding an exceedingly abundant yes.

Produce fruit in keeping with repentance. (Matt. 3:8, NIV)

Love, Reconciliation, and Identity

He who dwells in the secret place of the Most High shall abide under the shadow of the Almighty. . . . Because he has set his love upon Me, therefore I will deliver him; I will set him on high, because he has known My name. (Psalm 91:1, 14, NKJV)

God protects us by hiding us in His secret place. This secret place is the identity of God Himself. Jesus addresses this in John 17. In the following excerpts I have exchanged the word "name" with "identity" for ease of understanding:

I have revealed Your identity
to the men You gave Me from the world. . . .
While I was with them,
I was protecting them by Your identity
that You have given Me. . . .
I made Your identity known to them

and will make it known,
so the love You have loved Me with
may be in them and I may be in them. (John 17:6, 12, 26)

In Ephesians 3 Paul says that when we fully comprehend God's love we are filled with all the fullness of God—His identity. Paul is explaining a paradox here. On one hand, Paul says that the love of God surpasses knowledge—it is beyond our ability to comprehend. But then Paul says God is able to do above and beyond all that we ask or think.

In Jesus, God is named and His identity broadcast. Through Jesus we know the previously unknowable eternal God. The place of our protection is unclassified in Christ, and all are called to come.

When we live under the truth of God's love for us, the value God places on our lives by dying for us changes our identity. We are not worthless as eternal value has been placed on us. Our thoughts, which act as a factory for our actions, are given new inspiration.

Love, Reconciliation, and Sacrifice

Just after Jesus's famous statement in John 3:16, He gives two thoughts: in John 3:17, that God does not desire to condemn the world; then, in 3:18, that we aren't condemned because of our unbelief—rather, we are already dead and by not believing we are rejecting God's offer to begin living. Jesus says that if we don't believe in His name we will continue on in our dead state and by our own choice default into eternal death and separation from Himself—hell. Fast-forward to John 18:28–40 and we see this choice playing out in real life.

"My kingdom is not of this world," said Jesus. "If My kingdom were of this world, My servants would fight, so that I wouldn't be handed over to the Jews. As it is, My kingdom does not have its origin here."

"You are a king then?" Pilate asked.

"You say that I'm a king," Jesus replied. "I was born for this, and I have come into the world for this: to testify to the truth. Everyone who is of the truth listens to My voice." . . . They shouted back, "Not this man, but Barabbas!" (John 18:36–37, 40)

Barabbas was the name of the man the people chose to free over Jesus. He was a captured freedom fighter, who had been involved in a revolution that was trying to restore Israel by force. Barabbas's name is rooted in two words, *Bar* and *Abba*, *Bar* meaning son and *Abba* meaning father. Thus Barabbas means, "son of the father." The people of the day knew full well that Jesus was claiming to be the true Son of Father God who would restore Israel. By asking for Barabbas to be released, they were mockingly chanting for a failed, violent revolutionary called "son of the father" to be released.

This choice between the real Son of Father God who offers faith-based salvation and the fake son of the father who offers manmade revolution is the same choice posed to each and every generation.

Humanly speaking, Jesus was crucified because He dared to contradict man's self-made religious system.[54] Barabbas offered a revolution based on religious fervor; Jesus offers a saving relationship based on loving sacrifice. The way of the Master is the way of testifying about heaven's love through the means of sacrifice. Let us never be found shouting a message of religious revolution at our culture. Instead, let us lovingly sacrifice in order to make known heaven's offer to participate in the life of God through Christ.

The church is the community of the voice of God. It is the business of the church to open the Bible and let the voice of Christ speaking in and through it be heard all over the world.

Thomas Torrance, 1957[55]

3

··•·◆·•··

LET THE WORD BECOME
FLESH IN US

Therefore the Holy Spirit, of whom He hath given us, makes us to abide in God, and Him in us . . . when He has been given to man, inflames him to the love of God and of his neighbor, and is Himself love.

Through Him the whole Trinity dwells in us. This is the reason why it is right that the Holy Spirit, while being God, should also be called the gift of God . . . and this gift, surely, is distinctively to be understood as being the charity [love] which brings us through to God, without which no other gift of God at all can bring us through to God.

Augustine, c. 415[56]

Who Is the Holy Spirit?

The Holy Spirit has suffered greatly at the hands of many funny names, ideas, and misconceptions. Who He is and what His ministry is are very important questions. I pray that my thoughts in this section will add to the churches understanding of the Holy Spirit and encourage the emerging generations to think deeply about the things of God. To me it is never about being right—rather it's about being a contributor to the ongoing conversation that enables each and every generation to build God's glorious church.

Who is the Holy Spirit? This is one of the oldest questions in the Christian faith. At the Council of Toledo in 589 AD, a little phrase known as the *Filioque* was added to the global church's most accepted doctrinal statement, known as the Nicene Creed. The original creed read: "We believe in the Holy Spirit, the Lord, the giver of life, who proceeds from the Father, who with the Father and the Son is worshiped and glorified." The *Filioque* is a Latin phrase that in English means "and the Son." Adding this phrase to the Nicene Creed changed the definition of the Holy Spirit for the church.[57] Before adding it, the Holy Spirit was seen as coming (proceeding) forth from the Father only. Adding the *Filioque* meant that the Holy Spirit: "proceeds from the Father and the Son."[58] Simply put, adding this phrase means that Jesus is directly seen as being present in the Holy Spirit.

Jesus Christ did not come into the world to teach people how to be good. Instead, he came to save people who because of sin could no longer be good. Likewise, the Holy Spirit has not come into your very being to teach you how to be moral, instead He lodges in your heart to live the life of Jesus Christ through you.[59]

We assume the Apostles had it better. We assume that the grass was greener on their side of the ascension because they had Jesus with them in person. The Word of God, however, challenges this assumption. Jesus said, "It is for your benefit that I go away, because if I don't go away the Counselor will not come to you" (John 16:7).

While Jesus was living amongst the disciples they were constantly struggling to comprehend what He was saying and teaching:

> Therefore, when many of His disciples heard this, they said, "This teaching is hard! Who can accept it?" (John 6:60)

But they did not understand this statement, and they were afraid to ask Him. (Mark 9:32)

They understood none of these things. This saying was hidden from them, and they did not grasp what was said. (Luke 18:34)

These verses are a representation of the struggle the disciples had in comprehending all Jesus was teaching, saying, and doing. We see a transition in the way they understood Jesus and His teachings once Jesus left them physically and they were indwelled with His Spirit:

His disciples did not understand these things at first. However, when Jesus was glorified, then they remembered that these things had been written about Him and that they had done these things to Him. (John 12:16)

So when He was raised from the dead, His disciples remembered that He had said this. And they believed the Scripture and the statement Jesus had made. (John 2:22)

Jesus told us that the Holy Spirit comes to teach us all things: "But the Counselor, the Holy Spirit—the Father will send Him in My name—will teach you all things and remind you of everything I have told you" (John 14:26). It is clear that the disciples had much greater clarity once they were indwelled with the Holy Spirit. I am sure the physical presence of Jesus was very comforting because He was touchable and tangible, but Jesus left and sent Himself in Spirit form because the Holy Spirit is more effective for communicating divine information.

The difference between having a physical conversation with Jesus, like the Apostles did, and having Jesus inside of you via the Holy Spirit is like the difference between watching a documentary on TV about helicopters and having all the information about helicopters ever known completely downloaded into your mind. Remember that movie *The Matrix*? There is a scene where the character named Trinity needs to be able to fly a helicopter and doesn't know how. Her colleagues download a lifetime of flight experience into her mind in a few seconds and she flies away and escapes. This is an example of the difference between the connection we have to God through the Holy Spirit and what the Apostles had before the ascension. Watching the documentary is probably more enjoyable and even more real visually, but having an internal download is much more effective and powerful. With the latter, you become the very information being given to you; in the former, it is always somewhat external. Having the Spirit of Jesus inside gives us a much richer connection to God.

Once Jesus ascended and the Holy Spirit indwelled the disciples, they had much greater clarity and confidence. Instead of pulling out various verses, I would just put the New Testament forward as the ultimate example of the rich understanding that came to the disciples through the internal ministry of the Holy Spirit. Furthermore, Jesus Himself said that the indwelt church would do greater things then He had done on earth: "The one who believes in Me will also do the works that I do. And he will do even greater works than these" (John 14:12). I have always felt that this is one of those verses the church has struggled to reconcile and accept. This is because we often don't view this statement of Jesus in the context of Him knowing that He is going to dwell in us through the Holy Spirit. You could even say that Jesus is actually saying: you will do greater things because I will be indwelling thousands, millions, billions of people, and this is how I will carry myself into all the world.

In line with these thoughts, we should note that there are many examples of the disciples being powerless and faltering in faith while they were with Jesus: "Then the disciples approached Jesus privately and said, 'Why couldn't we drive it out?'" (Matt. 17:19). It is interesting that when indwelled with the Holy Spirit, there is no record of the disciples being powerless or really even faltering in faith. In fact, the complete opposite happened—they launched the worldwide expansion of the church. The truth I am driving at here is twofold: 1) We are not at a disadvantage through having the Holy Spirit instead of Jesus of Nazareth; 2) Jesus is living in us through the Holy Spirit.

"I in You and You in Me"[60]

"Have I been among you all this time without your knowing Me?" (John 14:9). This was one of Jesus's final statements to the disciples before He was crucified. The great I Am was saying to them: Have I been with you all this time in my Son Jesus, and you have not yet realized? The disciples struggled to comprehend the reality of the great I Am of Israel with them, walking and talking in His Son Jesus Christ (John 14:7).

In the same way, the church has struggled to grasp that Jesus is fully present in the Holy Spirit, and as a result fully present with us. Jesus directly talks about this process in these statements from John 14:

> Have I been among you all this time without your knowing Me, Philip?
>
> The one who has seen Me has seen the Father.
>
> I will not leave you as orphans; I am coming to you.
>
> The world will see Me no longer, but you will see Me.
>
> Lord, how is it You're going to reveal Yourself to us and not to the world?
>
> We will come to him and make Our home with him.
>
> You have heard Me tell you, "I am going away and I am coming to you." (John 14:9, 18, 19, 22, 23, 28)

When we combine three of these statements—"I am going away"; "I am coming to you"; "The world will see Me no longer, but you will see Me"—we arrive at an interesting point. Jesus is saying He is going away (in reference to His ascension), but then He says He is coming back at Pentecost. Likewise, Jesus says the world will no longer see Him, but that the disciples will see Him. Here Jesus is saying: The world won't see me any longer because the world can only perceive me in my physical form, but you as my disciples, who I will indwell at Pentecost, you will be able to see and perceive me spiritually in the Holy Spirit.

It is also worth noting the connection between the statements Jesus makes in John 14:17–18: the Spirit of truth "resides with you and will be in you. . . . I will not abandon you as orphans, I will come to you" (NET). The phrase translated as "will be in you" means that the Spirit's very being will be in you. There is a direct, intentional, connection between the idea that Jesus isn't abandoning us and that the Holy Spirit is coming to us. Jesus comes to us through the Holy Spirit—and through Jesus, the God of the burning bush also.

I want to pause here and list a few verses that directly share the idea of the Holy Spirit being the Spirit of Jesus (emphases added):[61]

> And because you are sons, God has sent *the Spirit of His Son* into our hearts, crying, "*Abba*, Father!" (Gal. 4:6)

> They inquired into what time or what circumstances *the Spirit of Christ within them* was indicating. (1 Pet. 1:11)

> . . . because the *Spirit's law of life in Christ Jesus* has set you free from the law of sin and of death. (Rom. 8:2)

> But if anyone does not have *the Spirit of Christ*, he does not belong to Him. Now if Christ is in you . . . (Rom. 8:9–10)

The idea that Jesus has gone and is coming back one day to take us to heaven is correct, but it is also incomplete. Jesus is coming back in His resurrected body to fulfill the prophecies of the Bible and take us home. But Jesus is also here now through His Spirit in His children.[62] It is a theological atrocity to teach that Jesus has gone and is only coming back one day in the distant future. Jesus left in the ascension and then came back through the events of Pentecost.[63] He has not left us as orphans. An orphan is one without a parent and all that the parent provides: protection, guidance, and love. You, Christian—yes, you—are not an orphan. Jesus is here now, abiding in you, in a way that is more intimate than what the disciples experienced during the earthly ministry of Jesus (James 1:21).[64]

The Holy Spirit of Love

The Holy Spirit proceeded out from the Father and Son. Augustine and Barth affirmed that what proceeded from the Father and Son was their nature of love, their very selves:

> *Augustine*: Love, therefore, which is of God and is God, is specially the Holy Spirit.[65] And, the Spirit Himself is God, who is love.[66]

> *Barth*: The Spirit outpoured at Pentecost is the Lord, God Himself.[67]

It is not some random characteristic of the Father and Son that comes together in the Holy Spirit, it is their very essence, being and nature. The essence, being, and nature of the Father and the essence, being, and nature of the Son came forth from within themselves and proceeded out. Remember that the essence, being, and nature of the Father and Son is love. So, the Holy Spirit is the love of the Father, joined with the love of the Son, to be the unique third member of the Trinity[68]—one who, as Augustine said so well, inflames us to the love of God.[69] Christian, you have living in you the love of the Father and Son in the Holy Spirit. God literally loves you.

If we are to add a thought to this, it is to bring in the idea that God's love is active and reconciling. The Holy Spirit is a Spirit of active reconciling love. He is by His very nature always seeking and desiring to bring you closer to God.

The Holy Spirit of Fatherly and Brotherly Love

Respectfully, out of the major world religions only Christians can say that God is love with confidence, as only Christianity has a Triune God. Love requires two; love must be shared to be experienced; love is impossible for one. John 1:2 in the TPT captures the literal rendering of the apostle's words: "They were together—*face-to-face*, in the very beginning."[70] Jesus and Yahweh, Father and Son were face-to-face loving each other for all eternity. The Holy Spirit is sent to bind us up into their eternal loving relation (1 Cor. 13:12; 1 John 3:21).

The Holy Spirit is the commonness between the Father and the Son.[71] He is the togetherness or the communion of the Father and the Son.[72] The Father, Son, and Spirit are not three different Gods or one God in three ways. They are, as Karl Barth said, three modes of being, of the one divine Lord.[73] The Holy Spirit stands in the middle between the Father and Son. The Holy Spirit's distinctiveness exists in the fact that He is the commonness between the Begotten Son and Unbegotten Father.[74] He is the common essence, the common subject—dare we say it, the common personal love.[75]

If we say the Holy Spirit is the commonness between the Father and Son, what we mean is that the Father loves the Son and the Son loves the Father, and that in this reciprocal exchange of love the Holy Spirit is found. The Holy Spirit's divine mode of being is comprised of the fellowship between Father and Son.[76] The Holy Spirit is unique in His mode of being because He is the mutual exchange of love between Father and Son.[77] The Holy Spirit is the very act of Father and Son imparting the gift of love, but He is not just an act or effect, He is God Himself as the gift God gives is His very being which we have come to know is love.[78] To be indwelt by the Holy Spirit is to be caught up in the middle of this giving and sharing of love. When we say we live in

Him, we mean that we live in the middle of the Father and the Son's exchange of love. Barth struggled to call the Holy Spirit the third person of the Trinity; rather, he said, He is the third mode of being of the one divine Lord.[79] The Father and the Son fellowship, and in this act of love the Holy Spirit is found. He is fully unique, fully eternal, fully God, and fully love, and because of that you are completely loved.[80] He is deeply personal. He is the personal love of the Father and Son and thus He is a He and never an "It."[81] As a mother would say to her child, the Holy Spirit is God's big loving bear hug—with the Father on one side, the Son on the other, and you sandwiched in the middle.[82]

It is rather safe to say that Tertullian (circa 200 AD) was the first to use the word "person" for the Holy Spirit; it is not a word used in the New Testament.[83] We are affirming that the Holy Spirit is a "He," that He is personal, but when we come to the word "person" we must define this term—carefully. This is not a definition of "person" in the way humanity uses the term, "person," for humanity, means a completely separate individual.[84] The reason for carefully defining the term "person" is that we want to avoid the idea implied through this modern usage of the word.[85] "Person" and "individualism" are fused in the modern western mindset; we cannot accidently drop this into the Trinity.[86] Left unchecked, we end up in the place where the common term "third person of the Trinity" equals "completely separate person within the Trinity." The Holy Spirit is not separate from Father and Son; He is in eternal loving communion with them. He *is* them.

Barth wrote that the Holy Spirit is the third divine mode of being of the one Lord.[87] In the modern world, saying "the Holy Spirit is the third person of the Trinity" inadvertently fosters the idea that the Holy Spirit is different in His identity from Jesus and the Father.[88] The Holy Spirit is a third person of the Trinity in the sense that He is a person who proceeds forth from two others, Father and Son. In this He is fully God in substance and completely unique in identity.[89] "Person," when used for the Holy Spirit, should describe the unique personal Spirit who is found through the Son and the Father's loving.[90]

God has sent the Spirit of His Son into our hearts, crying, "*Abba*, Father!" (Gal. 4:6)

My goal here is for you to have a revelation—and if needed, reformation—of who is in you. It is not some weird abstract identity-lacking Holy Ghost; it is the Holy Spirit, who is the Spirit of the Father and Son, known clearly to humanity as Jesus Christ. He is alive and living in you. Death could not hold Him, and ascension could not limit Him. He is in heaven at the right hand as well as in you now—say hello, just like the disciples did, because He is with you right now! The resurrection is a two-thousand-year-old historical fact, but it is also a present reality. Jesus is resurrected in you today. He walked out of the tomb and into your heart.[91]

When we demystify the Holy Spirit and know Him as Jesus (and Jesus as the Father), the Gospels pulsate with life. We enter the story, as it is alive in us. *He* is alive in us. He is not some long-gone (ascended) Savior. He is here, now, an ever-present help in time of need. When we know the Holy Spirit as the Spirit of Jesus, the haze lifts, the fog of time clears, and Jesus, who was a present fact for the disciples, becomes our daily reality.

I pray that "the Messiah may dwell in your hearts through faith. I pray that you, being rooted and firmly established in love, may be able to comprehend with all the saints what is the length and width, height and depth of God's love, and to know the Messiah's love that surpasses knowledge, so you may be filled with all the fullness of God" (Eph. 3:17–19).

The Messiah's love we are called to know is the Holy Spirit.[92] The Father walked before us, the Son walked with us, now the Holy Spirit walks in us. God was incarnated in Jesus of Nazareth to save you; now, through the Holy Spirit, the Word becomes flesh in you, to seal you, empower you, and make you see.

The Holy Spirit "is no other than the presence and action of Jesus Christ Himself," He is the outstretched arm of Christ, reaching forward in time.[93] Through the Spirit the resurrection is released from the confines of time and comes to us. To enter into relationship with the Spirit is to enter the upper room, the mountain sermons, and the discourse of the disciples. He is not an aspect of Christianity—He *is* Christianity. He *makes* Christians, Christians.

> As Jesus Christ calls us and is heard by us He gives us His Holy Spirit in order that His own relationship to His Father may be repeated in us…*Those who live in this repetition live in the Holy Spirit.* The gift and work of the Holy Spirit in us is that Jesus Christ should live in us by faith.
>
> Karl Barth, 1957 (emphases added) [94]

The Holy Spirit of Adoptive Love

It is almost endless what you can pull out from the idea of the fullness of God dwelling in us through the Holy Spirit's presence. But looking at the current state of our world and church I am convinced that the most relevant truth to draw out at this time in history is the same one Jesus brings out in John 14, that being: *we are not orphans.* Belonging is a core need of humans, and a particularly important issue as our modern societies promote connection without community. Knowing that Jesus is in you and with you welds you to God and removes the abandonment that so many people feel.

John 1:14 says "The Word became flesh and took up residence among us. We observed His glory, the glory as the One and Only Son from the Father, full of grace and truth." The word translated as "took up residence" is more literally "tabernacled." The word carries the idea of pitching a tent and talks about a temporary or movable dwelling place. In John 14:23 Jesus says, "If anyone loves Me, he will keep My word. My Father will love him, and We will come to him and make Our home with him." The word translated "Our home" means to abide. Jesus of Nazareth came to tabernacle among us, to dwell temporally, but in the Holy Spirit Jesus abides and takes up permanent residence with humanity. This permanent residence is the inner working of what is best called Jesus's adoption of humanity.[95]

It is almost certain that when Jesus refers to us as orphans who have been adopted, He is referencing the Roman concept of adoption.[96] In Roman society the adopted child had more rights than a birthed child. Sir William Ramsay noted that the Syro-Roman law book "lays down the principle that a man can never put away an adopted son, and that he cannot put away a real son without good ground. It is remarkable that the adopted son should have a stronger position than the son by birth, yet it was so."[97] The rationale behind this was that an adoption involved knowing all there was to know about a child before accepting it, thus the child could not be abandoned, ever. Under Roman law adoption was more binding than a birth. This brings out the idea that what you are adopted into through the exchange of the Cross, is more binding on your identity than what you were born into.[98]

Jesus is not holding off to accept you until you finally fit the image of what He expects of you. Jesus looks upon you, sees all, and chooses to take you into His household, forever. Just like a father who binds his estate up with his son and then cannot undo the arrangement, God's acceptance of you runs through His Son. It is so deep that you are literally bound up into Jesus's life and identity. To deny you would be to deny Himself and He cannot do either: "if we are faithless, He remains faithful, for He cannot deny Himself" (2 Tim. 2:13).

While discussing this adoptive-abiding Karl Barth wrote, "[Jesus] abides in the love of the Father so that to be obedient to the Father His own are required only to abide in His love."[99] Barth builds this phrase from John 15:10: "If you keep My commands you will remain in My love, just as I have kept My Father's commands and remain in His love." Barth highlights that Jesus interacts with the Father personally for Himself and also as the representative of us. Jesus abides in the Father's love on our behalf and does so in a way that enables us to live through this representative abiding. We are not orphans because Jesus is not an orphan, and we abide in Him. To be at peace with God we must abide in the Father. The only way to do this is to be made of the same perfect divine eternal nature that the Father is made of—perfect divine eternal love.

We possess an imperfect mortal terminal nature. Through His incarnation, death, and resurrection Jesus transforms our imperfect mortal terminal nature by bringing us into a symbiotic existence. We share His perfect resurrected eternal humanity, and through this we can partake in the Father's eternal nature. We are adopted into eternal divine love through Jesus's humanity, and in this realize that we have been seized by the power of a great affection.[100]

> May the grace of the Lord Jesus Christ, and the love of God, and the fellowship of the Holy Spirit be with you all. (2 Cor. 13:14, NIV)

4

····•◆•····

ULTIMATE CONCERN

So here we are: we have surveyed the inner essence being and nature of God. We have come to see that through the Holy Spirit we have the love of God actively dwelling in us. We have discussed how to take these points and inject them into our culture. These are wonderful truths and lovely to ponder, but the thought remains: *Who cares?*

I can hear a broken person, one really struggling, shouting this in their mind as they hear a preacher eloquently deliver points like the ones discussed here. "My pain is strong and my sorrow unending. Who cares about all your clever doctrines and fancy words? I am hurting, and I need relief."

Let me stop for a moment and share something personal about myself—my motivation in writing this book. I have been a caregiver for twenty-five years; my dad first got sick two decades ago and he has been disabled ever since. I honestly cannot remember my dad walking freely. It has been a long journey of care and patience for dad and our family. During this time, my mother was also diagnosed with ovarian cancer, and battled it for an entire decade before finally passing on. Mum was the holder of the most unwanted record imaginable:

according to her doctors, she was the national record holder for the woman to live the longest with terminal ovarian cancer.

During these decades I attended hundreds of chemotherapy appointments and hundreds of additional medical appointments, and made most major life decisions centered around this responsibility. Through this journey I have looked for God to intervene in my parents' pain, but also for Him to intervene in my own pain as I gave up my life and youth in caring for my parents. I tell you this because theology is useless if it cannot connect with the everyday realities of human life. Theology that can only speak of hope and not apply it has failed; it is actually devoid of hope.

I want to introduce here an idea that theologians have discussed called "Ultimate Concern."[101] We each have an Ultimate Concern in our lives, and if Christianity can speak into this area in a meaningful way we are likely to take it seriously. For example, consider a single mum who is really struggling to make ends meet. For her, the Ultimate Concern is getting financial security. Another example is a sick person, whose Ultimate Concern is their health and having this sickness healed. For a young child being bullied, the Ultimate Concern is having this bullying alleviated. Our Ultimate Concern is that which concerns us most. It is our most pressing need. It is what consumes our minds.

The Christian faith needs to be able to speak into the Ultimate Concern of each of the billions of people on the globe. The way we do this is by acknowledging that *we* can't—this is a function of the Holy Spirit. Only He can know and help the Ultimate Concerns of billions of different people. Our role in this is to seek to meet the Ultimate Concern of the one person we meet day to day, week to week. I have learned from my personal Christian witnessing, as well as from my experience as a caregiver, that people are not necessarily looking for a complete answer to their area of Ultimate Concern. Rather, as a doctor injects anesthetic, people are looking for Christians to inject God's loving reconciliation into their situations of hurt. Understanding, compassion, love, generosity, kindness, and gentleness—by injecting these we are injecting God and speaking into that which concerns people most. We are not necessarily answering their questions; we are presenting an alternative way of engaging with their problem, resulting in the cessation of a conflict of a lifetime.[102]

5

······◆······

THE LAZARUS DISCOURSE

The teachings of Christ have served as my inner light.

Queen Elizabeth II[103]

Mary and Martha: Lord, *the one You love is sick.*

Jesus: This sickness will not end in death but is *for the glory of God*, so that *the Son of God may be glorified through it.*

John: *Now Jesus loved Martha*, her sister, and Lazarus. *So when He heard that he was sick, He stayed two more days* in the place where He was.

Jesus: Aren't there 12 hours in a day? Jesus answered. "If anyone walks during the day, he doesn't stumble, because he sees the light of this world. If anyone walks during the night, he does stumble, because *the light is not in him.*

Jesus: *I'm glad for you that I wasn't there* so that you may believe. But let's go to him.

Jesus: Your brother will rise again.

Martha: I know that he will rise again in the resurrection at the last day.

Jesus: *I am the resurrection and the life. The one who believes in Me, even if he dies, will live. Everyone who lives and believes in Me will never die—ever. Do you believe this?*

John: When Jesus saw her crying, and the Jews who had come with her crying, He was angry in His spirit and deeply moved.

John: Then Jesus, *angry in Himself again*, came to the tomb.

Jesus: Didn't I tell you that if you believed you would see the glory of God?

Jesus: I know that You always hear Me, but because of the crowd standing here I said this, *so they may believe You sent Me.*

(from John 11:3–6, 9–10, 15, 23–26, 33, 38, 40, headings and emphases added)

Sometime before these events in John 11, Jesus made this statement:

Very truly I tell you, whoever hears my word and believes him who sent me has eternal life and will not be judged but has crossed over from death to life. Very truly I tell you, a time is coming and has now come when the dead will hear the voice of the Son of God and those who hear will live. (John 5:24–25, NIV)

Putting this together with the above statements in John 11, we can extract the following points:

- Mature allegiance to Christ allows Jesus to work in us in a fruit-producing way
- The indwelt Christian has Christ, and therefore life within

- Suffering is the gateway to clarity
- Life is not something God gives—it is who He is
- Jesus was angry at humanity existing in a life-vacuum because of sin
- Jesus identifies perpetual belief as the key to perpetual life

Resulting from this, we can see stages of the Christian life emerging:

- Christ's life beginning to form in ours
- Learning to see in the dark
- Enduring the byproduct of Christ's life forming the death of our self (James 1:18)
- Learning true life is not earned but received
- Comprehending that Christ's life living in and through us is the form God's love takes to humanity
- God's glory is observed when we believe

Imagine for a moment that you ordered a coffee in a cafe and they gave it to you without a cup. Imagine the cafe owner was some sort of genius and somehow managed to suspend gravity around the coffee so that you were given a floating ball of coffee like you see the astronauts have in outer space. Then imagine that this gravity wore off after a few seconds and you just had to try to catch the coffee and drink it. Far-fetched, I know, but my point is that the cup is essential to the coffee being usable. In this analogy, Jesus's life is the coffee and your life is the cup. Jesus has planted Himself, His love and life, in you through the Holy Spirit. Jesus's life is the form God's active love takes in your life; life and love are synonymous (John 10:10). Being a good cup to His life is our everything; the Christians who are powerful and effective are essentially good cups.

Love in the Form of Life

I said above that Jesus's life is the form God's active love takes in human existence. The process whereby God implants His life into us, and then brings us to the full realization of this new reality, is worth more discussion.

There are countless scriptures (and Bible books) centered on this theme; I will list two well-known ones here for diligence's sake:

> I no longer live, but Christ lives in me. The life I now live in the body, I live by faith in the Son of God, who loved me and gave Himself for me. (Gal. 2:20)

> But these are written so that you may believe Jesus is the Messiah, the Son of God, and by believing you may have life in His name. (John 20:31)

Christ's life being fully formed in you = resurrection. If you participate in the death of Christ, through surrender, you will also participate in the life of Christ through being raised up with Him. When Jesus said that through believing we will pass from death to life, he meant that when we believe in Him, He comes and lives in us through the Holy Spirit. The Holy Spirit immediately brings new life, and the byproduct of this is the death of our old fleshly life.

Believing = reconciliation initiated

Obedience begun = reconciliation progressing

Obedience completed = reconciliation realized

Reconciliation completed = resurrection

Resurrection = God's love fully known

God's love fully known = His glory seen

Holiness is just consistent obedience. The moment we believe, reconciliation is initiated; this is known as the process of sanctification. Sanctification means being set apart; it is the process whereby God makes us in practice what we already are in status. We are saved and secure for all eternity, but this is not yet our daily reality. We have been told we are loved, but accepting this is normally a rather long journey. One of the primary things I am seeking to build in this book is the idea that God's love is not an arbitrary feeling—it is a person. It is Jesus Christ.

I feel quite strongly that "love" is a very confused word. In a family, a child experiences love through his or her parents. It's inbuilt to us to experience love through relationship, and when this doesn't happen in our childhood love becomes clouded and unclear. So many of us see love as an ungraspable concept, kind of like trying to catch air—you can feel it and perceive it, but you can't grasp it. Thankfully this is not the Christian reality. Love is not a concept, emotion, or feeling; it is a person, specifically Jesus Christ. Jesus can express His love for us through feelings, emotions, and even media like art or music, but it is imperative to know that these are expressions of Jesus's personal love for us arising from the cross. There is a real personal God behind every act and expression of love. Love is known in and through Jesus. Love has a name.

When Christ is fully living in and through you, love is fully known and experienced by you. The following is an excerpt from a previous chapter:

> In Ephesians 3 Paul says that when we fully comprehend God's love we are filled with all the fullness of God—His full identity. Paul is explaining a paradox here. On one hand, Paul says that the love of God surpasses knowledge—it is beyond our ability to comprehend. But then Paul says God is able to do above and beyond all that we ask or think.

I repeat this paragraph to illustrate how all this fits together. Jesus reveals the love of the Father and implants this divine eternal love in us through the Holy Spirit. The life of Jesus living in and through you is the form God's love takes in your life. If through belief and obedience you partner with God and allow His Son to live through you, you will know, feel, and experience true love (1 John 4:18).

Jesus being *in* you is not something you have to partner with God to have; it is the gift of conversion. Allowing Jesus who is already *in* you to work *through* you is what we are partnering with God to see happen. He wants to bloom *through* you. It is a sad thing for a saved Christian to live in defeat and never allow the majestic gift of Christ *in* them to move forward and become Christ living *through* them. It is in the "through" that we experience and know Jesus's life and perfect, personal love.

To make this real, let me give a case study: A young pastor steps out in faith, but never becomes surrendered and obedient. This young pastor struggles on, trying very hard to build a ministry, but he entertains private unbelief—which is the breeding ground of defeat—thus sin continues and no power flows. He is *in* Christ, but through compromise he is not allowing Jesus to work *through* him.

Likewise, consider another young pastor who is surrendered to belief and obedient in lifestyle. Through him God's power flows, and he sees fruit and abundance in His ministry and life. This young pastor is experiencing the Christian life as it was intended; he is allowing Christ who is in him to work through him. This young pastor experiences love in the form of abundant life.

This small case study highlights how the stages we looked at above work together. If a young pastor doesn't understand that the fruit of suffering is completed obedience, then he will get discouraged and give up. But if he can view suffering as part of a wider process of fruit-bearing, he can endure and then attain. Love is not an intention; it is an action. If I say "I love my wife," I have to be loving toward her. God doesn't *intend* to love you—He loved you at Calvary and offers to make this love real through acting in you to grow the life of His Son.

After all that we have covered I am comfortable saying that we can look at the Trinity through love:

Father God—love

Jesus—loving

Holy Spirit—loved

Father God is love. In the Son we see this love active toward humanity. Finally, through the Holy Spirit we are loved. The eternal love of God and the active redeeming loving of the Son, has come near through the Holy Spirit indwelling us. We are, literally, loved.

In the opening part of this section we looked at the Lazarus discourse. I want to revisit this to draw out the meaning of probably the weirdest thing our Jesus ever said (even weirder than the John 6 lines about drinking blood and eating flesh!).

Jesus: This sickness will not end in death but is for the glory of God, so that the Son of God may be glorified through it.

John: Now Jesus loved Martha, her sister, and Lazarus. So, when He heard that he was sick, He stayed two more days in the place where He was.

Jesus: I'm glad for you that I wasn't there so that you may believe. But let's go to him. (from John 11:4, 6, 15, headings added)

For a long time I saw this sentence, "So when He heard that he was sick, He stayed two more days in the place where He was," as just plain weird. Jesus is meant to be compassionate and super-loving, and leaving His BFF to die miserably is seemingly irreconcilable with His character. However, this line gives us Jesus's primary objective in our lives: Jesus seeks to facilitate death in order to bring new life. He articulates this principle in John 12:24: "I assure you: Unless a grain of wheat falls to the ground and dies, it remains by itself. But if it dies, it produces a large crop."

God the Father, Jesus the Son, and the Holy Spirit are all working to the end of seeing your old life dead and your new life through Christ arise. For Jesus love has two distinct phases: death and birth. God is not condemning sinners; He is trying to eradicate sin. Sin is new-life poison, and God will at times allow extreme hardship in order to get us to let go of it (Deut. 8:1–10). Spiritual growth isn't measured by how much we know about the Bible but by how obedient we are to what we've learned; obedience, not prestige, is the barometer of Christian spirituality (Isa. 53:5). Obedience materializes the power of the New Testament into our today—one act of obedience is better than one hundred sermons.[104]

Through obedience Christianity moves from being theory to reality. Through obedience we perceive Christ as He is. Without obedience He remains a distant figurehead, talked about but never talked to.

I opened this book with the idea that right information empowers right living, if we can know what God is up to in our circumstance then we can partner with Him to move forward. God wants us to move forward, and to do that we need to understand that God's love seeks death in order to bring new life. All of this leads us to the axiom of the Christian life:

God: I give you Myself.

Man: I give You my self.

This axiom is the code of life. Through it we flourish and know love, when we grasp that love is personal and that it is seen through the life of Jesus living through us. When this happens, love comes alive; it becomes real, personal, and graspable. It is no longer determined by human role models but by our Father in heaven, who comes to us through His Son and is known and felt through the new birth (1 Pet. 1:22–23)

As a final thought, try reading through the "marriage passage" in 1 Corinthians 13 and exchange "love" with "Jesus's life":

> Jesus's life is patient, Jesus's life is kind.
> Jesus's life does not envy,
> is not boastful, is not conceited,
> does not act improperly,
> is not selfish, is not provoked,
> and does not keep a record of wrongs.
> Jesus's life finds no joy in unrighteousness
> but rejoices in the truth.
> It bears all things, believes all things,
> hopes all things, endures all things.
> Jesus's life never ends. (adapted from 1 Cor. 4–8)

The Hope of Science

I began this book with the following quote from Augustine: this book "may be too much for some, too little for others. Of both these groups I ask forgiveness", I feel this section embodies this sentiment well. These thoughts are one of three areas I considered leaving out of this book, after looking at *47 Tucanae* in the early hours of the morning I decided to include it, in order to assist Christians to engage science and science Christians.

In our time we are mainly influenced by human thought in the form of science, making scientific reasoning critical to any talk about faith in God. Many people will disregard faith in Christ as a meaningful way of living because it cannot be scientifically proven. Yet, without hesitation we will do any number of activities that science tells us not to do. For example, we will without objection follow our self–will and eat takeaway food on a daily basis even though science tells us this is very bad. Likewise, we will believe that a certain musical performance is far better than another and hold this position passionately even though we cannot give any scientific evidence to make this claim verifiable.[105] This shows that we will happily disregard science if it suits us, likewise, we will wholeheartedly embrace science as a tool for disregarding relationship with God if this suits us.

Christianity does not need to be at odds with verifiable scientific observations and we do not need to dimmish science to build up our faith. I personally believe people would be amazed at how strong the scientific case for faith is. A short example is that the primary scientific objection to faith is that the Kingdom of Heaven cannot be seen—e.g., Hitchens Razor. However, life on earth is literally sustained by invisible forces: light, air, gravity, magnetism and time (water translucent)—we perceive these only when they interact with another object. Furthermore, according to NASA, the entire visible universe is only 5% of the matter in the cosmos, invisible dark energy and dark matter makes up over 95% of the universe, similarly, we cannot see a black hole, only its effects—i.e., gravity, hawking radiation, quantum hair.

Do we not believe in the singularity inside of black holes because we can only see the accretion disk? Do we not believe in 95% of the universe because we cannot grasp it? Do we not believe in the critical sustaining elements of life on earth because we cannot see them? Do we not believe in light, air, gravity, Earth's magnetic field, time, dark energy, dark matter and black holes because we can only measure there effects? Likewise, there are studies that have measured drops in crime rates when faith is embraced in a society.[106] The point here is that we do not strictly follow the science, we use science to pick and choose what we want to follow. We so often profess science as absolute, but do not practice it as absolute. Likewise, we profess faith as illogical, but it would puzzle us to prove this.[107] Leading to the understanding that it is actually our human will that drives our decision making, not science— a human will that seeks self–satisfaction, regardless of consequences.

Faith is different, it seeks purity, but engages God's implanted will via the Holy Spirit to make this achievable. We could say the Holy Spirit is the singularity and the new lifestyle the accretion disk of sorts—the surrounding measurable element.

To make a sure statement that the Kingdom of Heaven does not exist through *empirical evidence*, we would firstly have to quantify the visible 5% of the universe. Secondly, we would have to not just perceive and measure the unseen 95% of the universe, but rather fully enter it and discover every single corner of it—which is akin to measuring infinity. Leading to the logical statement that *absolutely* discounting the Kingdom of Heaven is antilogical. Put another way, consider the scientific argument that measuring the age of the universe, 13.8 billion years, is akin to measuring the distance from New York to Paris. We can tangibly travel from New York to Paris, meaning that we can measure this distance with undeniable certainty. However, we cannot traverse the distance of the universe, making the 13.8 billion number an assessment, it is a very well–educated assessment and one hard to bypass, but an assessment nonetheless. Standing in New York and using technology to peer across the expanse to assess the distance to Paris is very different to traveling this distance and tangibly measuring it. For example there is a difference between a ground journey and an 'as the eagle flies' trip, also a difference in the time it would take to travel across water as opposed to land. Meaning that we must distinguish between a scientific assessment and a scientific absolute.

Christianity that operates with a frustrating stubbornness in the face of scientific absolutes and scientific assessments is not advisable. Likewise, science undertaken from a single galaxy, and therefore without the ability to develop another set of control data from an additional vantage point in the universe should always be honest about this limitation (the estimate at the time of publishing this book is two trillion, that's two million millions or 2000 billion, galaxies in the universe[108]— ruffly 250,000 Milky Way galaxy's for each person on earth, with an average one hundred billion stars in each galaxy; and that's only 5%).

The theologian Anselm of Canterbury advanced a way of approaching the world called "faith seeking understanding"—in Latin: *fides quaerens intellectum*. Using faith as a reference point in a practically infinite universe is not as illogical as we have been led to believe. Furthermore, one could say with certainty that just as we cannot scientifically *prove* God, we cannot scientifically *preclude* God—there is still mystery in the universe.

It can be rationally argued that empirical science doesn't point to a mathematical solution to the question of existence, but rather, to a mysterious hope at the heart of the universe, one the Bible teaches is revealed through Jesus Christ living in you.

PART TWO

FINDING GOD
IN CHRISTIANITY

6

·····•◆•·····

HOPE AS IT SHOULD BE
(PART ONE)

Jesus wants us to thrive in our everyday lives, not just the mountaintop experiences. It is the everyday, mundane elements of life that attack our hope. After mountaintop experiences we are sent back into the everyday and so often struggle to believe. An ordinary day changes history. When we learn to see God in our non-Instagram-worthy moments hope has sunk deep roots and we become "like a tree planted by water: it sends its roots out toward a stream, it doesn't fear when heat comes, and its foliage remains green. It will not worry in a year of drought or cease producing fruit" (Jer. 17:8).

I pray that through this next section the reality of your union with God begins to come alive in your mind. It is my intention that this section will reveal the inner workings of how Christ's life lives in and through us. I pray that this section helps to form hope as it should be—hope that buds, becoming touchable and tangible.

The opening part of this section contains a few theological thoughts that are like the foundation of a house, not super-exciting but needed. If you find them a bit much, you can skip to the next chapter; you will not be overly disadvantaged.

Hope through faith

The word "hypostatic" comes from the Greek word *hypostasis*, which is used five times in the New Testament: Paul uses it twice in his letters to the Corinthians when addressing pastoral issues; in these two instances it is normally translated "confidence." The word is then used three times in the book of Hebrews, in 1:3, 3:14 and 11:1. We will focus on 1:3 and 11:1 here (emphases added).

> The Son is the radiance of God's glory and the exact expression of His *nature*, sustaining all things by His powerful word. (Heb. 1:3)[109]

> Now faith is the *reality* of what is hoped for, the proof of what is not seen. (Heb. 11:1)

The words "nature" and "reality" here are both the Greek word *hypostasis*, formed by two root words which mean "under" and "to stand." The honest truth is that this word is a tough one to translate into English. The word carries a few ideas:

- An underlying giving reality or substance
- Being bound to and holding another to a legally binding agreement
- Assurance and confidence
- Person or being

Hypostasis is used to describe the union of Jesus Christ's two natures: His human nature and divine nature. These two natures of Jesus dwelling together in one person is called the "hypostatic union" of Jesus. This should not be something we allow to confuse us. The second member of the Trinity, the Word of God, descended from the majesty of heaven and dwelt among us. God came to humanity in a way that we could understand; the fullness of God came into a human body.[110]

The same word is used by theologians to describe this truth of divinity and humanity existing together in Jesus Christ (1:3), as well as to describe what faith is (11:1). When we say we "put our faith in God," we are literally trusting Him to bring us into a form of hypostatic union. Jesus's hypostatic union was self-contained, His perfect humanity dwelling with His eternal divinity. Ours is different; it is our humanity being redeemed and then dwelling in Jesus's divine humanity.[111]

The Scottish theologian T. F. Torrance observed that Jesus is the one who knows God from within God's very heart. Jesus becomes man to translate the knowledge of God into the heart, mind, speech, and actions of man.[112] Jesus repositions humanity into close proximity to God, He is the living center of salvation, the living bond between God and man. Torrance translates *hypostasis* as meaning "person."[113] Using this translation, we can say that the hypostatic union of Jesus is the union of Jesus's person—His human and divine natures.[114] We can also say that our faith takes the form of a personal union with Jesus. Meaning humanity receives redemption through union with Jesus's divine humanity. Jesus's divine humanity is in personal union with Father God and we are in personal union with Jesus's divine humanity. Through this twofold union, divine life comes down into humanity and redeemed human life goes up into divinity. Without Jesus, there is no other transport to the higher life.[115] We are only divine in the sense that we are in personal union with Jesus. Jesus and Jesus alone brings us through to God.[116]

Faith is essential for union with God, so it is important to understand what it is. It is not a weird mystical substance that we try to grasp, like trying to grasp a cloud. Faith is the mechanism Jesus gives that facilitates salvation.[117] I want us to understand that faith is personal and that it is synonymous with Jesus.[118] This is why Christians say they are saved by faith and saved by Jesus; these two sayings explain each other. Hebrews 11:1 says, "faith is the reality [or person] of what is hoped for, the proof of what is not seen."[119] Faith is the personal union with Jesus that bridges the divide and proves the unseeable claims of the Word of God. As Martin Luther wrote, "Faith connects you so intimately with Christ, that He and you become as it were one person."[120] Faith is union with Jesus, and Jesus is the game-changer who guarantees this union is real and as advertised.[121] We can paraphrase Romans 1:17 and say that the saints will live by union.[122]

> Clearly, God's promise to give the whole earth to Abraham and his descendants was based not on his obedience to God's law, but on a right relationship with God that comes by faith. (Rom. 4:13, NLT)

Hope through the Word of God

We are not called to have a relationship with the Bible only; we are called to have relationship with God through the Bible. The two seem similar but they are vastly different. One results in a religion, the other a relationship—or more specifically, a participation in the life of God through Christ.

The Bible as we have it is a recollection of past events. To fully experience the Bible's value, we must understand how it is constructed. I am not talking about its practical construction, such as the Old and New Testament or its composition of sixty-six books and language variations like Greek, Hebrew, and Aramaic. I am referring to that which makes the Bible divine, that which makes it a gateway to relationship with God and entry into eternity.

The Word of God was revealed to various prophets, priests, kings, and everyday people. We see this in the Old Testament; people like Moses, King David, and Isaiah received revelation, proclaimed it to others, and then recorded it. This process repeated itself in the New Testament. Luke highlights this at the beginning of his Gospel: "I myself have carefully investigated everything from the beginning, I too decided to write an orderly account for you" (Luke 1:3, NIV). When you hold your Bible, you are holding a threefold book:

- The revealed word of God
- The written word of God
- The preached word of God

This threefold Word of God is what the Bible is "made of," and it is correlative to the Trinity:[123]

- Father God—the revealed word of God
- The Son—the written word of God
- Holy Spirit—the preached word of God

These can also guide us in our understanding of each Trinity member:

- Father God—love
- The Son—loved
- The Holy Spirit—loving

All this is sitting in the Bible. It is more than a mere publication; it is the *love* of the Father revealed, the final statement that humanity is forever *loved* through the life and ministry of the Son, and the assurance of the continued *loving* of humanity through the Holy Spirit.

What we are speaking about is three different forms of the one Word of God that comprise the Bible: revelation, written and proclamation.[124] For the ancient generations it started with revelation; this revelation was shared verbally and then the verbal account was written down. They began with revelation and ended with the Bible. For us, we begin with the Bible and then share this message verbally, which produces revelation—in the sense that people receive a personal revelation of Jesus through Christian proclamation.[125] Just as the Word became flesh and dwelt among us, the revelation of God became word and was recorded for us in the Bible. When the church proclaims this message, the written words take root in a recipient's life, becoming flesh in them.

The Bible is the very Word of God, the exclusive record of God's dealings with and instructions to humanity. When you come to the Bible you are coming to the reliable record of God's revelation in human existence.[126] When you know the Bible, you know facts and knowledge that you can use to a variety of ends. When you know the loving God whom the Bible reveals, the end is a foregone conclusion: a love-based relationship outworked as a life of sacrifice.

The point I am driving at here is that we are called not just to preach and proclaim biblical facts, but the God of love revealed in the biblical account. You can preach biblical facts without knowing God personally (Acts 19:13–16). You can only share the message of loving reconciliation when you possess a personal relationship with God. The best sermons are not constructed through commentaries; they are fruit found in the bosom of the Father.

Eternal Hope

What we experience when we come to God through the Bible is His eternal reality, and this is often at odds with our daily experiences. I am aware that this is a concept that can be hard to take in, so allow me to explain it through a real-life example.

When my mother died, she had already had cancer for a decade. It slowly claimed her life, by small stages of advancement within her body. Occasionally the chemotherapy would work a bit and the cancer would be pulled back a little, but its advancement was ultimately inevitable. My mother's sickness followed a straight, linear timeline. It was progressive, one stage after another, a straight sequential series of events. Event after event piled together, which resulted in an outcome. However, in contrast to this earthly linear reality that my mother was stuck in, she was also experiencing something else—she was experiencing the results of the active Word of God in her life. My mother was a strong believer; she would read her Bible often and stand on the promises (or revelation) within it. She would then, by faith, proclaim these promises to herself as well as others. What my mother was experiencing was the alternate or competing reality of the Word of God. You see, mum had a battle in her body, but she also had one in her mind. The medical world said this was the end, but the Bible said it was the beginning. One viewpoint pronounced death, another proclaimed that death was not the dissolution of life but rather the consummation of it. One looked at the sequential events of my mother's cancer and pronounced that there was no hope. The other looked at the actions of Jesus in our existence and declared wholeness when home.

Karl Barth wrote that we do not come to faith; faith comes to us. Faith, as a change agent, is granted to us through the Word of God and it enables us to see another version of ourselves, one that without the resurrection power of Christ we would be powerless to become. We are given a picture of the life of Jesus fully alive in us and we are drawn to choose it.[127]

Mum had a choice and so do we. You may not be facing cancer, but you are facing the declaration of death that comes from some circumstance in your life. The Bible confronts that declaration with the events of Jesus's life, and through the Spirit Jesus's life is applied to you. Your human body may be dwelling on this earth this day and in these circumstances. Your redeemed spirit is stationed in an endless loop of the redeeming cross, life-giving empty tomb, and power-infusing day of Pentecost.[128] God sees us as fully redeemed; He gives us a vision of this wholeness and draws us toward it.

Hope in Our Time

You pore over the Scriptures because you think you have eternal life in them, yet they testify about Me. And you are not willing to come to Me so that you may have life. (John 5:39–40)

The Bible is not a mere book; it is the living language of God and it is capable of a temporal event. The great lie of the enemy is that the timeline of history puts us at a two-thousand-year distance from our Lord. You are not only redeemed but you are repositioned; you live in Him and He lives in you. Your house is a geographic location on this earth; your home is in Him.

In his *Confessions*, Augustine makes the following statement:

> My own childhood, which no longer exists, is in past time, which also no longer exists. But when I remember those days and describe them, it is in the present that I picture them to myself, because their picture is still present in my memory.[129]

The point Augustine is making is that a moment in time may cease to exist physically, but it can continue and even be recreated emotionally and mentally. If you think about it, this really is true. Out of nowhere we can remember the embarrassment of a past life event and be overcome with anxiety. Likewise, we can remember a hilarious event from the past and be overwhelmed with joy. Events pass away physically but can remain emotionally, mentally, and spiritually.

With this in mind, I want to pause for a moment and talk about the suffering of Jesus on the cross. It has been said many a time that the spiritual pain Jesus endured is what separates His suffering from the two thieves and other martyrs throughout history. The connection Jesus has with the Father was broken and He was separated from Father God.[130] The hell Jesus endured was not a geographical place—it was the absence of His Father's presence. A modern-day way of explaining this is to imagine your most horrific life experience—the worst moment of your life, the time when everything crashed around you. I am not talking about the hard days; I am talking about the moment when the entire world as you knew it smashed into a million pieces. When this happened you felt exposed, scared, and unsafe. At this moment of vulnerability, God stepped in. Now, if you are anything like me, you are probably prone to a bit of self-pity and this can sometimes make us feel like God wasn't there. But the reality is that through the promises of the Bible, the comfort of the church, and the love of family and friends you felt hope in the form of acceptance, understanding, and comfort.

Now, imagine that you went through this horrible thing and all your friends, church, and family abandoned you. Imagine that in your darkest hour of trauma everyone turned away from you and you belonged nowhere. There wasn't even an option for you to get a drop of comfort—not even a local church you have never previously walked into but could have if desperate enough. There was nothing at all; you were completely rejected and unaccepted. You belonged nowhere, and felt nothing but abandonment. This is what Jesus endured: complete absolute abandonment, pure and utter rejection. He belonged nowhere and with no one.

You cannot relive physical events, but you can relive the emotional, mental, and spiritual elements of the past.[131] When we realize that we can relive the nonphysical parts of historical events, we come to the idea that while we cannot experience the physical, historical act of Jesus's redemption we can experience the salvation that happened through His spiritual, mental, and emotional abandonment.[132] The resurrection is a universal offer to every human to live in the wake of Jesus's actions. The work of the Holy Spirit is to manifest the offer of renewal, one which takes the form of obtaining Jesus's personal history in place of ours.[133] In relation to this A. W. Tozer wrote:

> Let me exhort you to take this seriously. It is not to be understood as mere Bible teaching to be stored away in the mind along with an inert mass of other doctrines. It is a marker on the road to greener pastures, a path chiseled against the steep sides of the mount of God. We dare not try to bypass it if we would follow on in this holy pursuit. We must ascend a step at a time. If we refuse one step, we bring our progress to an end.[134]

When we talk about Jesus's personal history replacing ours, we are not talking about a denial of our life's reality. The biblical call to adopt the history of Jesus is not a replacement of your past circumstances. We can't say that we didn't live through these hardships or that they don't affect us. Adopting the reality of Jesus means to realize that the circumstances you lived through ran parallel to the kingdom reality that Jesus designed for you from the moment you entered this world (Jer. 1:5). Adopting the reality of Jesus is a clearing of the fog and a realization that your life journey has not been an aimless wandering, lost in the woods of hard knocks. Your life has been a Spirit-orchestrated journey up a path chiseled against the steep sides of the mount of God—which is unquestionably a road to greener pastures. Your life's value comes from Jesus's activity in it. You may feel like your life has been worthless. Maybe this is somewhat true in the natural reality, but it is not true in the divine reality. You are valuable and the place that value arises from is Jesus's past and present work in your past and present life.

We are not primarily talking about a change of circumstances, in the strictest sense. We are not even talking about a change in our perspective of our circumstance. We are talking about us seeing what God sees—not a journey of sin and failure, which has led us to ruin and purposelessness, but rather a heaven-constructed pathway that leads to the exchange of the cross and then upward to the city of God. This parallel journey is only made possible by the redemptive acts of Jesus Christ. His redemption begins at the cross and tomb and shoots out into the past, present, and future of our lives, grabbing our ruin, failure, sin, and pain and causing them to become subservient to His restoring power. Your past should be seen as a journey of renewal, your present renewed and your future determined by your participation in this process.

Think of it this way. If a father dies and leaves an inheritance for his young children, those children are not much better off than slaves until they grow up, even though they actually own everything their father had. (Gal. 4:1, NLT)

Hope in Our Mind

The standard understanding of the book of Romans is that the apostle Paul climaxes his argument in 7:21–8:4. I want to push against this a little and say that 7:21– 8:4 is *a* climatic point, but that the main climax of Paul's thought is found in 12:1–2 (BLT):

> Therefore I exhort you, brothers, through the compassions of God, to present your bodies as a living sacrifice, holy to God, well-pleasing, which is your reasonable service. And do not be conformed to this age, but be transformed by the renewing of the mind, for you to prove what is the good and well-pleasing and perfect will of God.

Here Paul presents his doctrine of change; he gives us the tool needed to tangibly change. Initial saving faith changes our eternal destiny; enacting the truth of Romans 12:1–2 will change your earthly destiny. Paul is telling us that we change by altering our mental identity. He is telling you to stop trying to form new habits, and to form new thoughts. Once your thought life changes your actions, habits, and very life will be renewed.

Below are some representative scriptures for thought-based change (emphases added):

> Do not be conformed to this age, but be transformed by the *renewing of your mind*, so that you may discern what is the good, pleasing, and perfect will of God. (Rom. 12:2)

> *Set your minds on what is above*, not on what is on the earth." (Col. 3:2)

> Therefore, I say this and testify in the Lord: You should no longer walk as the Gentiles walk, in the futility of their thoughts . . . you are being *renewed in the spirit of your minds*. (Eph. 4:17, 23)

> Therefore, *with minds that are alert and fully sober*, set your hope on the grace to be brought to you when Jesus Christ is revealed at his coming. (1 Pet. 1:13, NIV)

> Let this *mind be in you* which was also in Christ Jesus. (Phil. 2:5, KJV)

> But we have *the mind of Christ*. (1 Cor. 2:16)

Can I ask you to do something practical? Get a piece of paper, draw a four-sided square, and then next to that a three-dimensional cube. These two objects represent the difference between the Bible as a published book and the Word of God. Now on the same piece of paper, directly under the four-sided square, draw the man and woman images you see on bathroom doors. Then, underneath the cube, place a picture of your favorite person in the world; you can just use your phone screen.

Can you follow the progression, specifically the development from the square all the way through to the photo? This visual tool demonstrates the difference between a one-dimensional reading of the Bible and the living relationship we are called to have with the Word of God.

So often we see the Bible as a book of wisdom and knowledge only. If we do come to a richer understanding of the scriptures, we tend to see it as a relationship with a two-dimensional person. What I mean by this is that we tend to see the identity revealed in the Bible as a mystical Spirit, a holy ghost who embarks on somewhat weird and often rather random activity in our lives. When we come to see that the Bible is a book containing the Word of God and that this Word of God births and forms the life of Jesus in us, we have arrived at a healthy view of the Bible.

The disciples met Jesus through physical conversation; we meet Jesus through prayer-based conversations. The goal of the daily devotional life is to meet Jesus through His Word. Leading to the idea that "Christianity is not to offer culture another religion but the gift of life...

in Christ."[135] This gift of life begins in the beachhead of our mind and it works by bringing us through to the kingdom of God here and now on earth. In the following chapters I will develop this idea in detail.

> We cannot see Jesus just by piecing together picturesque historical detail about Him. Flesh and blood cannot reveal Jesus. Something else must happen. We must allow the sublime majesty of Jesus to break in upon our vision. Jesus must be transfigured before our very eyes. It is through His Cross that He pierces like that into our souls, and then it is in the power of His resurrection that He stands before us, shows the wounds in His hands and side, and says "Peace be unto you."
>
> Thomas Torrance, 1957[136]

7

HOPE AS IT SHOULD BE
(PART TWO)

A Kingdom of Hope

In the ESV, "kingdom" is mentioned 126 times in the Gospels and thirty-four times in the rest of the New Testament. Clearly it is an extremely significant theme in Jesus's teaching. Beyond the volume of usage, it is important to highlight the importance the theme is given in Jesus's teaching (ESV, emphases added throughout).

1. *The kingdom is the defining element of the good news Jesus brings*:

   And he went throughout all Galilee, teaching in their synagogues and proclaiming the Gospel of *the kingdom* and healing every disease and every affliction among the people. (Matt. 4:23; cf. 9:35)

   And this Gospel of *the kingdom* will be proclaimed throughout the whole world as a testimony to all nations, and then the end will come. (Matt. 24:14)

"Now after John was arrested, Jesus came into Galilee, pro-claiming the Gospel of God, and saying, "The time is fulfilled, and *the kingdom of God is at hand;* repent and believe in the Gospel." (Mark 1:14–15)

2. *The kingdom is the opening truth conveyed in Jesus's explanation on how to pray:*

Pray then like this: "Our Father in heaven, hallowed be your name. *Your kingdom come,* your will be done, on earth as it is in heaven." (Matt. 6:9–10)

3. *Just a little further in the above chapter, the kingdom is also Jesus's answer to worry:*

But seek first *his kingdom* and his righteousness, and all these things will be given to you as well. (Matt. 6:33)

4. *The kingdom was the message Jesus passed onto His disciples as their preaching content:*

And he called to him his twelve disciples and gave them authority over unclean spirits, to cast them out, and to heal every disease and every affliction. . . . "And proclaim as you go, saying, *'The kingdom of heaven is at hand.'"* (Matt. 10:1, 7)

After this the Lord appointed seventy-two others and sent them on ahead of him . . . and say to them, *"The kingdom of God has come near to you."* But whenever you enter a town and they do not receive you, go into its streets and say, "Even the dust of your town that clings to our feet we wipe off against you. Nevertheless know this, that *the kingdom of God* has come near." (Luke 10:1, 9–11)

5. *Finally, the kingdom of God was the centerpiece of John the Baptist's message as the appointed forerunner of Jesus:*

> In those days John the Baptist came preaching in the wilderness of Judea, "Repent, for *the kingdom of heaven is at hand.*" (Matt. 3:1–2)

There is great consistency here. John the Baptist comes to prepare a way for the Lord and His message of the kingdom. Jesus Himself affirms that the kingdom is His message (Mark 1:14–15). Jesus then gives this message to His twelve disciples (Matt. 10:1–7), then again to His seventy disciples (Luke 10:1–11). Jesus affirms that the kingdom of God is the content of His good news—the Gospel (Matt. 4:23; 9:35; 24:14; Mark 1:14–15). Jesus also affirms that the kingdom of God coming to humanity is the primary thought in prayer (Matt. 6:9–10).

Are you seeing a pattern here? The kingdom of God is our message. All added up, it is mentioned over 150 times in the New Testament. It is the theme of Jesus and His ministry.[137] So, what does it mean?

To answer this question, I will break down Mark 1:15 (ESV): "The time is fulfilled, and the kingdom of God is at hand; repent and believe in the Gospel." Below is an explanation of the key words:

- *Kingdom of God.* Greek *basileia*, meaning kingdom, royal power, domain. This word has the idea that the kingdom is connected to the King Himself. In Jesus's case, His kingdom is Himself.

- *Is at hand.* Greek *eggizó*, to make near, to come near, extreme closeness[138]

- *Repent.* Greek *metanoeó*, from two root words: *meta*, meaning "after with," implying change, i.e,. an after effect; and *noeó*, meaning "mind" and "understanding"

- *Believe.* Greek *pisteuó*, meaning to "believe" or "to be persuaded"

- *Gospel.* Greek *euaggelion*, from two root words: *eú*, meaning "good and well"; and *angellō*, from the root of *aggelos*, meaning a supernatural messenger of God

I want to highlight two points here. First, if you look closely you will notice that Jesus uses the term "kingdom of heaven" and the "kingdom of God" interchangeably. This is because the kingdom of heaven is not like earthly kingdoms. An earthly kingdom can exist without the king; King David lived and died, but the kingdom of Israel went on for many centuries. The kingdom of heaven is vastly different. It is not defined by geography or cultural traditions; it is defined by King Jesus. With an earthly kingdom you have to visit it to know it; you have to travel to enter its borders and experience its life and culture. The kingdom of heaven is not a place you visit—it is a person you meet. The kingdom of God and heaven is defined by Jesus. Wherever a Christian lives as Jesus would, Jesus is present and in Him His kingdom.[139] King Jesus comes into your heart and once you are occupied, your life becomes a border of His kingdom. The kingdom of heaven is not a place you enter when you die; it is a person whose life enters yours and causes you to live.[140] Its borders are measured by the expansion of God's love through His children. Where we love in Jesus's name, the kingdom advances. The world would call it an ideological kingdom, one identified through a way of life. We call it Jesus in us, the hope of glory.

When His life enters ours, our identity and purpose changes. We are no longer beings of flesh living and working; we are ambassadors of Christ and His kingdom. In this we see the eternal invade the temporal; we see His kingdom form. Streets once characterized by crime become places of heath and joy; families ruined by the vices of this world are set free and become renewed. Jesus is the landmass we live in, and when we allow Him to rule our lives we become an expansion of His occupied territory (Luke 17:21).

> The kingdom is God as man's salvation and therefore the meaning and goal of His encounter with man.
>
> Karl Barth, 1958[141]

Repentance as It Should Be

The second thing that needs highlighting is the meaning of the Greek word that is translated as "repent "in the English Bible. I want to spare you a long story here, but it would be irresponsible of me to not inform you of the history behind this word, so grab a cup of tea, rub your eyes a bit, and then read away at this short historical overview.

The early Christian church was founded by the Hebrew disciples, and mainly through the activity of Paul it moved to occupy the Gentile world. The early church spoke and wrote largely in Greek, with the Gospels themselves being written in koine Greek, which was the language of the everyday people.

The early church was badly persecuted; to become a Christian came at great cost. Christianity existed within the Roman Empire whose God was Caesar. Becoming a Christian meant entering into a minority group, one that was shunned from gaining positions of prominence such as high-paying powerful roles within the Roman government. In AD 312 all this changed. The Roman Emperor Constantine was riding into battle and believed he saw a vision of an early Christian symbol, with the words "by this conquer" underneath.[142] Constantine ordered all his troops to paint this symbol on their shields. Constantine won the battle, seized full control of the Roman Empire, and made this faith called Christianity the Roman state religion.

With this the tables turned within the church. To be a Christian was no longer a social, financial, and physical disadvantage. From this moment on to be anyone of social, financial, and political repute a Roman citizen was required to conform to this new religion of their emperor and nation. With this came corruption; people flocked to be baptized not because they believed by faith as commanded by Christ but because they wanted the worldly advantage that came with this "conversion."

The other critical thing that happened as a result of these events is that the Scriptures became dominantly written in Latin. They were translated heavily from Greek (the original language) into the language of Rome, Latin. From the time of Constantine until the time of the Reformation the Bible was locked away in the hands of the Latin-speaking Roman priests. The laity were not allowed to read it, only the clergy. One of the many changes that happened through the Reformation was that everyday believers were given access to the Bible. Critically, the original Greek Bible was also rediscovered and read, as opposed to the clergy-only Latin Bible.

The Greek word *metanoia*, which is translated as "repent" in the English Bible, is a linguistic manifestation of this religious and political tussle. When John the Baptist called people to repent and be baptized, and Jesus followed with the instruction to "repent, for the kingdom of God is at hand," the original Greek word they used was *metanoia*. *Metanoia* (noun) or *metanoeo* (verb) is a compound word comprised of *meta,* meaning "after" or "after with," implying change; and *nous,* "mind." This word carries the idea that change happens after we meet something new. If you read the word in the context of the Gospels you realize that the something new is the Word of Life, Jesus Christ. In the late nineteenth century Reverend Treadwell Walden, an Episcopalian (Anglican) minister from Boston, wrote the following:

> Meta is a preposition which, when compounded with Nous, means after [signifying change or transformation]. Metanoia is the After-Mind: perception, knowledge, thought, feeling, disposition, will, afterwards. The Mind has entered upon a new stage, upon something beyond. If the prefix were *pro,* "pronoia" it would mean perception before, thought before, a state of mind before experience. But Metanoia is a state of mind after experience; the mental condition which has developed itself after an entirely new set of circumstances has encompassed and invaded the consciousness.[143]

Reverend Walden was getting to the very heart of the Gospel message. If *metanoia* means to be changed after encountering something new it is presenting a Gospel of salvation by faith and God's grace. If it was presenting a Gospel of salvation by faith *and* works, it would have to contain the adjusted prefix of *pronoia,* which means to change before the experience—which it doesn't.

Essentially, we change as a result of meeting Jesus. We never change as a result of our own efforts and then add Jesus in after we have worked at it a bit. Christian change comes about as a result of encountering the living Word of God, Jesus Christ. He Himself is the entirely new circumstance that Rev. Walden writes about; His presence coming to us is the catalyst for change. *Metanoia* also carries the idea that it is a mind or thought-based change, hence Romans 12:2: "be transformed by the renewing of your mind."

Metanoia is a difficult Greek word to translate into English, as the English language does not contain an equivalent word.[144] The combination of the political and religious views of the Roman Catholic Church and the difficult task of bringing this Greek word to another language caused the Catholic Church to translate the Greek *metanoia* into the Latin Bible as *poenitentiam agite,* which means "do penance"— in other words, do good works to make up for bad. For hundreds of years people understood this Greek word, which means "change of mind" after encountering Christ, as an instruction to "do penance" for your sins.

The next chapter in this story is centered around the life and work of William Tyndale, a central figure in the Protestant Reformation. Tyndale is best known for being the first person to translate the Bible into the English language for the everyday Christian to read. Tyndale provides the origin of the English word "repent" that we have today in our Bibles.[145] Tyndale looked at the Catholic Latin translation of *poenitentiam agite* and was not convinced that it accurately conveyed the meaning of the original Greek *metanoia;* thus he changed it. Tyndale changed the word to "repent" because he knew "do penance" was not accurate. Tyndale was looking to move away from salvation by faith and works and to faith alone. Tyndale provided the first, and badly needed, correction of this term. The issue we have lingering today is that a second correction is still needed. Adjusting from "do penance" to "repent" somewhat cleans up the issue of doctrinal salvation, but the word "repent" doesn't accurately convey how this faith-based salvation changes us.

The English word "repent" is derived from the Latin *repoenitet*—which itself is derived from the root word *poena (poenitentia),* meaning "pain and suffering in view of being liable for punishment."[146] Latin Christianity has presented the idea that Christ's core command signifies pain, grief, and distress rather than a change of thought and purpose. The English translation of "repent" inherits the fault of the Latin words *repoenitet* and *poena*. It keeps the New Testament concept of a change of mind out of sight, making grief over sin the principal idea, as opposed to the constructive abandonment of sin via *metanoia*.[147]

Repentance carries the idea of having grief, and through its prefix instructs a looking back to the past with grief for what has been done wrong, or as Rev. Walden wrote, repentance "intensively communes" us with our past.[148] Mark 1:15 (ESV) says to "repent and believe in the gospel." "Gospel" means "good news." Jesus is instructing us to believe in Him and as a result see our mind changed—or more specifically, to have our mind changed by Christ through His Word and prayer. The word "repent" implies pain and entering into grief for past actions. If Jesus was saying this—which the Greek shows us He wasn't, but for the sake of the argument, if He was saying it—one questions looms: How is this good news? To believe by the renewal of your mind that salvation has been brought close to you through Jesus is good news. To enter into pain and grief and to focus on your past isn't good news. Just as Tyndale adjusted the translation to remove the idea of salvation by faith and works, we need a further adjustment in our time to remove the idea that pain and grief are primary elements of conversion.[149] Finally, an adjustment like this must produce doctrinal clarity on how Christian change is accomplished, that being: through the renewing of our minds.[150]

While this conversation may be foreign to many modern-day believers, it is not a new one. Rev. Walden wrote the book *The Great Meaning of Metanoia* a month after the Revised Version of the Bible came out. Walden and many other prominent clergy of the day, including members of the Revised translation publication committee, had hoped that the Revised translation would be a corrective update from the KJV, which had followed the Tyndale Bible in translating *metanoia* as "repent." Walden held that the nearest phrase in the English language to the Greek *metanoia* is "change of mind."[151] Walden also cites Archbishop Trench, a leading figure of that day who defined *metanoia* as meaning "that mighty change in mind, heart and life, wrought by the Spirit of God, which we call repentance."[152]

The most recognized word related to *metanoia* in the English language is paranoia (*para-nous*). Paranoia means to be beside-mind, beyond-mind, or in our common tongue, out of your mind. Paranoia is not being in a right mind, having a mind that is off—that is, not where it should be. If you compare *metanoia* and *paranoia*, you get the idea of what the New Testament call for *metanoia* is—it is a command to change your mind and get it where it should be.[153] Other great minds have weighed in on this throughout history:

> In Greek, Metanoia is not a confession of sins but a change of mind. (Tertullian, 198 AD)[154]

> For he who repents of that which he has done, understands his former error; and on this account the Greeks better and more significantly speak of metanoia, which we may speak of in Latin as a return to a right understanding. (Lactantius, c. 300)[155]

The Greek word metanoeite itself, which means "repent" and could be translated more exactly by the Latin trans-mentamini, which means assume another mind and feeling, recover one's senses, make a transition from one state of mind to another, have a change of spirit… as the Apostle says in Rom. 12, "Be transformed by the renewal of your mind." By this recovery of one's senses it happens that the sinner has a change of heart and hates his sin. (Martin Luther, 1518)[156]

Metanoeo, "to take an after view;" or more strictly, to change one's mind as a consequence of, and in conformity with, a second and more rational view…The English word "repentance" is often used to express regret, remorse, sorrow, etc., and is used in so loose a sense as not to convey a distinct idea, to the common mind, of the true nature of evangelical repentance. (Charles G. Finney, 1846)[157]

As you let the truth of the Gospel have its way with you, you will find the very shape and structure of your mind beginning to change. That is indeed what the Gospel is about, a metanoia, a radical repentant rethinking of everything before the face of Jesus Christ . . . a radical changing and transforming of your mind that comes through dying and rising with Christ. (T. F. Torrance, Lectures 1952–1978)[158]

Punishment, which "repent" conveys, comes from the Latin word *punire* and means to penalize, chastise, castigate, inflict harm, or humiliate. Considering that *metanoia* is the core command of Christ that lays the foundation for church discipleship and mission, the textually unsupported association of punishment with it is concerning. Penalty is reserved for those who consciously refuse Christ (Rev. 20:15), not those who come to Him (Matt. 11:28-30).

Bishop Westcott, in response to Rev. Walden's book, commented that just as the Reformers had transfigured faith and grace (*fides* and *gratia*), the preacher and the scholar must transfigure repentance. Bishop Westcott's words are wise. To rage against a term like repentance is not realistic. Whether it is accurate or not, repentance is part of the global Christian vernacular and cannot be removed. But as Bishop Westcott rightly said, it must be transfigured. The word "repent" must not be defined by its (etymological) Latin origin; it must be transfigured to draw a fresh (historically correct) meaning from the term sitting behind it in the Greek New Testament: *metanoia*. This is a critical element of Gospel proclamation as it ensures the words of John 3:17 are fulfilled— that Jesus comes not to condemn but to save.

This word goes to the very nature and being of God. If repentance is not transfigured to mean that which Jesus actually said, it will continue to misrepresent the Gospel by infilling it with pain and grief over one's past. This goes to the very kind of God we are ambassadors for. I said earlier that Jesus's name means "loving reconciliation," and that His name reveals the very nature, essence, and being of God. A call to change one's mind as a result of encountering the loving reconciliation that is Jesus Christ is good news. Jesus is not a God who comes to us to induce regret and pain; Jesus comes to us through His Holy Spirit so He can transform our minds to loathe the sin we loved and love the God we once loathed. To change the message is to change the messenger. Our God is one of love, His message good news, transfiguring our understanding of the English word "repentance" to accurately represent the original statement of Jesus has the capacity to transfigure our generation's view of Christianity, the church, and most importantly, Jesus Himself.

I want to be clear here that the Bible does talk about conviction for sin, confession of sin, and even sorrow and mourning over a sinful lifestyle (Jas. 4:8–10).[159] Second Corinthians 7:10 says: "For godly grief produces a repentance that leads to salvation without regret, whereas worldly grief produces death." When God utilizes our grief, He does so for a constructive purpose. God doesn't cause our grief, but He does work in us to make it constructive. God moves our grief to become remorse instead of shame. Remorse is constructive and induces a change in our thinking—*metanoia*. When grief is not combined with a belief-based change of mind, it produces death, not salvation.

Pain, shame, and grief are elements in salvation, but they are elements provided for by Christ. Jesus took our pain, shame, and grief on Himself at the cross. This brings us back to one of the great paradoxes of Christian doctrine: salvation by faith requires work. But it is Christ who works on our behalf, Christ does the working, we do the believing. It is not our works, rather the works of the Son, that faith joins us with. We believe in His work on our behalf. In relation to the specific area of putting effort into punishing ourselves for our past sins, we must—absolutely must— understand that the death and resurrection of Jesus is the once-and-for-all punishment for our sin. Jesus offers Himself as a divine substitute for us, He took what we deserved; He took our shame, our sorrow, our eternal consequences: "the punishment that brought us peace was on him" (Isa. 53:5, NIV).

It is God's kindness that ushers in salvation: "God's kindness is intended to lead you to repentance" (Rom. 2:4, NIV). In light of so great a salvation we live not in fear of God's wrath for our sin, but in awestruck gratitude that Jesus, the righteous Son of God, would step in and in His very body take our punishment. This is a hard thing for a religiously conditioned culture to grasp. To help make this point, I want to invert the argument. Most Christians would agree that it is not right to pray about something God has already commanded us to do. We don't want to use procrastinating through prayer as an excuse for delaying obedience. In the same way, I ask: Is it right to punish yourself for something God has already forgiven, and forgiven at great cost?

Once forgiveness has been applied, punishment is not necessary. The battle in this case is to renew our minds and accept that we are forgiven. In this scenario punishing ourselves is not even about remorse; it is a result of not accepting God's forgiveness. In this case punishing ourselves is about lifting guilt, which is something we are called to accept Jesus has achieved for us. Accepting forgiveness is a critical element in accepting Christ. In Him our new identity is as redeemed, renewed children of the living God.

We must remember that the call to *metanoia*—to change your mind—carries the idea of looking forward with Christ in anticipation of new life, not looking back in pain and sorrow to canvas our past. When salvation begins with regret, it continues in regret. We end up living confused and with a dual identity, the old and the new. Hebrews 6:6 talks about not subjecting Jesus to "public shame"—meaning, to live in a way as to suggest that His salvation is not adequate and needs a boost in the form of us chastising ourselves for our failures.[160] If as a matter of good mental health and personal healing someone needs to vent past sin, that is perfectly healthy and fine.[161] But it is important to note that this is different from Biblical confession and thus isn't necessary for us to be saved. Jesus paid it all.

> Surely he has borne our griefs
> and carried our sorrows;
> yet we esteemed him stricken,
> smitten by God, and afflicted.
> But he was pierced for our transgressions;
> he was crushed for our iniquities;
> upon him was the chastisement that brought us peace,
> and with his wounds we are healed. (Isa. 53:4–5, ESV)

I know that some will misunderstand my comments here. I am not in any way saying that sin should not be paid for. Sin produces sorrow, pain, grief, destruction, and many other horrific things. Sin must be paid for and it must be publicly put to shame—sin is that bad. The issue here is not if sin needs to be paid for; again, this is a confident yes. The issue is: Who pays for it? Do you pay for it through regret, shame, grief, self-loathing, and overapologizing? Or does Christ pay for it on the cross by taking on himself your guilt, pain, and shame?[162]

If we acknowledge that Christ pays for our sin then the correct response to salvation is not self-chastisement, pain, shame, and regret—it is thankfulness. You do not respond to a gift with self-chastisement, pain, shame, and regret—you offer gratitude. And in the case of salvation the gift is so immense that we respond with dedication and commitment to the Gift Giver. I would favor a genuine "thank you" being encouraged at the time of conversion: a "thank you" to Jesus for taking upon Himself our pain and shame. God does not want us to swell our minds with regret, pain, and shame over our past, but rather be full of thankfulness and gratefulness for the gift of the Savior—our best friend, Lord, and eternal defender.[163]

> Enter His gates with thanksgiving, and his courts with praise. (Ps. 100:4)

The Light of Life

> He knows what is in the darkness, and the light dwells with Him. (Dan. 2:22)

The Word of God (Jesus) must come. This brings something to contrast against the old life, which causes change. We are called to believe in this new reality and accept it as good news. We are not offered a doctrine of change; we are offered the *author* of change. It is important to note that Jesus is not just the messenger; He is the message.[164] The time that is fulfilled, is fulfilled in Jesus. Jesus has not come to just share a message of good news like a prophet or an angel; Jesus literally is good news. Jesus didn't come to "do ministry"; Jesus is ministry. In His body Jesus purchases a beachhead of reclaimed humanity, and from this place His Father puts on notice all that is failing and foreign. From this staging post the kingdom of heaven advances; its light shines forth and cuts down every corner of darkness that will allow it entry. Christ is the answer. He

is the truth that sets us free and sets our churches on fire. When a generation remembers the origin of glory, the generation sees glory.

As I have been writing this book, I have been struck by the supernatural and miraculous task that the church has been given. We tend
to think of miracles and the supernatural activity of the Holy Spirit as
being exclusively attached to extraordinary providential activity, such
as the healing of incurable disease. While this can be true, I wonder
how often we think of regular "old-fashioned" salvation as a miracle?

Adjusting the thinking of people is a billion-dollar industry. Physi-
ology, psychiatry, counseling, law enforcement, and politics all have at
their center a goal of changing people's lives through adjusting their
thoughts. The culture wars that so much of the world is engulfed in
centers around the desire to either change the opposing side's view or,
in extreme cases, enforce one's chosen ideology. The adjustment of the
mind is a central tenet of our culture.

I mentioned before that the word *metanoia* is difficult to translate
into English because there is no equivalent word. The apostle Paul actually gives us a clear and unambiguous answer to this translation issue in
Romans 12:2: "Do not be conformed to this age, but be transformed
by the renewing of your mind." The Greek word behind the English "be transformed" is *metamorphóō*. Notice the *meta;* it has the same
prefix as *metanoia*. The second part is *morphóō*, which means taking on
the form that properly embodies a particular inner essence.[165] The final
thought here is that the second part of the word *metanoia* is also present
in this verse—*noia,* which is the English word "mind." Paul adds the
term *morphóō* between *meta* and *noia*; this gives us the idea that repentance equals transformation centered on the renewing of one's mind—a
renewal comprised of not conforming to the world, but instead presenting your body as a living sacrifice through renewing your thought life.
There is nothing here even remotely talking about religious rituals, rules,
or regulations. This is a call to adopt the "mind of Christ" and in this
have your whole being renewed as a newly born citizen of the kingdom
of heaven – the continuing city (Heb. 13:14, NKJV). To truly worship

is to present your body as a living sacrifice. This presentation is not seen through public displays of religiosity; it is the inner worship of the mind. What we give our thoughts to, we love.

The word *metamorphóō* shows up in another place in the New Testament and from this occurrence we get a vantage point into the goal of the Gospel:

> And he was *transfigured* before them, and his face shone like the sun, and his clothes became white as light. (Matt. 17:2, ESV, emphasis added)

The word translated as "transfigured"—or "transformed," depending on your chosen translation—is the same word Paul uses in Romans 12:2 for "be transformed." Matthew says that Jesus's face shined with brilliant white light. Isaiah 53:11 gives striking insight into this redemptive process:

> After he has suffered,
>   he will see the *light of life* and be satisfied;
>   by his knowledge my righteous servant will justify many,
>   and he will bear their iniquities. (NIV, emphasis added)[166]

On the cross Jesus paid for our sins. Somehow, somewhere in the timeline of this redemptive act Jesus looks within Himself and sees that He, as God, is satisfied that payment has been made. The catalyst for this satisfaction was Jesus seeing that His glorious "light of life" had conquered the sin of humanity's generations.[167]

I am more than happy for others to obtain better wording to explain this miraculous redemption, but for me I get the picture of Jesus's light being swamped by our sin, light wrestling with darkness in the most magnificent of contests. I wonder if this was in the mind of John, the only disciple recorded to have been at the cross, when he wrote, "the light shines in the darkness, yet the darkness did not overcome it" (John 1:5). Jesus came to Galilee and shone in the darkness of the communities of Israel, but on the cross His light literally entered the darkness of mankind and completely overcame it. Upon seeing His own victory, He was satisfied that humanity could now abide in union with the Triune God again; our Lord then gave up His Spirit and was resurrected to walk again amongst the race He redeemed.

> For God who said, "Let light shine out of darkness," has shone
> in our hearts to give the light of the knowledge of God's glory
> in the face of Jesus Christ. (2 Cor. 4:6)

Jesus was transfigured in Matthew 17:2; He then purchased transfiguration for all humanity on the cross. This is good news: to be transfigured by the renewing light of Christ flooding your mind. Our activity is dependent prayer, asking God to renew our minds daily. We pray this because we believe it; we trust that the prayer of dependent faith will see Christ's transfiguration occupy our minds and lives. Our transfiguration is different from our Savior's, though. He shone with His own light; we shine forth His radiance into the darkness of the world. This is not a physical light but illuminated thinking. His light enters us and then, through us, the world—love into pain, kindness into hostility, peace into war, gentleness into rage, sacrifice into entitlement, self-control into excess. Through this the fruit of the Spirit germinates in our lives, communities, and culture; light enters darkness and transfigures it.[168] Interestingly, the word *metamorphóō* is the root of the English term "metamorphosis." This is the easiest example of this divine mystery: just as a caterpillar morphs into a butterfly, we are transformed from our lowly place into all God has for us.

A Gospel of Repentance in All the Earth

Depending on your Christian background you are probably familiar with one of two approaches to the Gospel. 1. The Gospel means to repent, believe and confess Jesus is Lord. 2. The Gospel means to accept God's loving act for you and to then live in grace, freedom and truth. Both of these have theological and doctrinal value, and both give rise to very different views of God and the Christian life.

If we look at the New Testament there are several key passages that evangelists regularly utilize that will probably be quite familiar (emphases added):

> "Sirs, what must I do to be saved?" So, they said, "*Believe* on the Lord Jesus, and you will be saved." (Acts 16:30–31)

> If you *confess* with your mouth, "Jesus is Lord," and *believe* in your heart that God raised Him from the dead, you will be saved. (Rom. 10:9)

> If we *confess* our sins, He is faithful and righteous to forgive us our sins and to cleanse us from all unrighteousness. (1 John 1:9)

> Therefore *repent and turn back*, so that your sins may be wiped out, that seasons of refreshing may come from the presence of the Lord. (Acts 3:19)

> For God *loved* the world in this way: He gave His One and Only Son, so that everyone who *believes* in Him will not perish but have eternal life. (John 3:16)

> But these are written so that you may *believe* Jesus is the Messiah, the Son of God, and by *believing* you may have life in His name. (John 20:31)

To help analyze these statements I will define the key terms.

- *Believe*: to trust Jesus is God, His ability to save, and His loving nature[169]
- *Confess*: to agree with God; to be in total agreement that we need saving and to accept God's plan for this (You can believe of sorts in God, but refuse to confess; note the former archangel Lucifer.)

- *Repentance*: a change of mind which changes our actions[170]
- *Love*: This is not something we do; it is something that happens to us. For our purpose here, I will say love is encountering Jesus. (1 John 4:10)

Salvation is a work of God in us, which we respond to.[171] Believing, confessing, and repentance are all responses to God's love. Repentance is an overall term used to describe a change of mind that God initiates. Saving belief manifested as a confession of Jesus Christ is the first stage of repentance—with the last stage being maturity, seen as a completed surrender (abiding, John 15; the presentation of Romans 12:1).[172] To be technically correct here: our belief, confession, and repentance don't save us; God does. The Father designs salvation, the Son purchases it, and the Holy Spirit applies it. Our part is to agree that we need it. In other words, we need to accept the free gift. We do this through belief. The form our belief takes is a wholehearted confession, and the fruit of this confession is a changed mindset, equaling a changed life.

Biblical confession does not require us to *dwell* on our past failures, rather, Christian confession is forward looking. Essentially, confession has two movements: a belief that *I* need saving due to sin and then a belief that Jesus is this salvation—initially and then daily (Matt. 6:11, John 4:14). We confess our sin to acknowledge it, which mentally marks a moment of departure from the sinful lifestyle—like an Old Testament memorial stone or pillar. Then we come to what Peter calls the "living stone" or living pillar, which is Jesus Christ (1 Pet. 2:5). We confess Him and His power to move us forward, upwards towards Heaven and away from the old life. Confession is the chief activity of *metanoia*, it is a forward (*meta*) mental (*noia*) movement. One that involves 'turning our minds' to be filled with the King and kingdom thoughts.

Martin Luther remarked in his lectures on Romans in 1515–1516 that "According to God, righteousness precedes works and works result from it."[173] Jesus triggers our belief. Once we have confessed

Christ, He occupies us and enables behavioral change to begin. Jesus in us brings change, nothing else. To put behavioral change before the indwelling of Jesus that comes through confession is to require change without Christ's provision; this sweeps the cross, resurrection, and Pentecost aside.[174] The primary activity of repentance is Scripture-based confession of Christ's lordship and prayer-based requests to have God act in us to achieve initial as well as lasting daily change—drinking daily (John 4:24).[175] Repentance is not about us changing our behavior; it is about us accessing Jesus's righteousness which changes us.

It is important to grasp that believing is necessary as it gives substance to confession. Confession is necessary as it enacts our will and conquers "Sean." Ongoing repentance is necessary as it forms Christ in us through our minds, ensuring genuine change is achieved. Remove one, and none work. When Jesus said a Gospel of repentance would be preached in all the earth, He was saying that there is good news; God has come near, and after you have been with Him you will be changed. A Gospel of repentance is a Gospel with teeth, a Gospel with punch and power, a Gospel that unlike its Old Testament law-based counterpart is able to actually produce true change, because it is based on the premise of Jesus living in us doing the changing (Gal. 2:20).

If someone thinks they need to have mastered behavioral change to be saved (or accepted), this is salvation by works and means you can only belong in Christ once you have changed—scary stuff. The byproduct of this kind of evangelistic practice is a generation bound by condemnation, legalism, and a view of God as an old man who is "up there" ready to pounce! The opposite—a Gospel so loose that it bypasses confession and personal responsibility—means that people are not saved. God's love is mixed in with His holiness; a conversion that lacks confession of our need for God, because of our rebellion, isn't acknowledging that we need saving at all—it's just *vation*, with no *sal*. It's meaningless.

An Act of God in Us

> For it is God who works in you to will and to act in order to
> fulfill his good purpose. (Phil. 2:13, NIV)

> By His doing you are in Christ Jesus. (1 Cor. 1:30, NASB1995)

The idea that salvation is a work or act of God in us was rediscovered through the Reformation.[176] Leading up to the Reformation,
salvation was seen as an activity of God that we partner with through
our own efforts or willpower.

In Martin Luther's time the Bible was only available in Latin, and
as noted earlier the Latin Bible translated the original command of
Jesus in Matthew 4:17 to *metanoia* as *poenitentiam agite,* which means
"do penance." Luther read Erasmus's newly published Greek New
Testament and saw the word *metanoia* in the Greek text. Luther knew
enough Greek to realize that the word did not mean "do penance,"
and as a result Luther began his ninety-five thesis by addressing this
word and issue; Luther's first three points were:

1. When our Lord and Master Jesus Christ said, ``Repent" (Matt.
   4:17), he willed the entire life of believers to be one of repentance.

2. This word cannot be understood as referring to the sacrament
   of penance, that is, confession and satisfaction, as administered
   by the clergy.

3. Yet it does not mean solely inner repentance; such inner repentance is worthless unless it produces various outward mortifica-
   tion of the flesh.[177]

The meaning of *metanoia* was at the forefront of Luther's argument, as it represents the core Christian message. As it was the central
command of Christ, it also largely defines each and every generation's
perception of Jesus Himself. Luther knew that the message and the
messenger would be viewed through the lens of the church's language

around the idea of *metanoia*. Our understanding of the word "repent" goes to the heart of the message, mandate, and mission of the church. This was true for Luther and it is true for us. Essentially, it is a battle to have either Jesus-power or our own willpower define the Christian message (Heb. 10:9–10). If we retain the idea that repentance involves pain and looking to the past with grief for what has been done wrong, we are affirming that our effort is needed for salvation. This is another dressed-up version of the same old thing: faith plus works.[178] Salvation is an act of God in us,[179] hallmarked by Christ and confession meeting in the mind (Matt. 16:16–18).

> Jesus, a radiant beacon of hope, affecting "that mighty change in mind, heart and life, wrought by the Spirit of God, which we call repentance.
>
> Richard C. Trench, Archbishop of Dublin, 1881[180]

Soren Kierkegaard championed the idea that "the consciousness of sin is the expression of absolute respect."[181] This section has been about reforming our concept of repentance, away from ideas that man has attached to it and back to what Jesus said and the Apostles relayed. If anyone has gotten the idea that as a result of this "reforming" we don't have to acknowledge that we have sinned, then I am sorry, but you have misunderstood. Sin is bad. Misrepresenting the connection between sin and *metanoia* is bad. Acknowledging sin in order to move forward and receive salvation is good.[182]

Metanoia and the Metaverse

In Luke 24:47 (NIV) Jesus said, "repentance for the forgiveness of sins will be preached." It is the marriage of the word repentance with Jesus Christ that makes New Testament salvation so effective. *Metanoia* (repentance) in its simplest form is the forward–mind, when we combine this forward–mind with Biblical confession, it pulls us out of the sheer terror of our sinful state and delivers us to God's eternal kingdom. Without this forward–mind, the call to confess and believe would birth utter despair, since we would see our sin (through confession) and God's glory (through belief) but be unable to move. Without the forward–mind we would join Lazarus, stuck on the other side of a great gulf (Luke 16:19-31), tortured by the ability to see freedom, but not attain it. It is the introduction of the forward–mind, the 'metamind' (repentance) that brings the joy of salvation. This is in contrast with the metaverse of contemporary society.

The metaverse is a false forward move, it is not a move in a forward direction as it does not lead away from our current station, rather it leads deeper into our internal self. The metaverse cannot construct anything new as it is simply recycling our dreams and making them into a virtual reality. There is no new content as nothing from outside of this existence has been used to build. *Metanoia*, however, calls us forward to adopt the "mind of Christ" (1 Cor. 2:16) that has come from the kingdom of heaven. The metamind of New Testament repentance is foreign to this world and as such is often rejected and devalued, but it is exactly this difference that proves its authenticity. If you enter the metaverse all you see is your highlight reel come to life, if you adopt the meta–forward–mind of Christ you see the eternal, primary existence— the kingdom of heaven.

Respectfully, it is an odd thing for God's salvation—which terraforms the diseased human mind into the mind of Christ—to be dismissed as it is not tangible, in an age where a virtual metaverse is normalised. Recently my study supervisor corrected me as he said I had written a "meta–sentence," this is a sentence that comments on your own work. The metaverse—while ok for causal fun—is the equivalent of commenting and liking your own Instagram post, it is an inward affirmation of our own fantasies and desires. New Testament *metanoia* is us entering and living in God's real, tangible, *"metaverse"*—the kingdom of heaven.

8

---- ··· + ♦ +··· ----

THEOLOGY OF CRISIS

Religion, and an awareness of the Divine, exists indeed in every part of the world, but there is only one place at which God challenges man to decision, because He Himself confronts man: Jesus Christ.

Possibly today few are willing to listen to this truth, perhaps, however, there are more than we in our desponding moods are inclined to believe. But it may be that the majority have never heard of this Christ at all. In any case, one who knows this truth has no right to hold his peace because he feels unworthy to speak.

Emil Brunner, 1927[183]

I live in Sydney, Australia, and here in my hometown research shows that when you get past generalized perceptions and digest the raw data on real people's thoughts about Jesus, the *local* Church and Christians they interact with personally, an interesting and not necessarily negative finding emerges. What becomes clear is that far more people are open to the Gospel and favorable to the church and its mission than are actively involved in the church.[184]

Essentially, there is a large gap between people who come to church and those who:

1. identify as Christian.
2. identify with Jesus's message.
3. are open to Christian spirituality.

In summary, Christianity is in decline within a group of people who are open to its message—some of them very open. There are literally millions of people in my home county of Australia who are not as closed to Christianity as we would necessarily think.

The research gave one powerful indicator on how to reach these millions of people who are "warm" to our faith: the greatest attraction to investigating spirituality and religion is by observing people who live out a genuine faith; 61% say they are attracted by this.[185]

My reason for mentioning these figures is twofold. First, I feel Australia is a good case study for the western world; what is happening in Australia is a snapshot of what is happening within the wider world. The second reason is that this is not a new problem. Before WW2 Germany was on the rise and the German church in crisis, a line swiftly grew between the German State Church, which largely sided with and sanctioned the rise of Adolf Hitler and the Nazi movement, and the German Confessing Church, which stood firmly with the Gospel and in the end stood in martyrdom. Karl Barth and Dietrich Bonhoeffer developed a strong friendship throughout this battle. Barth urged Bonhoeffer on as the standard bearer for the Confessing Church, while Barth himself was exiled in Switzerland waging war with his pen on the ideology that undergirded the Nazi movement.[186]

It was during this time the Swiss theologian Emil Brunner developed the term "theology of crisis."[187] This term was used to define the literal crisis the local pastor was in when he arose on Sunday to speak the Gospel within this context. In this setting the minster had to do a number of things well to survive and then be fruitful. He had to resist the nationalization of Christianity that was compromising the message and identity of the church. He had to avoid controversy to ensure his flock's chance of martyrdom was minimalized, while not comprising the core Gospel truth. Apart from the fusing of Nazi ideology with Christianity, there was also a large liberal theological movement that was causing a whole other set of problems; the pastor had to avoid this also. You can see why they called this a crisis and you can see why so many members of the Confessing Church, including Bonhoeffer, were martyred.

I want to be clear here: I am not drawing a parallel between the extreme situation that the German Confessing Church faced and the culture wars of modern-day western society. I am, however, drawing on the experience of the German Confessing Church to speak into the current degradation of the identity of Jesus and His church. We do not have the same situation of large groups of Christian leaders sanctioning the fusing of a Nazi-like ideology with Christianity. However, we do have widespread confusion around the identity of Jesus Christ and the purpose of his church. We are in a crisis, a crisis centered on who Jesus is and what His church is.

We need a reformation, one centered on our culture understanding the true heart and message of both Jesus Christ and His followers— a reformation within our culture of what Christianity is meant to be: namely, that Jesus's message is one of love and not division; the church an institution that protects and doesn't harm; the Gospel a truth essential to daily life and spirituality.

I mentioned before that Christianity is in rapid decline among a group of people who are open to its message. There is a large part of our culture that is open to Jesus and the church but which is confused as to who Jesus is and what the church stands for. I opened this book with an anecdote from the life of Bill Cunningham, where I said the following:

This book is a journey into why the cameras are down on the church in this generation, and how we get them up again. It is easy to blame society for turning away from the church. In some cases this is true—sin is sin, and there are those who have chosen a path of rebellion over the one Jesus offers. But I don't feel this is the norm. I truly believe that if Christians were to evacuate all other concerns and share the how and why of the core Christian message in a way our culture can digest, if this was to happen at large, I firmly believe the cameras would go up. Let's have faith for a church so true and strong that the culture would "get dressed" for its message.

The answer to this question, the way to get the cameras up again, is found in Jesus Christ Himself. Jesus needs no embellishment; He doesn't need a marketing strategy to be made more appealing. What He needs is to be presented—Him only.

In preparation for the next sections, below is a small overview of some key truths we have mined out so far:

- Just like you and I are composed of flesh and blood, God is literally composed of love.

- Jesus's name means "loving reconciliation."

- In order to share the Gospel properly, we must bring the ideas of love and reconciliation together in unison: love leading to reconciliation, reconciliation happening through love.

- Christianity is not a religion; it is participation in the life of God, through Christ.

- Comprehending that Christ's life living in and through us is the form God's love takes in humanity.

- Jesus seeks to facilitate death in order to bring new life.

- The kingdom of heaven is not a place you enter when you die; it is a person whose life enters yours and causes you to live.

The Way to Truth and Life

Depending on your Christian background you are probably familiar with one of two approaches to the Gospel.

1. The Gospel means to repent, believe, and confess that Jesus is Lord.
2. The Gospel means to accept God's love for you and to then live in grace, freedom, and truth.

Both of these have theological and doctrinal value, and yet both give rise to very different views of God and the Christian life. I said above that for something to be sharing the Gospel it must bring the ideas of love and reconciliation together in unison: love leading to reconciliation, reconciliation happening through love. When we combine this with the ideas that Christ's life living in and through us is uniquely made possible through the cross and also the form God's love takes to humanity we are approaching a clear understanding of what is meant as good news.

Religion is not good news; it is sterile works designed to modify behavior and culture. Jesus said He is the way, the truth, and the life. Early followers of Jesus were not called Christians; they were called followers of The Way, followers of the path to obtain true life. Reconciliation makes life with Jesus possible and this life is the way and the truth. It is comprised of God's love living in us, in the form of His Holy Spirit planting and growing divine life.

Currently my wife is pregnant; it has struck me that my wife doesn't know how to make a child, but she does know how to grow one. This is the difference between works and grace. We can't make the new life in us, but we can partner with the Holy Spirit to grow the new creation of Christ's life in us. Growing symbolizes grace; working symbolizes religion.[188]

The Gospel of Truth and Life

We can look at the New Testament as giving us two things: the historical events that gave rise to Christianity, and then, the outcome that arose from these historical events. I point this out as I want us to have biblical clarity on what the Gospel is. In 1 Corinthians 15:1–8 Paul says:

> Now brothers, I want to clarify for you the Gospel I proclaimed to you; you received it and have taken your stand on it. You are also saved by it, if you hold to the message I proclaimed to you—unless you believed for no purpose. For I passed on to you as most important what I also received:

> that Christ died for our sins
> according to the Scriptures,
> that He was buried,
> that He was raised on the third day
> according to the Scriptures,
> and that He appeared to Cephas,
> then to the Twelve.
> Then He appeared to over 500 brothers at one time;
> most of them are still alive,
> but some have fallen asleep.
> Then He appeared to James,
> then to all the apostles.
> Last of all, as to one abnormally born,
> He also appeared to me.

In this passage Paul is clarifying the historical events that comprise the Gospel. This is important for us to grasp. It may seem somewhat silly to say but you cannot have Christianity without the historical truth of 1 Corinthians 15:1–8. This is necessary to say, as there is currently a theological movement designed around the idea that you can have the outcome of a changed life without necessarily believing in the historical reality of Jesus's life. Theologians who hold to the same belief that Paul outlines here—that Jesus died, was buried, and was raised to life—call this believing in the "historical Jesus." Simply put, this means that Jesus is real; the events of the Gospels and Acts are real historical facts.[189]

Alongside 1 Corinthians 15:1–8 the apostle John gives a different summary of the Christian Gospel: "But these are written so that you may believe Jesus is the Messiah, the Son of God, and by believing you may have life in His name" (John 20:31). John calls us to believe in something that Paul doesn't list here, but rather infers: life in Christ. Or as John himself put it, "In him was life and that life was the light of men" (John 1:4). Paul gives us the historical events that the Gospel is composed of; John gives us the outcome of someone accepting these historical events, that being the full formation of the life of Christ within them (Gal. 4:19).

When we look at the sharing of the Gospel message within our culture we must understand that the Gospel has these two complementary sides. To see someone experience the life of Christ, that person must come to a knowledge of the true origin of this life: the historical life and ministry of Jesus. They must also come to understand the outcome of this historical truth: the full formation of the life of Christ within them.

Our culture is familiar with the historical "story" of Jesus's life, death, and resurrection, but there is little comprehension of the outcome of this "story." Most people think that the goal of this historical story is behavior correction, culture modification, or the advancement of institutional religion. This point of confusion is a large part of the perception problem Christianity currently has. Through the above-cited research, we found that Christianity is unpopular within a large group of people who are in fact open to its message. These people are not the mockers and scoffers of Psalm 1. To borrow a phrase from sales: these people are "warm leads"; they are interested in Jesus but confused about the relationship between Jesus and religion.

And yet, the researchers provided the answer: these people are most moved by genuine and authentic representations of Christianity. The words "genuine" and "authentic" both carry the idea of returning back to the original. For something to be genuine and authentic it needs to accurately carry the image of the original thing it is seeking to represent. For a Christian, allowing the founder of their faith to live in and through them equals genuineness and authenticity. The true Christian is not just a close copy of Christ; he or she is an imitator of His life. When this kind of Christianity rises, religion is exposed as the fake it is.

We do not need to petition heaven for another move of God. We need to properly stand in the provision of the foundational move of Christianity, the crucified and risen Christ who comes to our hearts at Pentecost.[190] Jesus said the work of God is to believe in the one He has sent. Our work is not to induce revival through spiritual effort. Our work is to believe the Gospel—that the kingdom of heaven has come, and that this kingdom is seen in its King, a King who through His very actions disabled death and made the way for all to have redemption from sin and reconciliation with the source of life itself. Jesus living in us is life and peace. It is also the only way to showcase the true image and heart of Christianity to an awaiting culture. Jesus doesn't need a billboard—he has you!

First Corinthians 15:1–8 gives a clear summary of the historical events that must be believed to obtain the real-time outcome of life in Jesus. The outcome itself is a bit harder to pin down, as there are so many statements in the New Testament that give insight to it. To me, Paul's pastoral letter to the Galatians contains an excellent summary statement: "My children, I am again suffering labor pains for you until Christ is formed in you" (Gal. 4:19). This is not a doctrinal creed designed to enforce the historical events of Jesus's life—1 Corinthians 15:1–8 does this well. This is the cry of a pastor's heart. It is a cry for people to move beyond the religious red tape and experience the pure truth of the Gospel, the fully formed life of Jesus Christ within.

Additionally, the "I am" statements in John's Gospel give us a neat list of things that Jesus Himself is and that He then grows in us:

Sustenance: I am the bread of life. (6:35, 48, 51)

Illumination: I am the light of the world. (8:12; 9:5)

Entrance: I am the door of the sheep. (10:7, 9)

Goodness: I am the good Shepherd. (10:11, 14)

Resurrection: I am the resurrection and the life. (11:25)

Directional clarity: I am the way, the truth, and the life. (14:6)

Supply: I am the true vine. (15:1)

With this all said, we end up with a Gospel message that has three distinct movements to it:

1. 1 Corinthians 15:1–8: historical events that need to be believed
2. Seven "I am" statements that show us what is being formed through belief
3. Galatians 4:19: the outcome of points 1 and 2[191]

It is important that we comprehend the process new Christians must travel in order to become fully formed in Christ. First, they must believe in the historical truth of Jesus's life, death, and resurrection. Second, they should understand what Jesus's life, death, and resurrection produces. Finally, they must know the goal: the full formation of the life of Jesus Christ within them. It may seem like a small difference, but we are not called to only have knowledge about Jesus's death and resurrection; we are called to be changed by receiving the life that arises from it. The Gospel is the process whereby we receive the very life that resurrected Jesus from the dead.

We are to know, by faith, the life of Jesus daily. We are saved for eternity and we are saved in this life through the new exodus—an exodus out of the wilderness of sin, insecurity, and hopelessness, and into the promised land of His presence. The Gospel is a matter of being brought into belonging with God. In human relationship belonging is purchased through relational collateral. In our relationship with God belonging is a gift purchased by Jesus's sacrifice. You confess that you belong with Him; this confession is a statement of what you hold true, what you believe. It is comprised of a rejection of any past places you belonged that were unrighteous and an acceptance that belonging with God is love-centered and based on His faithfulness as seen at the cross. Confessing this the first time saves us; confessing it continually renews our mind.[192]

> While wrestling with Paul's epistle to the Romans in the conventual tower, Luther was suddenly struck by the words from the prophet Habakkuk cited by Paul in Romans 1:17: "He shall gain life who is justified through faith" (NEB). It then dawned on Luther that the righteousness of God is not a prize that can be earned by works of love but a gift that enables man to do such works. Salvation is not a matter of working one's way into heaven but of being received into the favor of God.
>
> Donald Bloesch, 1980[193]

Glory Known

"God has not a name as men have."

Alexander of the Iron Chair. 177 AD[194]

I began this book by looking at the name of Jesus and how this name reveals the inner essence, being, and nature of God. I have used the phrase "essence, being, and nature" as a way of describing the mystery that is revealed through the name of the Lord Jesus Christ. This phrase—essence, being, and nature—is OK for everyday conversation, but it is worth clarifying more accurate language.

In his work *Paul and the Faithfulness of God*, N. T. Wright discusses the work of Richard Bauckham that deals with the identity and nature of God: "Identity concerns who God is and nature concerns what God is."[195] Who the God of the Old Testament is, is a mystery until Jesus arrives. What Yahweh is, was also a mystery until the coming of Jesus. In Jesus we see who God is: He is love. We also see what God is: He, as love, is reconciling by nature.

The Old Testament looks forward to the coming of Jesus and is then defined by Jesus. Jesus is the primary statement of who God is in the Bible.[196] Jesus is the exact representation of the eternal God to humanity, and His ministry on the cross is the exact representation of God's identity and nature.

As we've discussed, Jesus's name means "loving reconciliation." Using Augustine and Karl Barth's writings we came to understand that God's being essence and nature is one of active love, giving us the loving part of loving reconciliation; with reconciliation itself coming from the "saves" present in Jesus's name and 2 Corinthians 5:19.[197] Now that we are a little deeper into this journey together, I must cover with greater depth how the name Yahweh represents God's being as love. I don't want any gaps in this critical area.

The name Yahweh is somewhat like the word *metanoia* in the sense that it has a long and interesting history. The name YHWH is millennia old, but the words used to describe it in the English Bible—LORD, Yahweh, or Jehovah—are younger variants. It is essential that we understand this word correctly, as it is the initial revelation of who and what God is to humanity: a precursor to the complete revelation in Jesus Christ.

YHWH (sometimes written in the older style as YHVH) is known as the tetragrammaton, meaning "four letters." The four Hebrew letters that comprise it are *yodh, he, waw,* and then *he* repeated. YHWH is mostly translated as Lord or LORD (all caps) in the English Bible. The Jewish people feared taking the Lord's name in vain to the extent that they refused to pronounce the name at all. They substituted the name YHWH with the less revered Adonai, which is a more general term for Lord. Eventually, the vowels from Adonai ("Lord") and Elohim ("God") found their way in between the four consonants of YHWH, thus forming YaHWeH. Around the sixteenth century the Y was substituted with J; this, along with a few other changes, resulted in Jehovah. The key thing to understand here is that the words Yahweh, LORD, and Jehovah are not translations; they are substitutions. A translation seeks to form an interpretation based on the meaning of the original word. A substitution has other motivations, such as solving the Jewish fear of speaking the name of God.

Earlier on in this book I mentioned that in older cultures like the Jewish one someone's name is attached to their identity. The Lord's answer to Moses was not designed to simply name Himself, it was a revelation of His being or identity. The French reformer John Calvin said the following in his commentary on Exodus 3:14:

> *"I am who I am"* in the Hebrew is in the future tense, "I will be what I will be"; but it is of the same force as the present, except that it designates the perpetual duration of time. This is very plain, that God attributes to himself alone divine glory, because he is self-existent and therefore eternal.[198]

The connection between the name YHWH and God's being as love is seen in God's answer to Moses in Exodus 3:14–15, where God reveals a name descriptive of His identity.[199] In the above commentary John Calvin outlined that God's statement "I Am who I Am" reveals that God is self-existing and therefore eternal; this statement is given by God to interpret the name revealed in verse 15, YHWH. The French Geneva Bible of 1535 chose to translate YHWH with a name that represented the original meaning. In French this was *L'Éternel*; the English would be "The Eternal One."[200] The phrase *L'Éternel* is not perfect, but it is much more accurate than the English substitution of LORD, as it brings out the original idea behind the name YHWH and its connected phrase *"I Am who I Am."*

Just as God gave the connecting statement of "I Am who I Am" to help explain the meaning of His name YHWH, Jesus, as God, gives us the connected phrase "God is Love" to help us understand who He is, as God.[201] Jesus revealed this truth to John, and John revealed it to humanity through his New Testament writing. Moses stood before the burning bush; John walked with the God of the burning bush. It is interesting to note John identifies himself as "the one who Jesus loved." John defined Jesus through love, just as Jesus defined the entire Old Testament through love (Mark 12:28–31). In 1 John 4:8 and 4:16 the apostle gives us the statement "God is love." I mentioned previously that we can use this statement for understanding God's essence, being, and nature. In verse 8 John tells us that if we do not have love, we do not know God. From this we can confidently reverse the statement of verses 8 and 16 "God is love" and say that "love is God."[202] God and love are one in the same.[203] For John, love was the substance of God's being; to know love was to know God's eternal nature.[204]

It is worth adding to this thought that John's Gospel emphasizes Jesus's adoption of the name "I Am." Throughout the seven "I Am" statements, the incident of John 18:6, and through Jesus's critical exchange with the high priest and the Sanhedrin, He clearly and repeatedly identifies with YHWH, the great "I Am."[205] In John 14

Jesus identifies as the great "I Am" and connects this identity with the coming Holy Spirit.[206]

YHWH is a description of God's being. This revelation is dimly lit in Exodus 3:14–15, but in Jesus people saw it face-to-face. The open truth is that YHWH is difficult to translate, as it does not give one single clear thought as to the meaning of God's name. Jesus knew this, so He chose to define His name and identity with love. Anyone who has done any higher education will know how remarkable this is. One of the most advanced things in education is to take an extremely difficult idea and translate it into a basic truth that a child can comprehend without losing the more complex concept. Jesus as love, God as love, is a simple truth that a kids' church leader can explain to a child, but it is also a deeply complex truth that theologians, scholars, and senior pastors can develop for a lifetime.

The name Jesus is the oldest known Hebrew name containing the tetragrammaton (YHWH). [207] Through taking this name Jesus directly links Himself with the God of the burning bush.[208] Jesus is the exact representation of God's being, the full revelation of God's identity and glory to the human race. Jesus is the physical manifestation of God's being in our space-time. Jesus is YHWH incarnate, He is love incarnate; and through the Holy Spirit, the God of eternal divine love lives in you. The post-Pentecost Christian is the recipient of the full revelation of God's being that began thousands of years ago with Moses.[209] God gave initial revelation to Moses, complete revelation in Jesus, and implanted revelation to us through the Spirit-filled life—glory fully known.

God is not anonymous. He has an identity. He has made himself a name from this identity. He has made His identity known through this name; that is why it is holy.[210]

Your throne has been established
from the beginning;
You are from eternity. (Ps. 93:2)

PART THREE

JESUS ALIVE IN YOU

9

······•◆•·····

CITIZENS OF ETERNITY

This is an invitation to men and women who are exhausted with the search for truth, Jesus said you have been searching for truth, you are tired—I Am the way the truth and the life—you found it, the search ends with me.

Billy Graham, 1980[211]

It has been well documented that Jesus did not come to establish a physical earthly nation; instead, he came to establish the kingdom of heaven among men. When you look at Jesus's teaching there are two distinct concepts He brings out: first, the kingdom of heaven; and second, the church. The church is one part of the kingdom of heaven; alongside the church, which is also called the "Bride of Christ," is the Jewish nation. There is also the heavenly host, angels and other divine beings; these are all a part of what Jesus called the kingdom of heaven. It is helpful for modern-day Christians to remember that the church is one part of a larger whole. In an earlier section I said this about the kingdom of heaven:

The kingdom of heaven is not defined by geography or cultural traditions; it is defined by King Jesus. With an earthly kingdom you have to visit it to know it; you have to travel to enter its borders and experience its life and culture. The kingdom of heaven is not a place you visit—it is a person you meet. The kingdom of God and heaven is defined by Jesus. King Jesus comes into your heart and once you are occupied, your life becomes a border of His kingdom. The kingdom of heaven is not a place you enter when you die; it is a person whose life enters yours and causes you to live.

The word "church" is utilized in the English Bible to translate the Greek *ekklésia*, which is used by Jesus and then the New Testament writers. The word "church" is not a direct translation; it is an English version of another Greek word, *kyriakos,* meaning "belonging to the Lord." Commentators highlight that *kyriakos* is interlaced with the idea of a house or building as opposed to people, bringing in a possible meaning of "the Lord's house."[212] The Greek word *ekklésia* means "assembly" and is sometimes translated that way in English Bibles. *Ekklēsía* is a compound word; it is comprised of *ek*, "out from" and "to," and *kaléō*, "to call." The idea of *ekklēsía* is a people, not a building, a people who assemble together in the kingdom of God while on Earth. These people are, as *Strong's Concordance* puts it, "called out from the world and to God, the outcome being the church."[213]

The kingdom of God is the cause—it is the thing the church is to build. The church that has forgotten this becomes inward-focused. The church that knows its function is forward-oriented and looks to the establishment of the kingdom of heaven in the hearts of humanity. We are called out of the kingdoms of the world and into two things: an identity centered around being a citizen of heaven's kingdom, and the cause of establishing the kingdom of heaven. This all comes about through a relationship with the King, a relationship founded on His act of loving reconciliation.

Most scholars agree that the apostle Paul was the most effective establisher of the kingdom of God in history. Paul's strategy has been well covered over the years. To put it simply, Paul built the kingdom of God through the establishment of local churches. This process has been the bread and butter of evangelism for two thousand years. While writing about the apostle Paul's evangelistic mission, theologian N. T. Wright said the following: "He saw his vocation in terms of bringing into being 'places'—humans, one by one and collectively—in which heaven and earth would come together and be, yes, reconciled. God was reconciling the world to himself in the Messiah: the Messiah is the new temple where heaven and earth meet."[214] Paul saw himself as a dual citizen of both the kingdom of heaven and the earthly "kingdoms" of Israel and Rome. Paul understood the nature of the worlds he inhabited; one was resource-giving and one resource-consuming. The need Paul was called to meet was in the earthly kingdom of men, but the resource to meet this need came from the kingdom of heaven. The core of Paul's effectiveness was that he didn't try to draw provision from the resource-consuming world; he knew to draw resource from a place of strength, the kingdom eternal.

In Acts 9 Jesus sends Ananias to Paul; He tells Ananias who Paul is and what Paul's purpose was: "But the Lord said to him, 'Go, for he is a chosen instrument of mine to carry my name before the Gentiles and kings and the children of Israel'" (v. 15, ESV). The word "carry" here is also translated as "bear," "proclaim," and "take"; it means to take up and carry the name (identity) of Jesus. Paul is to be the message through the messenger living in him. Paul is to take this new message, embedded in His very own life, and boldly proclaim it to the world. Remembering that the power to achieve this comes from the kingdom of heaven, in the form of the King of Heaven living in Paul. Jesus is both the message and the power to see the message received.

The character (as opposed to identity) of Paul's carrying of the name is given in the very next verse: "For I will show him how much he must suffer for the sake of my name" (v. 16, ESV). Paul, like his

Master, was to build the kingdom through self-sacrifice, as Jesus Himself said in Mark 10:45: "the Son of Man did not come to be served, but to serve, and to give His life a ransom for many."

This sacrificial suffering must be contrasted with the call to abundant life of Jesus in John 10:10. Romans 8:2 reconciles these two seemly contradicting thoughts: "the Spirit's law of life in Christ Jesus has set you free from the law of sin and of death." The call of Jesus is to operate your life here on Earth from the orientation of the kingdom of heaven. The suffering we are called to enter into is best seen as birth pains associated with us being born into the kingdom of heaven—birth pains that produce momentary light affliction but cause us to be born into a far greater inheritance. Paul put it this way in 2 Corinthians 4:16–17 (ESV):

> So we do not lose heart. Though our outer self is wasting away, our inner self is being renewed day by day. For this light momentary affliction is preparing for us an eternal weight of glory beyond all comparison.

Nearly 1,600 years ago Augustine, who is somewhat universally seen as the father of theology, wrote his timeless work *The City of God*. In it Augustine argues, among many things, that Christians should live mindful of their place in the City of God. For Augustine, the citizens of the City of God are known by their love for God, which often takes the form of sacrificing themselves. Likewise, citizens of the Earthly City are known for their love for themselves, which often takes the form of sacrificing others. Augustine saw that "two cities have been formed by two loves"[215] and "life will only be happy when it is eternal."[216]

Fast-forward to nineteenth-century Copenhagen, and we see Soren Kierkegaard use the same theme to seek reformation in the Danish State Church. Kierkegaard outlined two ways of living: the aesthetical life, which is self-centered and pleasure-driven; and the ethical life, the life that upholds society's cultural and moral standards—the aesthetical life being a life led by one's senses, and the ethical life led by intellect. Kierkegaard's book *Either/Or* is a tough one to digest, but arrives at the idea that neither the pleasure-driven aesthetical life nor the morally higher ethical life are close to comparing to the "religious life."[217] Kierkegaard uses the term "religious" to present the Christian life as Christ intended it: as a personal living faith.

Kierkegaard extended this theme and wrote about the knight of faith. He explained that Abraham's decision to obey God and sacrifice Isaac, even though he knew it was ethically wrong, made him a knight of faith. Kierkegaard explained this through what he called the "teleological suspension of the ethical"—stay with me! "Teleological" means to understand an action based on the outcome it produces, rather than the means it uses; it is similar to the saying "the end justifies the means."[218] A teleological suspension of the ethical is an action that doesn't conform to the ethical standards of the world because it has a higher eternal purpose in mind. Kierkegaard also put forward the idea that the knight of faith is someone who passes through what he called infinite resignation, or absolute surrender. For Kierkegaard there are two key "movements" to this; embracing these enables someone to see a situation as Abraham did and then act as Abraham did, making them knights of faith:

1. Accepting the loss of that which one loves
2. Accepting a seemly unethical task because they believe there is a greater eternal purpose involved

As I write this section, my eyes are drawn to a biography of Hudson Taylor, founder of the China Inland Mission, sitting on my bookcase. Taylor's life embodies this twofold absolute surrender, or as Kierkegaard called it, infinite resignation. Hudson Taylor accepted the loss of the life he loved in England as well as the seemly unethical task he was given in China—seemingly unethical because it cost the life of his wife, children, and friends—but had an eternal purpose that warranted this sacrifice:

millions of salvations. Hudson Taylor, like Abraham, walked forward in faith on the bases of what Kierkegaard called the virtue of the absurd—the seemingly absurd call of Scripture to accept that the impossible truly is possible. To set your life and that of your family solely on the basis that God will do the impossible is virtuous in the eyes of heaven, but absurd to the world of men—hence the idea that it is a virtuous but absurd thing to do. Through this, Hudson Taylor lost everything, but the result was not ruin; rather, it was abundant eternal blessing that also gave him abundant earthly provision, more than what he started with. In this, he joined Abraham and became a knight of faith.

Abraham and Hudson Taylor did not halt when confronted with the absurd request of God to bank on the impossible; they took what Kierkegaard called a leap of faith, even though it seemed absurd. They moved forward in faith, a faith that was not based on human reasoning but rather the eternal plan of God. This is nowhere better modeled than at the cross. Jesus was asked to do something that looked absurd in the eyes of mankind but had an eternal purpose that made it virtuous. Kierkegaard wanted us to understand that real faith, world-shaking and kingdom-constructing faith, begins with a leap into that which seems absurd. When Abraham stood on the edge of human understanding and leaped into the absurd plan of God, he performed the double movement required to become a knight of faith. Movement one was becoming indifferent to the fear of loss that holds potential knights back. Now freed to act independent of the world, Abraham made the second movement and leapt into the absurd plan of God, demonstrating such dedication that it gained him access to the storehouses of heaven—not just a ram, but a role as a knight of faith in the court of the King of Heaven.

The knight of faith has made the choice to choose, and through this process has learned to place complete trust in the King's ability to provide both resource and divine reasoning. That which once enslaved is now itself enslaved. God gives back that which He once demanded because the knight of faith can now master that which once mastered him. The knight of faith is resigned to that which once held him and held by that which he was once resigned to. The knight of faith accepts that the move toward certain faith in God involves absurdity in the calculation of men. He is so certain that the impossible is truly possible that he leaps forward in faith and proves God, becoming one who has experienced the certainty of faith.[219]

This is truly beautiful stuff, the transformation of ordinary human existence into a life that serves the purpose of heaven and gains the provision of heaven's Lord. The question that arises from this has to be: Why don't more Christians make this move and become knights of faith? Kierkegaard put forward Abraham, Mary, and Jesus as the three knights of faith, but theorized that there could be more. Kierkegaard tragically died young, stopping short of a full writing career, one I am sure would have developed this idea further. I feel that if Kierkegaard were alive today, he would almost certainly seek to develop the idea of the knight of faith through an interesting discussion that is taking place in the theological community, called the *Pistis Christou* debate.

The Just Shall Live by . . . ?

Pistis Christou is a Greek phrase translated as "faith in Christ" in the English Bible.[220] It literally means "faith *of* Christ," and depending on your interpretation you arrive at it meaning either "faith in Christ," "the faithfulness of Christ," or something in between like "the faith that is of Christ" or "the Gospel of faith, which is Christ."[221] This debate is long, wide, and varied but it essentially boils down to two views on salvation: we are either saved by faith in Christ, or saved by Jesus's faithfulness. Consider these examples from Scripture (emphases added).

Faith in Christ:

For in it the righteousness of God is revealed from *faith for faith*, as it is written, *"The righteous shall live by faith."* (Rom. 1:17, ESV)

But now the righteousness of God has been manifested apart from the law, although the Law and the Prophets bear witness to it—the righteousness of God *through faith in Jesus Christ* for all who believe. (Rom. 3:21–22, ESV)

We ourselves are Jews by birth and not Gentile sinners; yet we know that a person is not justified by works of the law *but through faith in Jesus Christ,* so we also have believed in Christ Jesus, *in order to be justified by faith in Christ* and not by works of the law, because by works of the law no one will be justified. (Gal. 2:15–16, ESV)

I have been crucified with Christ. It is no longer I who live, but Christ who lives in me. And the life I now live in the flesh *I live by faith in the Son of God*, who loved me and gave himself for me. (Gal. 2:20, ESV)

Jesus's faithfulness:

For therein is revealed the righteousness of God from *faithfulness unto faith*; as it is written, but *the righteous shall live from my faithfulness.* (Rom. 1:17, Barth)[222]

But now apart from the law the righteousness of God hath been manifested, being witnessed by the law and the prophets; even the righteousness of God *through his faithfulness in Jesus Christ* unto all them that believe. (Rom. 3:21–22, Barth)

We are Jews by birth and not Gentile sinners, yet we know that no one is justified by the works of the law but by *the faithfulness of Jesus Christ.* And we have come to believe in Christ Jesus, so that we may be justified *by the faithfulness of Christ* and not by the works of the law, because by the works of the law no one will be justified. (Gal. 2:15–16, NET)

I have been crucified with Christ, and it is no longer I who live, but Christ lives in me. So the life I now live in the body, *I live because of the faithfulness of the Son of God*, who loved me and gave himself for me. (Gal. 2:20, NET)

We either live each day in the Christian life by confessing faith in Jesus or we are carried by Christ's faithfulness. The debate in the theological community has been going on for some decades now, so much so that a third view has arisen that operates between the two main options. If faith in Christ centers on an individual's act of faith and Christ's faithfulness on God acting in us to redeem, the third view sits in between, with man partaking in what some have termed "Christ-faith." In support of this third view Wolfgang Schenk commented: *Pistis Christou* ("faith of Christ") "is not only the faith which Christ has, also not only that which he gives, but above all the faith which is himself."[223]

The theological debate is unresolved, and with many great and thoughtful arguments on each side the debate will remain that way until a solution is found. This is where the pastor can help lead the theologian. The theologian is able to leave this debate unresolved, as he rarely has the pressing need of the destitute and broken individual knocking at his office door. The pastor who may read a book like this does not have that reality. For the local pastor the debate on whether faith is God's action toward us—as in, God faithfully reaches out and passes to us the faith His Son purchased—or if faith is a human act of believing in Jesus's death and resurrection is of the utmost importance. For the local pastor this cannot be unresolved as he has the pressing issue of lives needing eternal salvation.

Maybe even more importantly for this debate, the local pastor has real people needing now-salvation, people who need hope today in their situation of pain, hurt, and hardship. I say the latter is more important as eternal salvation can be trusted for either way. The more pressing pastoral issue is how do we, as local pastors, train our people to obtain the power of God for the now-need? Is it through a human act of faith or through partaking in Jesus's faithfulness? The two are very different ways of praying and living the Christian life, and given that we discovered Christianity in the western world is declining within communities that are largely open to its message, we should look with fixed gaze at this issue. It is central to the type of salvation the church of Jesus Christ is presenting to the world.

Jesus personalized His teaching through parables, so to help resolve this debate we will do the same. Imagine the heartbreaking burden a local pastor has when he sees a congregation member whose mind is overwhelmed with anxiety, and desires to see her freed. Suppose the pastor truly believes the Bible's claim that through prayer and the Scriptures Jesus can enter that mind and renew it. Does the pastor tell her to pray prayers centered around trusting in Jesus's faithfulness to deliver her? Or does he tell her to pray prayers affirming her personal faith in God, and through this constant repetition the mind will be renewed and freed? This is the practical outworking of the *Pistis Christou* debate.

Neither method involves lazy faith. The first says that Jesus's work is finished and that it is a gift that they need to ask Him to come and apply to their mind. The second focuses of the fact that Jesus's work is finished but that they need to act to apply this "cure" to their own mind. So which one is right? Do we prayerfully ask Jesus to apply His finished work through the Holy Spirit? Do we apply Jesus's finished work through an act of human faith? Or do we embrace the third view of the *Pistis Christou* debate, as it has the idea that faith is not something we do, nor a thing we seek out—it is Jesus Christ Himself?

To answer this, we need to dig deeper into the actual act of salvation that the Father orchestrated, Jesus executed, and the Holy Spirit applies. Unfortunately, to do this I need to take you through the valley of the shadow of death, otherwise known as the doctrine of election and predestination. So, may I suggest that before you keep reading you grab a cup of tea and have a stretch!

Karl Barth lived centuries after John Calvin and Martin Luther and had the advantage of working with all the content of the Reformation age. Barth wrote that the core idea of this doctrine is that God has not elected or rejected you; you are not predestined to salvation or predestined to hell. God has elected and rejected His Son; God has elected Jesus to salvation and rejected Jesus to hell—on your behalf. Karl Barth removes man from the center of the doctrine of election and predestination and places the Son of Man, Jesus, at the center. Allow me to explain this further. Historically, Christianity taught that God predestines people to heaven but doesn't predestine them to hell; let's call this single predestination. Single predestination is very light on the details of how God can choose one person for heaven over another, and this not be a direct determination of God that some people go to hell. This is the cause of many arguments in Bible college classes. In an effort to solve this, the doctrine of double predestination was developed—the view that each human who has ever lived is predestined to either heaven or hell. Theologians don't like to accept this, as it is difficult to reconcile with Jesus's missional commands and scriptures like 2 Corinthians 5:19. You can see why Barth presented the idea that election is centered in Jesus; it makes a lot more sense, and since Barth published the idea it has been widely accepted—by those who can get their heads around it![224]

Barth took issue with the fact that historically the doctrine of election and predestination had been formulated without any mention of Jesus Christ. If salvation is accomplished once and for all by Jesus Christ, so too is election. Barth wrote that the doctrine of election operates off a twofold principle: 1) Jesus Christ is the electing God; 2) Jesus Christ is the elected Man. Election, like salvation, happens through Jesus Christ, not man.[225] God chose to use Himself as the organ and instrument of election.[226] Between God and man there stands the person Jesus Christ. He is the one who does the electing and the one who is elected. He chooses to elect Himself in the place of man and therefore takes upon Himself the rejection of man with all its consequences.[227]

"Predestination means that from all eternity God has determined upon man's acquittal at His own cost."[228] This is what John wants us to see in the opening of his Gospel (John 1:1–14). God is activating His predestined plan to incarnate into flesh, die in flesh, and then rise in this flesh all for the salvation of humanity. That God would hazard and abase Himself in this way is, then, the content of predestination.[229] God becomes man's friend in Jesus and elects to not just take our rejection on Himself, but to make it His own; it is no longer ours but His. He exchanges our failure with His conquest. He elects us to bear His identity of faithfulness and elects to exchange His Throne for our shame—this is how God loves the world. Solomon had a throne of golden splendor—"nothing like it had ever been made in any other kingdom" (1 Kings 10:20)—while the King of Kings a throne of bloodied cedar—nothing like it had ever been made in any other kingdom.[230]

God acquits man at His own cost and this exchange becomes irreversible because it does not take place through us, but through Him. Faith in Christianity involves disbelief in the rejection of mankind. Condemnation is not possible because it has been vanquished. Jesus Christ has absorbed it; He has taken it into Himself. He becomes a black hole of sorts, absorbing failure, sin, and shame into Himself. To be condemned would involve the overthrowing of this principle, or as Barth said, "it is clear that rejection does not concern us because God willed that it should concern Himself."[231]

Barth's doctrine of election is impressive, but the one thing I need to emphasize is that individuals have to choose to accept Jesus's "election to rejection" on their behalf. Each person must accept Jesus's death and resurrection and gain the consequence of heaven, or choose to reject it and gain the consequence of eternal separation.[232] Without this choice in place Barth's doctrine of election drifts dangerously close to universalism. Universalism is the idea that God will let everyone into heaven at the end of time and we don't really have to worry too much. D. L. Moody and Billy Graham would strongly disagree with this idea and so do I.

Barth's doctrine of election says that Jesus was predestined to hell for us (death) and also to life (resurrection) for us, without taking away personal responsibility.[233] To me, this is a winner. Entering the real world with a message that says "God loves you, but you could be predestined to hell so don't bother believing" is not only evangelistic futility; it is inconsistent with the heart of God in reconciling the world to Himself through Jesus Christ.

Before I end this section and move back to how Barth's doctrine of election gives insight into the *Pistis Christou* debate, I want to have a pastoral moment. When covering heavy areas like election, we must be careful to ensure our belief doesn't accidentally waver. There is a lot of mystery in the area of election, and the antidote to the unknown elements is faith. We know that Jesus died for us, we know we are called to make a decision to follow Him into death and life, and we know this happens through faith. C. S. Lewis summed this up well in his book *Mere Christianity*:

> We are told that Christ was killed for us, that His death has washed out our sins, and that by dying He disabled death itself. That is the formula. That is Christianity. That is what has to be believed. Any theories we build up as to how Christ's death did all this are, in my view, quite secondary: mere plans or diagrams to be left alone if they do not help us, and, even if they do help us, not to be confused with the thing itself. All the same, some of these theories are worth looking at.[234]

How God elects and saves humanity is important and we have covered it for a reason. But it is very much secondary to simple belief in Jesus's salvation. Educate yourself, obtain knowledge and wisdom, but never, ever, let your heart wander away from simple childlike trust.

The Just Shall Live by Faithfulness

So far in this section we have overviewed that we are citizens of the kingdom of heaven who dwell in the earthly world of men.

We learned that the kingdom of heaven is provision-giving and the earthly world provision-consuming. We then looked at the "knight of faith," and how through entering into the process of becoming knights we can make the impossible possible. We moved to look at whether we are called to "faith in Christ," "the faithfulness of Christ" or "the faith which is Christ"—or, as Soren Kierkegaard would say, we moved to look at whether we are called to be a knight of faith, a knight of faithfulness, or knighted by faithfulness. Finally, we just looked at how Jesus's election to rejection is the center element in salvation.

Karl Barth put forward the idea that it is divine faithfulness, not human faith, that lies at the heart of Paul's theology in the New Testament. For Barth, Paul's idea of divine faithfulness is a continuum that flows in three stages:

1. Being occupied by the faithfulness of Christ
2. Participating in the life of Christ
3. Stages one and two forming an entirely new creation[235]

Paul referred to this new creation constantly. A few examples are:

Galatians 4:19: "Christ is formed in you"

Ephesians 4:13: "attaining to the whole measure of the fullness of Christ"

2 Corinthians 5:17: "if anyone is in Christ, the new creation has come"

Just as we internalize our failures, sin, and shame and then allow these to become our identity and outwork a reality of continuing failure, sin, and shame. The call of Jesus, Paul, and the New Testament is to understand that the Holy Spirit comes to us to indwell us with eternal love (God's being). This indwelling of love outworks as the life of Jesus living in and through us. The form the life of Jesus takes in us is a new reality based on Jesus's faithfulness being imprinted over our faithlessness. Believing in Christ involves placing His faithfulness in your past and allowing that to determine your present. Jesus's faithfulness to God becomes your internal determining principle; it activates a belief that the best is yet to come because you have accepted that your past is now full of faithfulness.[236] We are called to partner with the Holy Spirit as He seeks to internalize Jesus's life in us. We partake in the death and resurrection in the sense that they cleanse us and give us a new personal history. The Holy Spirit then brings the new creation to fill us. This process produces a new identity based on Jesus's faithfulness, and this new identity enables us to live differently, creating a new reality for us.

God's love in us = Jesus life in us

Jesus life in us = new identity

The idea of man-centered election has always had an awkward relationship with the doctrine of salvation by faith that the Reformers gave us. This is because it just doesn't make sense. How can we be the objects of divine eternal love, but yet be predestined to either heaven or hell? When we accept that Jesus was predetermined to both death and life for us, it all becomes a lot clearer. Jesus is the source of salvation and we partake in His salvation through responding to His faithful call to us. To enable a response, we are given the gift of faith, drawn out from the bank of His faithfulness. Jesus gives us this gift and enables us to freely choose Him. When we say we have free will we are saying that we have the free will to choose Him because He chose to make the choice possible. We are set free for a faithful response to God's faithfulness, or as Barth put it: "He brings about the change which as a divine change only He can bring about—the change in which a man, in virtue of God's faithfulness to him, becomes faithful to God in return, and thus becomes a Christian."[237]

Jesus Himself went to the cross and lost all. He gave up His life in an act that humanly speaking was absurd; but in this absurdity, Jesus performed the double movement Kierkegaard spoke of and gained all back through His Father faithfully resurrecting Him. Jesus performed the impossible. He changed death and made it a transition. Through the power of God, it became an access point into the full inheritance of heaven.[238] This act of Jesus is the central truth of Christianity and its outcome the central promise.

Narrowing In

The phrase "faith in Christ" (*Pistis Christou*) must present the idea that faith is not something we conjure up and give to God—it is a gift Jesus purchases at the cross and then gives to us. It enables awareness of our sinful state by drawing a contrast between Jesus's perfect life and our troubled life. This initiates belief, resulting in salvation. The Holy Spirit comes and seals us with eternal love felt and known in the common tongue as faithfulness. The sayings "saved by Jesus" and "saved by faith" explain each other. Just as Barth moved election off man's shoulders and onto Christ's, we must move salvation off man's shoulders and onto Christ's. The argument over Greek grammar in the phrase *Pistis Christou* (faith in Christ) is superseded by an acknowledgement that only Jesus can save and therefore only Jesus can give what is needed for salvation. Jesus's actions at Calvary inform the *Pistis Christou* debate— all that is needed for salvation comes from Him, especially faith. If faith is the gift of God, then the origin of this gift has to be the faithfulness of Jesus Christ at Calvary.

Kierkegaard gave us the knight of faith; using Karl Barth's framework of Jesus–centered election we can confidently say that Jesus is the one great knight of faith in whose provision we partake. We are knighted when we bend our knee to His majesty and allow His faithfulness to become our story. The world considers this an absurd act, but moved by God's faithfulness the serious Christian bends all desires, habits, wants, and dreams. In this everything of the world is lost, but the inheritance of heaven is gained. The life in the body is lived by accessing the bank of faithfulness stored up in Christ. Through this one joins Jesus and becomes a knight of faith, knighted by the faithfulness of God.

My desire here is not to get bogged down in theological reasoning, but rather to free a generation from striving to obtain faith by resting in His faithfulness. Whether you see a few choice Christians as knights of faith, or see Jesus as the knight of faith who offers position to all who would partake in His faithfulness, is somewhat peripheral. The main issue is how you access Jesus's provision. Is it through summoning the faith to believe, or is it through acknowledging your inability to do this and dedicating yourself to receiving and resting in Jesus's faithfulness?

The Just Will Live by Jesus

My goal here is to address an issue that all local pastors confront daily, an issue that plagues the modern world: self-salvation. People are confused, really confused, about how Christian salvation operates. Perception becomes reality and the message the culture is hearing is not one of salvation by Jesus; it is a message centered around adherence to a moral code. This is not the call of Jesus, Paul, or the New Testament. Jesus is our Savior, and He is faithful. He does not grow tired or weary, and His patient, understanding nature no one can fathom. Jesus knows how bad our failure is and how stuck in a cycle of sin–effort–sin–effort we are. Jesus doesn't want us to come to him for some help; He wants us to come to him to be completely rescued. The prayer of the Christian is not "Lord help me be free of this thing"; it is "Lord, free me from this thing." The critical thing is an acknowledgment of our inability to save ourselves. This gives rise to a request, through simple Scripture-based prayer, for Jesus to completely take over.

Recently, I was talking to my wife's ninety-three-year-old Nan, who grew up in a place called the Eastern Suburbs of Sydney. The Eastern Suburbs have some of the most beautiful and iconic beaches in the world. Nan was telling me that when she was young and growing up on these beaches, the lifesavers would knock people in the head when they went out to save them. The reason for this is that the lifesaver didn't want the person they were saving to try to help them. If the person they were saving tried to help, it would often result in the lifesaver being knocked off his or her board—and then there were two people in rough waters and more lifesavers would have to go out and clean the situation up.

This is obviously illegal today, but the point is the lifesavers didn't need or want any help from the drowning person; this would just cause more problems. They knocked them out so that they could grab them, save them, and then sort out the bruised head (and ego) on the shore. The same is true of God—except for the punch, of course. God doesn't want our help saving ourselves. More than that, he knows any help from us will actually make the situation worse. Our role is to call on God to save us. He will do it. He has to, because He is faithful.

When it comes to the Christian life, so many feel like they are trying hard to serve God but keep getting knocked down. The problem is that we don't realize the person throwing the punches is us. We keep trying to be faithful, but when this effort is based, even partially, on our own capacity we inadvertently knock ourselves down time and time again.

God is not just faithful; he is faithfulness itself. He is the origin of faithfulness. In the garden of Eden Adam and Eve sinned and fell. Have you even wondered what it is they fell from and into? They didn't fall out of God's love; God is love so God always loves, even when we fail. Adam and Eve fell out of the ability, among other things, to perceive and comprehend God's faithfulness. Adam and Eve separated themselves from God, and from that moment God no longer walked with them; the proximity of humanity to faithfulness was no longer close.

In Jesus God walks with humanity again, deals with the self-inflicted disease that causes separation, and then through the Holy Spirit implants faithfulness in us again. We were once eternal humans who walked *with* God; now we are eternal humans who walk *in* God. God has taken the failure of humanity and not just fixed it—He has poured favor seven times over on the wound. We do not live by summoning faith; we live by dwelling with the faithful one and feeding off the faithfulness this relationship gives us. Or as the Psalmist said, "Dwell in the land, and feed on his faithfulness" (Ps. 37:3, ASV).

It is essential for Christianity to be founded in Jesus Christ's faithfulness at Calvary. We are saved by the faith God takes from His Son's faithfulness. We are filled and empowered by the faithfulness He transplants into our lives. This faithfulness transforms us by renewing our minds. It brings us into our right minds; it centers us in Jesus. Faith does not force belief but enables it to happen. Once belief happens, faith fills us with Jesus's faithfulness, and in this we are reborn. Jesus's faithfulness casts out our failures and enables more belief to happen—belief in a new day, belief in a new way, belief that it is no longer I that live but the Spirit of Christ living in me. We see this process in 1 John 5:4–5:

> . . . because whatever has been born of God conquers the world. This is the victory that has conquered the world: our faith. And who is the one who conquers the world but the one who believes that Jesus is the Son of God?

"Our faith" literally means "the faith of us." The idea here is that faith is offered to all humanity equally, but for reasons known only to God, some chose to activate this faith through belief and obedience.[239] When this happens, faith becomes personalized faith—"the faith of us."[240]

The other idea here is that this personalized faith is made available by the victory of Jesus Christ. The church conquers the world by the

faithfulness of Jesus Christ, by knowing it and showing it. The answer
to our current question, "What the just shall live by?" is simply: Jesus.
The just shall live by Jesus, as He is the source of faithfulness and the
identity of faith. Jesus brings faith to us, which draws us away from the
lust and pride of life, toward a choice to repent and believe in Him.
Once we believe, Jesus sustains us by the power of His own being,
which we know is a being of love. God's eternal being of love comes
to humanity wearing the garment of faithfulness. The point here is that
faith and faithfulness are things God enacts through Jesus. Jesus is the
common denominator to faith and faithfulness.

If we accept Barth's conclusion that long before Jesus came to
earth God had elected His own Son to die and rise for humanity, we
are left with a Jesus-centered salvation. This Jesus-centered salvation
informs the *Pistis Christou* debate with the knowledge that it is the
faith which is Jesus Himself that saves.[241] In Jesus we live and move
and have our being, just as Barth took predestination off man's shoulders and placed it on Christ. I am working here to see the spiritual
substance which saves us: faith, come from Jesus's faithfulness, not
our human willpower. Faith should be seen as a gift, or more specifically, as an act of God in us.[242] It is never something we generate
through effort.[243]

We gain provision for this life from the bank of faithfulness stored
in the body of Jesus Christ. We are bound to Him by the Spirit's law
of life in Christ Jesus, a law that sets us free from the sin and death of
this world by setting our mind on things above.

Faith in His Faithfulness

> Christian faith is not an inactive quality in the heart. If it is
> true faith it will surely take Christ for its object.
>
> Martin Luther, *Commentary on Galatians*, c. 1535[244]

The prayer of the genuine Christian is one of "Lord, increase our faith." Like the disciples, we so often stand by and wonder where the power is. We can blame culture for abandoning Christianity, but the real place to look is at our faith and its ability to be a vessel for God's power. If we have a broken faith-circuit, we must come to understand that faith needs to have an assuring substance; it needs a rational or reliable reason to warrant us trusting it. The assuring element of faith is Jesus's faithfulness. To have faith, we must first comprehend that faith is not unintelligent; it has an identity, which is Jesus's faithfulness. We are to trust that Jesus's faithfulness is the organic intelligence present in faith. By accepting this, we can have confidence that salvation by faith is achieved by trusting in Jesus to accomplish it. We are to have faith in His faithfulness. Jesus is the rationale of faith. He is the "thing" missing from so many Christians' faith-lives.

Somehow we have managed to construct a concept of faith that is separate from Jesus's person. Just as Barth reformed the doctrine of election by centering it in Jesus Christ and not mankind, we must reform faith. Faith is not something humans produce. If we accept that definition of faith, it amounts to salvation including works. Faith is the gift of Jesus's faithfulness at the cross. We are not to have faith, period; we are to have faith in His faithfulness. John Calvin translated Acts 20:21 as "faith toward our Lord Jesus Christ," and 26:18 as Jesus saying the "faith which is in me," concluding "that faith has all its stability in Christ."[245] What has been missing from faith for so many for so long is the object of faith: Jesus.[246]

Mothers of babies talk about object permanence. This is the idea that an object continues to exist even when we don't see it. A small child doesn't know that an object continues to exist when they are not looking at it; this is why they get startled when someone looks away and looks back quickly. As God's children, when we look away from God's Word, prayer, and Christian community we forget Jesus's faithfulness exists—we have an issue with object permanence. Jesus's faithfulness is permanent. If we believe this, we will never look away; and if we never look away, we will believe this.

In summary, the main conclusions for this section are:

1. Faith is not something we manufacture; faith is a gift crafted from Jesus's faithfulness.

2. Faith is not arbitrary. Jesus's faithfulness is the object of faith. Jesus's faithfulness is the thing we have faith from and in.[247]

This section has not been about redefining, reconstructing, or adding to faith. My desire is to inject Jesus back into the church's understanding of faith. If I was explaining this at youth group, I would use the example of social media. My social media pages are an extension of me. I am present in them, and my very being fills them out. Yet, they are separate from me as a living and breathing person. This, to me, is an example of what faith is. Faith is an extension of Jesus and He is present in faith. Jesus fills faith out and makes it capable.

Another example can be seen through marriage. When people accept Jesus's offer to enter into relationship with Him a third thing is formed: the Church, the Bride of Christ. Likewise, when a husband and a wife come together in union before Jesus, a third thing is formed: their marriage. Their marriage is 50% husband and 50% wife; it is a combination of themselves. If they are loving, gentle, and kind, then their marriage will have that aroma. If they are selfish, impatient, and hostile, then their marriage will have that aroma. In a previous section I commented that we can paraphrase Romans 1:17 and say that the saints will live by union.[248] This marriage analogy is an example of what faith is. Faith is the "thing" that comes into existence when God and humans enter into relationship.[249] I am calling it a "thing," as I don't want to slip into the trap of trying to define the indefinable.[250] The point I am making is that faith is linked to relationship with God.[251] To increase our faith, we increase our union, through walking in a consistent and faithful relationship with God.[252]

Jesus Christ Himself, and He alone, makes man a Christian. He Himself is the divine change in this man's life. In this work of His, *He calls for the corresponding and confirming answer of man*. A man becomes a Christian, and is thus freed for that response and summoned to it, on the basis of the initiative of Jesus Christ. Jesus Christ imparts not supreme insights, powers, directions, and tasks, but, Himself, as at once the guarantor, He baptizes him, as only He can with the Holy Spirit. He brings about the change which as a divine change only He can bring about—*the change in which a man, in virtue of God's faithfulness to him, becomes faithful to God in return, and thus becomes a Christian.*

Karl Barth, 1967[253]

10

THOUGHT WARFARE

The Devil . . . the adversary. He's working overtime. He blinds our minds. And I cannot lift that blind. No amount of argument, no amount of debate, no amount of proof, will lift that veil that he's put over your mind. Only the Holy Spirit can do it.

Billy Graham, 1985[254]

Jesus went to the cross and lost all, but instead of this being lasting death, through the power of God it became an access point into the full inheritance of heaven. This act of Jesus is the central truth of Christianity, and its outcome the central promise. We are not called to attain the impossible on our own; we are called to partake in Jesus's actions as if they were our own. The exchange Jesus purchased and offers to humanity makes the impossible possible, the absurd sensible, the leap of faith a walk in faithfulness. Jesus's life becomes a new world we inhabit, one marked by the availability of the impossible. In this framework the definition of impossible is based on your perspective.

To someone who inhabits a world of riches and wealth, paying twenty thousand dollars for a first-class airfare is the norm; it may even be considered a cost-saving measure if they normally charter their own personal jet. To another person who inhabits the middle class, this scenario is impossible to attain to or comprehend. If the middle-class person was offered this situation for a holiday, he or she would call it a miracle. In a similar way, Jesus's life is another world we inhabit; it is a place with a different level of ability and provision. With Jesus, the impossible is not a matter of a miracle happening; it is a process where we mature and live on a higher plane. A more literal translation of Jesus's famous statement: "what is impossible with man is possible with God" is "what is powerless with man is powerful with God." The words "impossible" and "possible" carry the meanings of "powerless" and "powerful."

Ephesians 1:18–20 (ESV, emphasis added) contains the following prayer from the early church:

> . . . having the eyes of your hearts enlightened, that you may know what is the hope to which he has called you, what are the riches of his glorious inheritance in the saints, and *what is the immeasurable greatness of his power toward us who believe, according to the working of his great might that he worked in Christ when he raised him from the dead and seated him at his right hand in the heavenly places.*

The word translated "power" in this prayer comes from the same root word that "impossible" and "possible" come from in Luke 18:27. The root word means a power that has the *ability* to perform.[255] The type of power the New Testament is presenting is a power that has the ability to perform certain actions. In the case of Ephesians, it is the power to raise Jesus to life again—and raise you to life again. God is offering humanity the ability to perform that which we are powerless to do in our natural state.

Mind-virus

> Blind Pharisee! First clean the inside of the cup, so the out-
> side of it may also become clean. (Matt. 23:26)

You cannot physically remove a mind-virus. A mind-virus cannot
be hit, talked to, or medicated; it must be fought with another mind-
weapon. When discussing the New Testament call to *metanoia* (repentance), we found that the call of the New Testament was not to just
change our moral conduct or feel sorrow and pain for our past, which
induces shame-based change. Again, the word *metanoia* is difficult to
translate into English because there is no equivalent word, but the
apostle Paul gave a clear and unambiguous answer to this translation
issue in Romans 12:2: repentance equals a transformation centered
around the renewing of one's mind.

Paul gives a few other phrases that offer insight into how this heavenly mind-weapon works:

> Ephesians 1:18: "I pray the perception of your mind may
> be enlightened" (HCSB); "having the eyes of your hearts
> enlightened" (ESV)
>
> Romans 8:6: "For the mind-set of the flesh is death, but the
> mind-set of the Spirit is life and peace" (HCSB); "For the
> outlook of the flesh is death, but the outlook of the Spirit is
> life and peace" (NET)

In Ephesians 1:18 Paul is praying for the part of us that forms our
identity to be illuminated with a new perspective. If this happens, then
the lens we look at the world through will change, and as a result our
outward behavior will change.

Religion operates only on the surface; it seeks to deal with moral
conduct by offering people a system of behavior management. The
call of Jesus is vastly different. To be religious means to seek salvation

through your own flesh, through self-salvation. The man enveloped in self-salvation never acknowledges that he cannot save himself, and as a result never seeks out the divine ability to perform the impossible. This man never asks the true question, "How may I be saved?" and as a result never obtains the answer.[256] In contrast to this is the man who acknowledges he cannot save himself, and in the poverty of this humiliation finds the "entrance into the eternal kingdom of our Lord and Savior Jesus Christ" (2 Pet. 1:11, ESV).

Thought Weaponry

I personally enjoy science fiction movies. If you are anything like my wife and passionately detest sci-fi, allow me to educate you a little. At its core, science fiction presents the idea of technologically superior races with advanced weapons that they use to project power—hopefully for good. The science fiction writer Arthur C. Clarke famously said, "any sufficiently advanced technology is indistinguishable from magic."[257] I feel there is a lot of value in this statement for theology. Many people in western society think that change based on a belief in Jesus is indistinguishable from myth, fantasy, or magic. Humanity has tried for thousands of years to change itself and never succeeded. The Bible presents a change process that is so "technologically advanced" that humanity at large is unable to perceive its power, and therefore labels it a myth. But as Clarke reminded us, what seems like myth or magic to the eye of mankind can be an advanced way of living from a level of existence beyond our comprehension.

The Bible presents the idea that humanity is infected with a disease called sin, which manifests as a mind-virus. A mind-virus cannot be shot at, blasted away, or even talked to; a mind-virus must be attacked with a mind-weapon. Satan didn't control Adam and Eve in the garden of Eden with a gun or sword; he deceived them with a mind-weapon, and the result was humanity becoming infected with a mind-virus. Jesus comes to humanity to offer a mind-weapon of his own: Himself.

We previously discussed how we are to have faith in the three-fold Word of God, and how the Word of God comes to humanity:

Father God—the revealed Word of God

The Son—the recorded Word of God

Holy Spirit—the preached Word of God

The Word of God is this mind-weapon. The Father is revealed in the Son; the Son is revealed to all generations through the Bible. Through proclaiming the Word of life that is in the Bible, the church operates in the power of the Holy Spirit, revealing Him to each generation.[258]

We have come to understand that in Jesus the eternal being and identity of God is revealed. We have understood that this eternal being of God is one of love and comes to humanity through the loving reconciliation of Jesus. We learned that the form God's loving recon-ciliation takes to humanity is the life of Jesus implanted in us through the Spirit of Jesus living in us: the Holy Spirit. Another key element we covered is that we obtain this life not through self-salvation and adherence to a religious moral code; we obtain this life through the gift of faith given from the storehouse of Jesus Christ's faithfulness. This faithfulness comes as we take on the past of Jesus Christ. Just as we internalize our failures, sin, and shame—and then allow these to become our identity and outwork a reality of continuing failure, sin, and shame—the call of Jesus, Paul, and the New Testament is to inter-nalize the exchange that Jesus offers—death for life, failure for victory, shame for confidence, anxiety for peace. The form the life of Jesus takes in us is a new reality based on Jesus's faithfulness being imprinted over our faithlessness. To walk with Jesus is to place His faithfulness in your past and allow that to become your internal determining principle.

The reason why Scripture talks about a mindset change is that the mind is where our identity is housed. For our outlook or mindset to change, our identity has to change. For this to happen, the prayer of Ephesians 1:18 has to be answered, particularly the request for our inner eyes to become enlightened. This inner eye is the mind's eye, the part of us that perceives who we are. Alongside this, the "mind of the Spirit" in Romans 8:6 is the innermost level of your personal thought—literally, the thought that is in your mind. Jesus, Paul, and the New Testament call for a war to be waged on the inner thoughts of fear and failure that default to sin and disobedience. This happens through the Word of God coming to your innermost level of reasoning and adjusting the lenses through which you see.

In Mark 1:15 Jesus says to "repent and believe in the Gospel." "Gospel" means "good news." Jesus is instructing us to believe in Him and, as a result, change our way of perceiving the world. This is not a call to moral betterment; it is a call to see the great King high and lifted up. It is a call to join Isaiah, Job, and Daniel in seeing the One Supreme of all eternity on the throne eternal, in the temple eternal. It is a call to join the disciples in beholding His glory, and as a result of such a vista have your inner mindset, your internal outlook, rewired. This rewiring causes you to be begotten by faithfulness and filled with the ability to wield the power of heaven on earth.

The early church leader Justin Martyr's account of conversion dates back to a time hard for the modern Christian to imagine. In his account of conversion, in the year 160 AD, Justin Martyr recalled a conversation with an old man who pointed him to the Old Testament Scriptures as they spoke of a man called Jesus Christ. Upon hearing this, Justin said, "a flame was kindled in my mind."[259] You exist in your mind; the innermost thoughts inside your mind form your mindset or outlook, and from this place your outward behavior is constructed. The mind-virus humanity contracted in the garden of Eden was transmitted by deception; it infected our identity, causing us to rebel against God (Col.1:21). The mind-weapon of the New Testament is none other than the original identity that humanity had in Eden—an identity mirroring God as we were made in God's own image (Gen. 1:27).[260] God implants His identity in us through His Spirit and compels us to fan this into flame through saturating our mind with the Word of God and saturating our environments with the preached Word of God. In this the eternal being of God is revealed to us afresh and anew. We become not so much new beings, but rather renewed beings—beings whose minds are reconstructed in the image of God. And once the control tower is won, the body and life follow.[261]

The word *phronéma*, the Greek behind the English word "mindset" in Romans 8:6, has the meaning of our innermost level of opinion or internal beliefs that regulate outward behavior. This word *phronéma* is from a root word *phren,* which is the origin of the English word "diaphragm."[262] *Phren* is an ancient Greek word for the center of one's thoughts, the mind, or in older times, heart. The diaphragm is the muscle in the middle of our body that regulates breathing. Just as the diaphragm regulates our breathing, the mindset regulates our spiritual breathing—recall that both the Hebrew and Greek words for "Spirit" also mean "breath." This mindset is comprised of the inner opinion of ourselves. This inner opinion is formed by the mind's eye, the lens we interpret life through, and it regulates our outward behavior.

To describe this process, I will coin the term "spiritual diaphragm." God implants a new spiritual diaphragm into us at conversion; this gift is the organ that formulates the new identity, reality, and creation in us.[263] If we partner with it, it becomes the primary organ regulating who we are. If we fight it, then we live in the place of frustration where we have two natures pulling us in two directions; Paul discusses this conflicted identity in Romans 7. Just like our breathing functions without us concisely willing it, the point where Christ is fully formed in us is when we operate in this new mindset and outlook without consciously willing it. It is no longer something we desire; it is who we are, which comes from knowing *whose* we are.

A critical step in accessing the full life of Christ is understanding that the enemy attacks our mind because it contains our identity. If he can take hold of this place, we will not even think to fight against it;

we will accept his dominion as the norm. In Jesus the Father purchases a beachhead of reclaimed humanity, and from this place He launches an offensive to take back what the enemy has stolen. Through Jesus's renewal of humanity, the Father draws His children to wholeness. He seeks to implant the restored human identity that Jesus purchased into our lives, and the place he implants it is in our mindset. From this stronghold our entire life is transformed and the spiritual diaphragm takes over, regulating our every moment on earth until we are called home to the kingdom of heaven, the City of God.

God does not fight wars with weapons that ignite an explosive powder in order to project small pieces of metal—He decimates the mind-virus that has destroyed humanity's ability to comprehend that it is a race formed by His love and formed to be in His love. Through the incarnation God forms a mind-weapon, and at Pentecost He fires it into the world. When Jesus says "I will be in you and you will be in me," He is talking about weaponizing His own life in order to redeem a race He loves but owes nothing to. That God would weaponize Himself in order to save me commands the highest level of allegiance.

Therefore Christ having suffered in the flesh, you also arm yourselves with the same mind. (1 Pet. 4:1, ESV)

The Seed

If the mindset is where our identity is housed, then the fruit of the Spirit is the "thing" that is housed. The fruit is the DNA of the new identity that the Word of God, the mind-weapon, forms in us. The Word of God is the seed of a new way of living; once planted it germinates in our mind and grows. The local church, Christian community, personal prayer, and the Scriptures are the growth agents. God will also take the opportunity presented by suffering to fast-track growth. In suffering our life-lens becomes dislodged and we are strangely open to new ways of living. God takes this unique open door to will us toward a mindset and outlook that is centered in Him and His king-dom. In this the weak become strong; hardship that was meant to destroy constructs. The old mindset is torn down and the new mind of Christ springs forth. That which is unpleasant facilitates new growth; it becomes a fertilizing agent. Like all fertilizers it can be unpleasant and even burn, but if applied in the hands of the master gardener, the unpleasant substance releases not burning destruction but the nutrients needed to bring new life to full term.

The fruit of the Spirit is the evidence that the seed of life has taken root. It is the substance that Jesus grows in us. The world will gravitate to the construction of wealth in the form of things. The kingdom of God constructs wealth in the form of a peace-filled life. The gift of God to humanity, a gift that Jesus brought and purchased, is peace. Gabriel tells us that the baby Jesus has come to bring peace:

Glory to God in the highest heaven, and *peace on earth* to people He favors. (Luke 2:14, emphasis added)

After His resurrection, the first thing Jesus says to the combined gathering of His followers was:

Then Jesus came, stood among them, and said to them, "*Peace to you!*" (John 20:19, emphasis added)

This seed is the seed of humanity's purpose. The war of the mind—anxiety, fear, insecurity, inadequacy—is the plague of a modern world that connects socially without building community. God wants us to believe for a purpose and the purpose is completed salvation that equals complete peace.

As a local pastor, I often get the question, "Why is God doing this to me?" Or, "What is the purpose of all this?" The sentiment in these questions is a heartfelt desire to know what God is constructing in us and through us. The thing being constructed is a new life and new way of living. It is the life and lifestyle of the kingdom of heaven, one hallmarked by peace. The world is fixated with obtaining a lifestyle of personal pleasure that produces pain. God is fixated on producing a way of life that produces peace: both personal peace and public peace. This peace is comprised of the fruit of the Spirit of Jesus. The individual fruits are the perceivable elements of Jesus's eternal divine love. To have them grow in us is to have Jesus grow in us. To have Jesus's life grow in us is to transcend time and be anchored behind the veil, in the eternal being of love, in God. This truth, this process, is the one entry point humanity has to the reality that sits behind ours, the kingdom of heaven. To enter it is to experience life on the highest plane, life as it was in Eden. God is calling individuals to life in Him, and humanity as a whole to its destiny.

As noted earlier, Augustine wrote, "two cities have been formed by two loves."[264] The citizens of the City of God are known by their love for God, which often takes the form of self-sacrifice. Likewise, citizens of the Earthly City are known for their love for themselves, which often takes the form of sacrificing others. The motivation for a life of self-sacrifice is an inner mindset change. When Christians and the church are transfixed on Jesus, they become focused on the implantation of this mind-weapon: the seed of life that germinates in individuals and communities, transforming them from people who sacrifice others in order to benefit themselves to people who sacrifice themselves in order to benefit others.

When the fruit of the Spirit hallmarks a church, the church tangibly shows the life of Christ to the community. The remarkable thing the church can offer society is not a religious moral code—it is the characteristics of heaven that are foreign to our race: love, joy, peace, patience, kindness, goodness, faithfulness, gentleness, and self-control. If these qualities are in a church and increasing, they will keep the Christians in it from being useless or unfruitful in the knowledge of our Lord Jesus Christ. The church that lacks these things is blind and shortsighted and has forgotten that they are redeemed and called to a heavenly purpose. They will become concerned with the religious preservation of their rights, not the life of God in men (2 Peter 1:8–9).

> If today's church does not recapture the sacrificial spirit of the early church, it will lose its authenticity, forfeit the loyalty of millions, and be dismissed as an irrelevant social club with no meaning for the twentieth century… Is organized religion too inextricably bound to the status quo to save our nation and the world? Perhaps I must turn my faith to the inner spiritual church, the church within the church, as the true *ekklesia* and the hope of the world. But again I am thankful to God that some noble souls from the ranks of organized religion have broken loose from the paralyzing chains of conformity and joined us as active partners in the struggle for freedom.

Martin Luther King Jr.,
"Letter from Birmingham Jail," 1963[265]

Seed Thought

The Bible uses the language of the fruit of the Spirit, as there is a difference between growing something and making it. I mentioned previously that my wife doesn't know how to make a baby but she can grow one. Likewise, the church is not asked to make Christianity in a society; we are asked to grow it, like fruit on a tree (Matt. 13:31–32). If we try to understand how to make the church, we end up lost in an endless discussion about something we weren't even meant to bother with. The faith life is different; it involves trusting the Lord with all your heart to grow the church. In John 15:2 Jesus said the following:

> Every branch in Me that does not produce fruit He removes, and He prunes every branch that produces fruit so that it will produce more fruit.

The word "produce" here is more literally translated as "bear." The Greek word translated as "bear" or "produce" is *pheró*, which has the meaning of carrying or bringing forth fruit. In this we see the difference between works and grace, faith, and effort. Jesus has not asked us to make something, He has asked us to *grow* something: His church. Making involves works and effort, growing is determined by the quality of the branches resting in the vine. As John Allan Wood once said, "the perfection of the branch is in the vine."[266]

Now how does a branch bear fruit? Not by incessant effort for sunshine and air; not by vain struggles for those vivifying influences which give beauty to the blossom; it simply abides in the vine, in silent and undisturbed union; and the fruit and blossoms appear as of spontaneous growth. . . . How, then, shall a Christian bear fruit? By efforts and struggles to obtain that which is freely given? No, there must be a full concentration of the thoughts and affections on *Christ;* a complete surrender of the whole being to him; a constant looking to him for grace. Christians in whom these dispositions are firmly fixed, go on calmly as the sleeping infant borne in the arms of its mother.

Harriet Beecher Stowe, 1851[267]

11

UNCOMMON CHRISTIANITY

God does not do His great works by large committees. He trains somebody to be quiet enough, and little enough and then He uses him.

Hudson Taylor, 1894[268]

The phrase "uncommon Christianity" is taken from an article written by the long-at-rest North American director of the China Inland Mission, Henry W. Frost, who lifted the phrase from a translation of John 10:10 by leading Bible scholar Dr. Robert Young: "I have come that they might have life, and that they might have it above the common."[269]

We must desire to front the presentation of Christianity to this generation not with a religious moral code, but with Jesus Himself. Adhering to a moral code is one outcome of Christianity, but it is not Christianity itself. It is uncommon for Christianity in the modern world to be hallmarked by Jesus and His life.[270]

To my mind there are two extremes operating in the western world today. One is a message of love that is surface-level only, which produces pleasant statements that have not been evaluated in light of their long-term consequences. The other approach is the lockdown. This is where people, fearful of losing their way of life, define themselves not with their values but with the expression of these values. This forms a religious mindset, one that has forgotten the real truth that sits within. This mindset protects the expression of the truth, as opposed to the truth itself—it is a subtle but huge difference, one that ends up destroying the very thing it has sworn to protect. In between these two extremes is the way of life, the way of Jesus.

As part of the preparation for writing this chapter, I spent a morning watching some recordings of various media organizations discussing the social and political debate that is raging in the modern world. In one recording the commentators were discussing how gatherings in universities across the western world needed hundreds of police officers to ensure that they could take place. A long and in-depth look at the culture wars that are burning across the world is not my goal here, but it is important to note that this is the context in which theology and church ministry is taking place. While committed Christians should be able to draw a distinction between a social or political position and the Christian faith, unfortunately the wider world cannot. "Jesus illiteracy" has swept across the western world, and this means that the vast majority of the unchurched population sees Jesus as a political position, social cause, or religious icon.

Between the end of the Old Testament and the beginning of the New Testament there is four hundred years in which the Bible records nothing;[271] scholars call this the four hundred silent years. It is interesting to observe that during this time God was not inactive; he was preparing the circumstances for the coming expansion of His kingdom in and through Jesus. One thing in particular that was developed in the four hundred silent years was something called the *Pax Romana*. This was a period in which the Roman Empire ruled with little challenge, and as a result of this relative calm there was a number of advancements, particularly in relation to engineering. The most notable of these was that the Romans built the first-ever road system, one that connected the developed world. These roads were extensive, paved, and protected—they are the origin of the saying "all roads lead to Rome." This road system would make the sharing of the Gospel possible. Paul and the other early church evangelists were able to cover vast distances safely on these roads. In the four hundred silent years God was, quite literally, making a straight highway for the message of His Son to be transmitted across the known world (Isaiah 40:3).

To my eye God is exiting a similar perpetration phase, one that has been preparing the world afresh to receive an expansion of His kingdom. The world is immersed in confusion on who Jesus is and what the church is. The world is also immersed in confusion about what truth is in society and what doing good looks like. This state of confusion produces frustration and fear (hence the need for hundreds of police officers to be present just to ensure ideas can be exchanged), but it also produces a hunger for truth itself. This hunger should not be underestimated; it is strong. The challenge the church at large has is to present the clear and full truth of Jesus to this confused but hungry culture. The question is: How does this happen?

Uncommon Message

To answer this question, I want to go to a passage of Scripture presenting a critical juncture in Jesus's life and ministry, John 12:44–50. It is worth noting that John wrote His Gospel long after the other three were penned. John looked at the accounts given in Matthew, Mark, and Luke and felt something needed to be added. John's Gospel begins with the statement that life was in Jesus and that this life was the light of men (1:4). John ends his Gospel by telling us that he has written it so that we may believe and that by believing we may have life through Jesus's name (20:31). In John 12:50 John records Jesus saying that the message the Father has given Him to speak is eternal life. John's Gospel begins, ends, and centers on the idea of life in Jesus. For John, life in and through Jesus is not a key theme—it *is* the theme. John 12:44–50 is Jesus's personal summary of his message and ministry, given after He has entered Jerusalem and just before the Last Supper takes place.

Understanding this passage is critical to grasping the mission, message, and expansive ministry of Jesus. John 12:44–50 has three key movements. I will cover them below.

> Then Jesus cried out, "The one who believes in Me believes not in Me, but in Him who sent Me. And the one who sees Me sees Him who sent Me. I have come as a light into the world, so that everyone who believes in Me would not remain in darkness." (vv. 44–46)

When Jesus says that we see the Father when we see Him, He is not talking about physical sight. Even the disciples who walked with Him couldn't physically see the Father in Jesus. They could see Jesus physically, but they saw the Father metaphorically. We looked above at how Ephesians 1:18 contains the statement "eyes of your heart" and how this statement is not talking about our eyeballs but the mind's eye—the lens we interpret life through.[272] We also looked at how the statement "the mindset" in Romans 8:6 means our innermost level of opinion or internal beliefs that regulate outward behavior. Here Jesus is talking about seeing Himself and His Father with our inner eyes and, through this, having our innermost opinion adjusted. When we see Jesus with our mind's eye our mindset is illuminated, and we no longer walk in darkness. Our days are no longer determined by the darkened desires of this world; our mindset is able to see something new as the light of God has made it possible.[273]

To fully grasp this concept, it is essential to understand how light works in relation to sight. Light comes from the sun and hits various objects; this same light then bounces from those objects to our eyes, allowing us to see them; maybe a better term is "perceive them." Our eyes can be working, the object we desire to view be present, but without light there is nothing to connect us to the object we desire to see. Light is the illuminator and connector. Light is not the object you see; it is the tool that allows you to see.

The same principle is true with our inner eyes. Light comes from the Son and it enables us to perceive and view the Father. This same light also lands on the kingdom of God in our world and enables us to perceive it and see it. The life of God is there, His kingdom is there, and our inner eyes are there, but without the Son's light we are oblivious to it all. John revolves his New Testament writing around the idea that Jesus is the life, light, truth, and way. John can see clearly and as one that sees, he is calling others to the marvelous vista unseen to the human eye but completely visible to the redeemed inner eyes. Jesus's first statement in this passage is one that deals with the illumination of the mind via the inner eyes beholding Jesus and the Father, the very glory of God.

If anyone hears My words and doesn't keep them, I do not judge him; for I did not come to judge the world but to save the world. The one who rejects Me and doesn't accept My sayings has this as his judge. The word I have spoken will judge him on the last day. (vv. 47–48)

If verses 44–46 give the purpose of Jesus's mission, message, and ministry, verses 47–48 give the scope, tone, and boundaries. Jesus is clear here that He has not come to judge—He even says in the following verses that the Father has given Him the command to speak about eternal life (not judgment). Jesus states that His Word is the standard and that the day will come when all will be judged by this standard.

This is an important point to note, as a truth is only received when it is communicated in the correct tone. Tone communicates the motive behind the content. Sharing the message of Jesus in a tone that is judgmental will produce zero reconciliation. This is something the early church understood well, and it is a key point of reformation for the modern-day dialogue between the Christian community and the secular world. Not only are we to love; we are to have the right motive. If our motive is to prove people wrong it will come through in our tone (Phil. 2:14-15).

Jesus is focused on the formation of the life of God in men. To interlace this message and mission with other motives is to leaven the dough and step outside of the boundaries of Jesus's sacrificial ministry, which is our model. Remembering that reconciliation is often described as divine humiliation for human exaltation.[274] In Philippians 2 we are told that Jesus emptied Himself of all that was His in His kingdom. Jesus's citizenship was not recognized in the world of men and instead of judging humanity unworthy to receive His kingdom, He sacrificed His life in order to open the way for us to enter in. Jesus sets a high bar for cultural engagement (1 Cor. 9:19-21).

Christianity has a clear and unambiguous moral code. This passage reminds us that adherence to this moral code is the outcome of the life of Jesus in an individual. To see the morality of a community reflect the Bible, the church must ensure the culture can accurately understand the way change happens. The church must offer people the opportunity to see a higher way of living, one that transforms the body by the renewal of the mind. We must make His message our life.

> For I have not spoken on My own, but the Father Himself who sent Me has given Me a command as to what I should say and what I should speak. I know that His command is eternal life. So the things that I speak, I speak just as the Father has told Me. (vv. 49–50)

The word I want to develop here is "eternal." In the western world the word "eternal" has become associated with the future. This is not the case in Jesus's use of the word in John 12:50. Here, it means God's timeless self-existent life. Earlier on I mentioned that to say something exists is to limit it; if something exists it has a start and finish and it is subject to the world it exists in. [275] God doesn't exist; He just is. God has no beginning and no end; He is eternal. In this way of thinking eternal life is not future life; it is life that sits outside of earthly reality.

Jesus offers His life through the Word of God.[276] When His Word enters you, it enables you to perceive elements and truths outside of your normal ability. When you know the Word of God, when you really know it, it opens eternity for you and delivers provision from outside of our earthly station.[277] Eternal life is life from another place. When it enters us, it enables us to perceive and experience life from a higher plane of living, specifically the life of the Father from the heavenly kingdom (Heb. 9:11). Eternal life is an offer to be caught up into the flow of God's life that operates inside our existence from a source beyond our physical and scientific sight. Eternal life is an alternate power source for our days in this body. It is the life of Jesus dwelling in the life of men. The command of the Father to His Son is to offer this life to humanity through the giving of His life to humanity. This framework is the model for the Christian and church alike. We are to offer life, through sacrificing our own lives.

N. T. Wright wrote that the redeemed Christian is "already in the new age," the "age to come has arrived even though the present age is still rumbling" along—this is the overlap of the ages. For Wright those who are in Christ are given a new status and declared "daytime people"; note these scriptures (emphases added): [278]

1 Thessalonians 5:8: "But since we *belong to the day*, we must be serious and put the armor of faith and love on our chests, and put on a helmet of the hope of salvation."

Colossians 1:13: "He has rescued us from the domain of darkness *and transferred us* into the kingdom of the Son He loves."

Acts 26:18: ". . . to open their eyes so they may turn from *darkness to light* and from the power of Satan to God."

1 Peter 2:9: "But you are a chosen race, a royal priesthood, a holy nation, a people for His possession, so that you may proclaim the praises of the One who called you out of darkness *into His marvelous light.*"

Wright highlights that this new status is the basis for new behavior.[279] Without giving us this new status God is asking for the impossible, with it He is enabling a new "possible." The redeemed Christian must move beyond surface-level attempts to mimic Jesus's behavior. They must allow the process to take place whereby the Spirit of God joins our mind with Christ's, resulting in a shared consciousness of sorts. The redeemed Christian must also move beyond surface-level attempts to change society. Placing Jesus in us changes us. Placing a group of people changed by Jesus in a community, changes a community.

When I first read this passage in John 12, I thought the middle section about not judging was almost misplaced; it seemed like an odd thing to highlight among the other thoughts. However, as I read it more and more, I began to understand that Jesus made these comments among religious leaders, Pharisees and Sadducees who were prone to judgment. In this climate Jesus wanted His followers to be armed with a powerful advantage when seeking to build His church, and the charge to not judge gives them that advantage. When we are not judging others, we are accepting others, loving others, and befriending them. This creates an environment that is supercharged with genuineness and authenticity, the two elements that we discovered earlier are key to winning our modern world.

The other thought here is that judgment almost always involves generalized condemnation of a particular group, way of life, or sin. This judgment is easy, as it doesn't have to deal with the individual person; it bypasses personal contact and makes a blanket statement. Jesus presses His church into personal engagement with individual people. I have found that addressing culturally acceptable sin is best done once relational collateral has been built. Personal conversations in local churches allow for localized and deeply personalized application of Jesus's way of living; public condemnation does not.

The call of God is uncommon. It is uncommon to the secular world and the religious world alike. It transcends both these world-views and presents a mindset of life on earth from the perspective of eternity. Jesus, Peter, Paul, and John, as well as the entire New Testament, present a worldview that is not based in Roman or Judean culture. The worldview of Jesus and the early church is that of the kingdom of heaven. The Apostles had the outlook of heaven implanted in their minds. They transcended space and time in the sense that their minds existed in what modern science would call another dimension. Their minds were caught up into the kingdom of heaven, even while their bodies remained present on earth. The Apostles were aware of earthly cultures and realistic about human circumstances, but they lived this life via the perspective and provision of heaven. Their minds were accessing the new age while their bodies dwelt in the current (old) age.

An example of this is when my friends from the United States leave Australia to fly home. Australia is a day ahead of the US; when my friends leave Australia and arrive home, they leave and arrive on the same day. They dwell in two different continents on the same day. While this is a limited example, the truth remains that one person can exist in two realities on the same day. We are called to have our minds operate in the daytime of the kingdom of heaven while our bodies dwell in the nighttime of this world. The Apostles' key mindset marker was this dual dwelling; it gave them an uncommon existence made up of an uncommon perspective and uncommon provision. It is uncommon in the modern secularized and religious world for someone to rise up and live life on the highest plane, life above the common.

The whole purpose of a reminder is to render itself superfluous. It is my sincere desire that as soon as possible this book will no longer be necessary; indeed, that people will hardly be able to understand why it was necessary to take so much trouble to say what every Christian knows; that the Church, as she proclaims the Name of Christ to the world, will do so with such mighty fervour, clarity, and conviction that she will convince the world.

Emil Brunner, 1927[280]

As a small aside, a key thought is for the church to not get the blood of David on its hands, the blood of war that stopped David from building the temple (1 Chron. 22:7–8; 28:3). With clean hands and a pure heart, the church must be armed and ready with the mind–weapon of heaven—Jesus's redemptive love and life. Just as the missionaries of old like Hudson Taylor fought religious mindsets to bring the Gospel only and not Victorian culture to China, we must fight to stay on message—to stay away from religion and judgment. We must approach our community with the belt and banquet of truth found in Jesus Christ, ready to serve life in Him to a starved culture, His life as bread and nothing else.

"When the church as a whole is no longer seen as speaking to questions that transcend politics, and when it is no longer united by a common faith that transcends politics, then the world sees strong evidence that Nietzsche, Freud, and Marx were right, that religion is really just a cover for people wanting to get their own way in the world."

Dr. Timothy Keller, 2020 [281]

The Immovable Ladder

To my mind, this is the front line for the church of Jesus Christ in the modern western world. To come with clean hands and a pure message to our culture takes great humility and a Spirit-empowered reformation. This is my primary prayer: "Lord change me"—take the beam of religion and tradition out of my eye so that I can help take the splinter of sin from my neighbors' eyes.

In the Old City of Jerusalem, the Church of the Holy Sepulchre sits on the site that is believed by some to be where Jesus was crucified and also placed in the tomb. This church has a long history, with its formation dating back to the time of Emperor Constantine almost 1,700 years ago. The church has been managed by various Christian orders throughout the ages and was even used as a mosque for a time. In 1852 the Ottoman Sultan issued a decree known as the Status Quo, which formalized the joint ownership of the church by six Christian denominations. This agreement is fragile and results in frequent physical altercations. The situation is so tense that two Muslim families have held the keys to the church for the last few centuries to ensure impartiality.

Within this situation there is an iconic monument to Christian religiosity, traditionalism, and disorder, known as the Immovable Ladder. An unknown person placed the ladder on a ledge in the church during the seventeenth century, and so strong is the fear of change that it has remained on the same ledge (outside) for around 250 years. In 1997 a mischievous visitor moved the ladder (probably a youth pastor), but it was found and put back and then protections were added to the window it sits near, to ensure it cannot be moved again.

This ladder is a rather amazing symbol of the power of traditionalism and religiosity in the Christian faith. The fact that such a ladder is held in place by various denominations' unwavering desire to not sacrifice their rights, in the very spot where Jesus is believed to have sacrificed all His rights for us, is the definition of irony.

I wonder what the "immovable ladder" of Christianity is in our generation, and how this metaphorical ladder gets moved. To my mind, the immovable ladders of our generation are the same as those faced by Jesus while He ministered on earth. People of faith have an uncanny ability to become attached to the expression of their faith above the actual faith itself. This forms a religious mindset, one normally comprised of comforting traditions. These traditions are not necessarily bad, but they become problematic when upholding them rivals the central act of faith. In this context they become idols.

The immovable ladders discussed in the above overview of John 12 and at other places in this book can only be dislodged by the power of God. They are in themselves a mind-virus at odds with the Gospel of Jesus Christ. Only one thing in the entire biblical teaching can remove them: prayer. In prayer we find the mechanism for the application of all we have canvassed and learned in this journey. Let us then move on to an overview of prayer.

12

························· ··•◆•·· ·························

LIFE ABOVE THE COMMON

Jesus went to the cross, but instead of this being lasting death, through the power of God it became an access point into the full inheritance of heaven. This act of Jesus is the central truth of Christianity, and its outcome the central promise. Through baptism and communion we remember this; through prayer we partake in it. Prayer is not a ritual or remembrance; it is a resource, one given by Jesus Himself to His church to enable the flow of power. This power is not abstract or mystical; it is the outcome of Jesus's ministry at the cross and tomb, a power given at Pentecost and accessed through prayer.

Jesus calls us to an uncommon life, a life above the common, and the power that enables such a life is prayer. Jesus stood in the midst of one of the most ritually charged societies in existence and taught a form of life and prayer that cut against the grain so hard that they literally crucified Him. Jesus taught life in Him, as opposed to religion. He also taught prayer as a resource, as opposed to ritual, and it caused an upheaval.

One of the main reasons for this is that religious leaders maintain control through maintaining rituals. Rituals are the substance of religion; remove the rituals and the religion is formless. Jesus removed ritualistic prayer, and in doing so He struck a deathblow to religion.[282] Jesus removes ritualistic prayer and replaces it with living prayer. In Jesus's time the purpose of prayer was to boost your social status. Jesus reinstates prayer's correct purpose. He offers prayer to humanity as a resource that draws provision, power, and peace.

The disciples directly asked Jesus how they should pray. The answer to this question is recorded in Matthew 6:9–13 and Luke 11:2–4. The Luke version is a bit shorter, but both prayers have the same basic outline:

- Honoring the name of the Father
- Asking for the coming of His Kingdom
- Request for provision and forgiveness
- Deliverance from temptation and the enemy

I recall having to recite the Lord's prayer at high school assembly, and I distinctly remember thinking that it was boring, old, and irrelevant. We want to rescue this marvelous resource from such a mindset and unlock its redemptive power afresh for our generation.

"Our Father"

In the Lord's Prayer Jesus gives the church an organized and somewhat systematic process for interacting with the full breadth and scope of His Father and the heavenly kingdom. "Our Father," or just "Father" in Luke's version of the prayer, gives the church a framework for understating God's nature and His intentions toward humanity. The word "Father" is placed at the beginning of this prayer for good reason. To understand this word is to place both feet in proper position before God.

Karl Barth culminated his theological life's work with the idea of invocation.[283] For Barth, Christians are to live their entire lives in invocation to "Our Father." Barth defines obedience as obeying God's command to focus always on the one action of invocation.[284] If we invoke our own will, efforts, and power, we seek to save ourselves (Jer. 5:30–31). This is not the vision the New Testament presents. We are to live as dependents of God, invoking His power, will, and kindness for our every need. To do this, we must know the one we are calling to. We must know that "Our Father" is full of fatherly goodness.[285]

Invocation comes from the word "invoke." To invoke something means to call on an authority to act on your behalf. It carries the idea of a higher authority, either a person or an institution that is called upon for help in a particular situation. On one side is a person who is being invoked for help; on the other side is a person who, without the requested intervention, is powerless to see the thing come to pass. Invocation involves enacting God's power into our powerlessness, His provision into our poverty. Invocation is the central activity of the Christian life.

I have sought, in this book, to translate theology into everyday language. With this in mind, I looked for some time to find another word to substitute for "invocation," as I feel it is largely unused and therefore not understood in today's world. Unfortunately, there is no other single modern English word that completely conveys its meaning. The reason for this is that "invocation" has two layers: it describes the action of asking or calling upon God, but also the confidence that you will receive or be able to draw out from God. Remembering that the desire to call and ask is initiated by the Holy Spirit (Pentecost). The source of our confidence is that Christ has taken away that which made us disqualified (the cross). The withdrawal is assured because we are drawing from Jesus "bank" of victory (the resurrection). This all said, the leading candidates for substitution are: asking, calling to, drawing from, and receiving. Within the following section I will use these terms interchangeably alongside "invocation" in order to modernize it.

The Christian life is not meant to be lived in obedience to a moral code; rather, it is a life lived in obedience to the command of God to invoke His provision.[286] The Christian life is a life of receiving from

God through prayer.[287] Barth looked to biblical commands such as Psalm 50:15's "call upon me" as the foundation of the Christian life; he saw the Lord's Prayer as Jesus's central command to call on God. This command is not a sacrament through which we remember like baptism and communion; it is a resource through which we experience. If a Christian lives with a mindset of calling upon God for everything, this Christian lives in absolute obedience to God.[288] To draw from God daily is to experience salvation by grace, as opposed to just studying it and discussing it.

This drawing begins with understanding the words "Our Father." A Christian who calls to God knows God as Father and nothing else. This is why Jesus puts these words at the beginning of His answer on how to pray. If we are speaking about the Father but not to the Father, we have adopted powerless prayer. In essence we are not praying at all, but rather discussing God, just as one discusses a present but lifeless object. Prayer should not be a confession about God, but rather a confession to God. Barth highlighted that "Our Father" is in the vocative case in the Greek; this means that it is a direct address. If I wanted my wife to bring me some tea, I would not talk to her indirectly but directly. I would say "Can I have a cup of tea?" not "I desire a cup of tea from my wife." The indirect clause in the second sentence is misplaced because I am directly addressing my wife.

The same is true for God. We are not to address Him indirectly with unbelieving vague requests; we are to directly address Him with confident petitions.[289] This asking is made before "Our Father," not an impersonal distant deity. We are directly talking to our actual good and kind Father and receiving our rightful inheritance. This inheritance is earned by Jesus and given to us, so much so that it becomes our full legal right. As a result of this status we come without a qualification of how underserving we are; such a practice is to make a mockery of the salvation of Jesus and subject Him to public shame, as it means His salvation was insufficient. The Christian who knows the truth of salvation comes not with self-chastisement, nor with pride, but rather with thankful confidence that he or she can directly withdraw from the Father's account because the Son has made their signature akin to His.[290]

We are called not to adopt a religious perception of God or settle to see God through the lens of our earthly father, no matter if he was good or bad. We are called to view "Our Father" through the lens in which He has chosen to reveal Himself, the name and person of Jesus Christ. In our above dig into John 12:44–46 we learned that to see Jesus is to see the Father. Our Father is seen when we see Jesus, when we pray:

> Our Father in heaven
> Your name be honored as holy
> Your kingdom come
> Your will be done on earth as it is in heaven.

When we pray this, we are not asking for it to happen for the first time; we are asking for it to happen afresh in our time. We are acknowledging that our Father has come in Jesus and that in Jesus His will was done on earth as it is in heaven. We are affirming that the disciples saw this prayer fully fulfilled in the first person and that we desire to continue to see it in the first person through God's direct action in us.

Our Father is seen in Jesus in the sense that Jesus's life and ministry is, as Luther said, "a mirror of the fatherly heart of God."[291] Through Jesus's loving reconciliation we see fatherhood displayed. The revelation that comes through Jesus's life and ministry is the great wonder of our lives, for in Jesus a fatherly goodness is seen and known.[292] This breaks through the propaganda surrounding God and brings into full view not only the fatherly goodness of God, but also that there is no distance between our orphaned self and our Father's fatherly goodness. When Jesus says "pray then like this," He is giving a foundation for relationship with God—a foundation based on receiving the goodness of the Father's heart into the void of humanity's self-built orphanage. Jesus is presenting this framework for approaching God: He is a good Father and we are His dependents.

Receiving from God is best understood in this parent-to-child dynamic.[293] Through speech children relate to their parents. Until they are of sufficient age the parents guess what they desire, but when speech becomes active the child can tell the parents their needs. Prayer is our speech to God. Jesus says, "pray then like this," and in this He says talk and relate to God as a child to a good and giving parent. Relationship, prayer, and communication outside of this dynamic is frozen and dormant. When we comprehend the command to pray to God as a dependent child coming to a good and giving Father, the warmth of His goodness melts all else away and we see the true intention of "Our Father."

"Our Father" is not a dry ritualistic statement; it is the framework for the entire Christian life. "Our Father" is a command to recognize His good fatherly nature and good fatherly provision and an invitation to call to this nature, receiving His provision through the means of living prayer. We choose where we live. We either live in sin, in our own efforts, or in invocation. Choose life; choose invocation.[294]

"Your Name Be Honored as Holy"

The Greek word for "name" is *onoma;* it means the manifestation or revelation of someone's character. As we have discussed previously, the Hebrew concept of the word "name" is inseparable from the person to whom it belongs. It is not a term used to identify someone; it is a term designed to bring out someone's identity.[295] The phrase "be honored as holy" is one Greek word, *hagiazó*; it means to regard something as holy because you understand it is special and set apart from the ordinary.

In the early twentieth century, using Kierkegaard's work, Barth developed a term called the "wholly otherness of God"—again, stay with me! This term is meant to emphasize the fact that God is far beyond the ability of humanity to comprehend. God is completely "other" to what humanity is.[296] Barth added to this idea that Jesus Christ is the bridge, or window; God comes bursting through the frame when we see and know Jesus.[297] Apart from Jesus Christ there is an unbridgeable gap between the ideal and the actual. The only way to realize the ideal is through an actual relationship with Jesus.[298] In Jesus God becomes comprehendible to man and man can relate to God.

I mention this here because the root word for *hagiazó* ("be honored as holy") is *hagios* and carries the idea of something being holy or sacred because it is different, or "other" to the ordinary. The idea of honoring God's name as holy is not only a matter of acknowledging that God is pure and sinless; it is an understanding that God is far beyond our ability to comprehend without Jesus. Understanding this makes the coming of Jesus absolutely essential to spirituality, and centers prayer in Jesus.

In his commentary on Romans, Barth wrote that in Jesus Christ the two worlds meet: the known and the unknown. The known world is the creation we live in; the unknown is the realm of the Father, the place where our creation arose from and where our final redemption will rest in. Barth wrote that the name "Jesus" is the point where the unknown world cuts the known world.[299] Jesus has one foot in the known world with His humanity and one in the unknown with His divinity; Jesus intersects both planes of existence.

Before Jesus the kingdom of God was something people talked about and looked toward but never experienced. Humanity no longer gazes from a deep distance. Through Jesus the morning light of the heavenly kingdom dawns on the horizon, opening the way and truth of this "other" reality, this wholly other way of living.[300] The daytime people from the work of N. T. Wright dwell in the dawn light of the kingdom of God on earth. Daytime people must live in the caution that daytime is difficult to explain, as the nighttime is not a state; it is the absence of another state, daytime. This heavenly dawn is induced upon another when the daytime people bring to bear the light of the heavenly kingdom through the resource of prayer.

This statement "Your name be honored as holy," or the older "hallowed be your name," suffers from great ritualization, resulting in meaning coming upon it that isn't there in the text. Often people will interpret it to be talking solely about God being sinless; they will then add to this the notion that they are not holy and therefore need to revere God in light of their own worthless sinful state. This is not only incorrect, but is completely devoid of any biblical basis. The opening line of the Lord's prayer is not a command to reverence God through a prism of His holiness, making us feel worthless. The command of this statement is to acknowledge that God is eternally good and that this goodness is fully visible in Jesus Christ. To honor God's name as holy is to honor the name of God we know as holy: Jesus Christ.

Jesus presents the founding element of prayer as honoring His name as a revelation of the previously unseen fatherly goodness. We acknowledge that through the phrase "our Father" God presents himself to us as a good and loving parent. We then accept that His coming is seen in Jesus Christ—that in Jesus's life and ministry the fatherly goodness of God is brought forth from the unknown eternal regions into humanity's full view. When prayer begins with an acknowledgement of this truth, prayer ceases to be a human ritual and transforms into calling on this name and receiving from the identity who sits within it. In Jesus we see the first human sitting before the Father in the morning watch, and through this daily habit live a life fully for the Father. Jesus embodies the fatherly goodness of God as His only begotten Son, and He models it as humanity's first Son.

To honor God's name as holy is to honor that He has adopted such a posture to mankind—that He has offered a wellspring of goodness and life and given us unambiguous instructions on how to access such a bounty. His name is holy because it is wholly good, wholly available, and wholly willing. We honor it not through repetitively reciting mere words but by repetitively partaking of His goodness and bearing much fruit. Prayer is not mere speech; it is a living calling on God and active receiving from Him. This is the Christian's highest obedience and easiest command, to "come to Me, all of you who are weary and burdened, and I will give you rest" (Matt. 11:28). Through prayer we receive rest from our restless religion. As the old missionary saying goes: "the work is Mine and Mine alone; Thy work—to rest in Me."[301]

When we pray and then wonder how God can possibly meet our need, we are affirming that the answer to our request is unknown. This answer is unknown because the provision to meet it is unknown; it is unseen to the human eye. We see Jesus, and He sees into the unknown and locks His divine eyes onto the provision coming to meet our need. When we say we trust Him we mean that we trust that He can see that which we cannot, and that His testimony of its approach to us is true. Jesus confirms that our unknown answer is coming, and it will in time manifest in our line of sight.

When we acknowledge and accept God as He reveals Himself to be in the name the Lord Jesus Christ, His name is made Holy among us.[302] His name is made unholy when His identity is distorted.[303] If we come to God with religious pride, we project our image of Him into this name and make in unholy. Likewise, if we come to God in disbelief, we project our impotence onto God and make His name unholy. Further to this process is the truth that the church is responsible to be the bearer of the name of God to humanity at large. When the name of God becomes unholy in society, the first place of examination is the church—is it making the name to be holy or unholy?

"Your Kingdom Come. Your Will Be Done on Earth as It Is in Heaven."

The coming of the kingdom is the coming of goodness to man and man to goodness. It is the coming of the orphans to their Father and the homeless to their home. It is a coming that happens in the beachhead of the mind; it is unseen to the natural eye but fully visible to the inner eyes. This coming cannot be written in the language of men or willed through the preaching of a pastor. It is invoked by prayer.

First, it is invoked by the parental prayer of the concerned Christian for those who will not concern themselves with such matters. God uses the prayer of the evangelistically minded Christian to awaken those who slumber. Once awakened, the child is drawn from darkness into the light. They perceive the coming dawn through their inner eyes, and the praying parental believer is able to explain the new vista as the scales begin to fall. This is the truth of the kingdom of God: that it is always coming. Each day is not a new day; it is day returning. Just as the earth turns toward the sun each day to receive her dawn, humanity turns each day to receive the dawn light of Christ's kingdom. All those who call to this Son-rise receive it. While we engage with this truth through the five senses of bodily existence, we are always speaking about it or around it but never to it. Only through invocation do we call directly to it and then receive it. We receive it through an illumination of our mind to the true nature of our existence; we re-see life as participation in the fatherly goodness of God.

I remember standing on Waikiki Beach in Honolulu and being transfixed by the stunning sunset with countless others from countless nations. To me, this is the picture of the coming of Jesus's kingdom: it is His church obeying the command to bring people to this dawn light and standing with them as its warmth lashes the scales from their eyes—just as the light of the King caused Saul's scales to fall. It is the picture of a great coming and a picture of a great bringing. If we would cease the endless religious debating and simply invoke them to come, the light of heaven's dawn will push into the distance the temptations of the material world.[304] No one who has stood on the shores of Waikiki has wanted to leave.

"Give Us Today Our Daily Bread"

"Give us today our daily bread" is an interesting phrase to understand, as the Greek word translated "daily" is not used in any other place in the New Testament and is not found in classical Greek. Scholars theorize that Jesus coined this word in an effort to explain—through human language—the divine truth of living off the presence of God.[305] The Greek word translated as "daily" is *epiousios*: it more literally means our being or existence receiving what it needs. The Rev. Campbell Morgan offered the following translation: "Give us today the bread we need for our existence." The idea here is that we receive the "bread" we need to exist in the kingdom of God while on earth. The question is, what is this "bread"?

Jesus quotes Deuteronomy 8:3 to the enemy in Matthew 4:4: "Man must not live on bread alone but on every word that comes from the mouth of God." John 1:14 tells us that this word of God is Jesus. Jesus also says in John 6:35, "I am the bread of life" and we learned earlier that the Father and the Son are the persons present in the Holy Spirit. From this we come to the truth that "Jesus," the "bread," the "Word," and the "Spirit" are synonymous. As a result, we can produce the descriptive paraphrase, "Give us throughout today an awareness of the Spirit of Jesus."

We must note that we have the Holy Spirit permanently as a result of salvation. Therefore, this is not a daily coming of the Spirit, but a daily drinking or eating. John 4:14 says "whoever drinks from the water that I will give him will never get thirsty again—ever!" Note that the word "drinks" here is plural. It is not a one-off drink; it is a daily drinking and eating (John 6:35) that passes to us what we need to exist in the kingdom of God while on earth. Consuming the Word of God and prayer each day raises our awareness of our citizenship in the eternal kingdom while physically dwelling on earth.

Second Corinthians 4:6 says, "For God who said, 'Let light shine out of darkness,' has shone in our hearts to give the light of the knowledge of God's glory in the face of Jesus Christ." From this verse we learn that God shines in our hearts. The Greek word translated as "heart" is *kardía;* it does not mean the muscle in our chest but rather the center of our being, the part of us that has the capacity to establish who we are.[306] In our time we have the benefit of modern biological understanding, and as a result we know that this is speaking more directly about our minds. The picture present here is that God lives in us by inhabiting our minds.

The idea of Christ living in us (Gal. 2:20) is often a hard one for humanity to grasp, but it is actually rather simple. My wife is currently pregnant; she quite literally has a physical person inside of her. Likewise, redeemed believers have the presence of Jesus inside them. The difference is that Jesus doesn't place His humanity into our physical body; He deposits His mind into ours (1 Cor. 2:16). A baby inhabits its mother's physical body; Jesus inhabits our mind through implanting His presence in us. James 1:21b says, "humbly receive the implanted word, which is able to save you." The words of Jesus enter our minds, and through this the presence of Jesus is alive in us. This presence comes permanently as a seed of new life at conversion, and then through the process of drinking and eating daily of the Word of God it grows, buds, and blossoms into a full new life.

The bread of our existence is the source of our existence, Jesus. When we come to Him each day (today), we are to call upon Him for power and strength to exist in the world of men as citizens of the celestial city. In Christianity, power is not abstract or random; it is the occupation of our lives by Jesus. Christianity is not a truth you learn, a behavioral code you adopt, or a power you charge through spiritual effort; it is a person you meet: Jesus.

> Our task when learning about Christ is to yield the obedience
> of our mind to what is given . . . in Jesus Christ.
>
> Thomas Torrance, Lectures 1952–1978[307]

"And Forgive Us Our Debts, As We Also Have Forgiven Our Debtors."

The forgiveness of what we owe and the forgiving of what is owed keeps us upright in the new life with God. It reminds us of how we entered and who we entered through. It keeps the disease of sin in the category God keeps it in and avoids worldly attempts to sanitize it, which in turn undermines the sacrifice of Christ and our need of it. The enemy could not keep the Son of God from Calvary, but if he can convince us that we have no debt he can keep *us* from Calvary.

Offence has been industrialized in our time. We are reminded here that forgiving those who have wronged us is an essential part of reconciliation. Forgiving wrongdoing once restitution has been offered is noteworthy, but the call of Christ is to forgive even when the perpetrators remain righteous in their own eyes. This is the way of Jesus. "Father, forgive them, because they do not know what they are doing" (Matt. 5:44; Luke 23:34). This, ironically, is the greatest change agent, as it results in masses flocking to one's character and then cause (Rom. 12:20).

"And Do Not Bring Us into Temptation"

Not bringing us into temptation is a strange one to the child of grace. It is a reminder that without Jesus, the Old Testament justice of God has no other place to land and would come to us. It is a prayer for God to not tempt us, but to rather place this temptation upon His Son as He alone can withstand it (Heb. 4:15). At its core, this request is the inner workings of the Gospel brought to the surface. "Do not bring us into temptation" is a prayer for Jesus to take the cup of Gethsemane, and in doing so be brought into our temptations (Matt. 26:39).

"But Deliver Us from the Evil One"

Why does God allow evil to persist? Part of the eradication of evil is the awareness of evil. Modern culture has an uncanny ability to see evil as good and that which is good as evil. We must reset. We do this by crafting our values from the values of Christ, His cross, and His life.

We need deliverance as we have an unseen but fully felt enemy. He seeks to drag us away from the uncommon life and back into the common. The enemy does not come with fiery acts; he enters the mind to initiate disbelief and from there he runs rife. The shield of faith is wielded when victory is expected. Soren Kierkegaard wrote, "an expectation of the future that expects victory has indeed conquered the future."[308] Kierkegaard employs a tool that Thomas Aquinas developed many years before him, one that undermines the evil one by fortifying the shield of faith. Aquinas taught that in certain situations the outcome of an action can determine its value and credibility, not the means it employs.[309] To the modern world faith seems unintelligent, as it is formless and unseen. For God to ask us to use this means for protection from our enemy seems unreasonable. But Aquinas and Kierkegaard show us that while the substance of faith is unseen, its end products are tangible and visible.

We are delivered from the evil one when we are delivered from a view that faith is ineffective. We must learn to judge faith by the victory it achieves, as opposed to the means it wins the battle by. Faith does not deliver us from the evil one through a standard shield of war. Like two waves that cancel each other out, faith is a living shield that protects by producing a force equal to the arrows of the evil one. Faith is an eternal means used by God in the world of men. It delivers us from the evil one because it is able to match his power. The shield of faith does not deflect the enemy's arrows; it disintegrates them.

It has been said that the end justifies the means; a more fitting statement is that the end *defines* the means. When the means God uses is defined by the outcome it achieves, belief rises and victory is ensured. The enemy enters in and bellows that God is unfaithful, because the journey requires faith. The enemy screams in our mind that the outcome of our stand of faith is uncertain. Faith is needed because there is an unmet need, and it is this unmet need that the enemy highlights.

To combat this we look to Jesus. He was stricken and killed for us. Jesus committed His Spirit to the Father, and the Father faithfully resurrected Him to glory and new life. This act of the Father is the foundation of faith and its outcome the rational of our confidence. At the cross Jesus becomes guarantor for us. Even if we stumble, we count the promise pre-fulfilled. In this the enemy loses his power to question the journey and we are delivered from his deceptive reasoning. As the apostle Paul said,

> if we are faithless, He remains faithful, for He cannot deny Himself. (2 Tim 2:13)

Faith is the substance that assures us. Faith is believing that you will see victory even though the way to victory is unseen. Faith anchors us to the outcome and pulls us in.[310] Faith gives entry into the eternal kingdom and a victory so profound that it brings an end worth struggling for. Aquinas said that anything that lacks intelligence cannot move forward; we must see that there are two intellects acting in our situation: God's intellect, manifested as faith; and the enemy's, manifested as despondency.[311] One of the greatest strongholds the enemy has over the world today is that he has convinced us to determine our actions based of how we feel as opposed to what those actions produce. If we were to act based of what each action would produce, we would never sin, humanity would rarely go to war, promises would bloom to provision much sooner, and the morality of the Bible would be understood instead of undermined. The Bible teaches us to sacrifice momentary pleasure to gain lasting peace. When we make a decision to believe, we are done with allowing our lives to be determined by the enemy's illusionary future.

Gospel faith gives us the capacity we need to stay faithful, obedient, and consistent when we cannot see Jesus active in our circumstances. In doing this, faith ensures that we don't enter into unbelief which produces sin, taking us off the path. Faith motivates us to take decisive daily action in line with God's commands, even when we can't see the evidence of God's promise in our daily circumstances. In this faith becomes the evidence of things unseen; convicting unbelief as a lie, passing down the verdict in our minds that we must continue to obey in the face of circumstantial uncertainty.[312] Through this faith breaks the cycle of failure, and walks us through the uncertain circumstance and into the promise. Faith injects Jesus's faithfulness into circumstances that scream "unfaithful," and in doing so faith enables victory. When everything seems lost, be the one who lets the victory of the cross beckon what you believe.[313]

13

············ •·•·◆·•·• ············

SPIRITUALLY COMPETENT

I'm Going to the Footy[314]

There is an unspoken powerlessness in the Christian community. I remember hearing one of the best Bible preachers in America say that he realized something was very wrong when the same people, week after week, year after year, came down the front each Sunday to unendingly rededicate. These people were not experiencing anything exceptional. They were experiencing the same thing any worldly change-system could give them and wondering where this power Christianity proclaims was.

Is it in the seminary? Let me go there. Is it in strict dedication? Let me try this. Is it in conforming to my local church's dress code, cultural form, and Bible translation? I'll try that. Is it in the new ministry that is down the road? I guess I should go there. Where is it? Oh, it is just Jesus. Well OK, I get that—but where is He? He is in His Word—but that is just a book? No, sorry, let me rephrase that with more theological nuance: it is through the written Word that we come to the living Word—oh, OK, well how do I do that? Through faith—OK, what is faith? It is believing—but faith and believing are the same word in Greek? Oh, then it's through prayer—I pray and nothing happens?

You need to pray in obedience—oh, OK, I'll do that? But nothing remarkable happened? Yes, it did, you just need to believe that it did—but isn't that just works and not grace? I'll get a theologian to come and talk to you—I'm going to the footy. . . .

In John 18:36, Jesus said to Pilate, "My kingdom is not of this world." This statement has inspired much theological thought. Augustine picked this theme up 1,600 years ago and penned a foundational work of Christianity, *The City of God*. Martin Luther picked up this theme with varying metaphors.[315] In Copenhagen in the nineteenth century, Soren Kierkegaard wrote about it; the final major voice was Karl Barth in his *Church Dogmatics*. Kierkegaard and then Barth unpacked Jesus's teaching on the kingdom of God with the idea that Jesus's eternal kingdom and our reality are infinitely different.

The quality of our existence and God's is completely different. In science fiction you hear about strange things like nebulas or gas clouds that are living entities with thought and personalities. While any analogy is limited when describing God's eternal being, this is the kind of imagery Kierkegaard worked toward (Ex. 13:21; 19:9): a God who is completely different in form and thought coming to humanity in Christ.

> "For My thoughts are not your thoughts,
> and your ways are not My ways."
> This is the LORD's declaration.
> "For as heaven is higher than earth,
> so My ways are higher than your ways,
> and My thoughts than your thoughts." (Isa. 55:8–9)

Kierkegaard wrote about three futile ways of bridging this infinite difference. The first was trying to enter into a state of ecstasy through cramming as much pleasure into your life as possible. The second was educating yourself into an ethically and morally superior person. The third was religion. Kierkegaard split religion into two categories.

Category A was the religious life that led you to an awareness of your need for salvation, through making you aware of the infinite (endless) distinction between yourself and God. In this place you become aware that uncontrolled pleasure leads to pain, ethical superiority leads to ethnic cleansing—whether through warfare or ideological enforcement. In this first category of religion you are aware that no human means can save you and that you need to travel an insurmountable gulf to reach the substance of salvation: the kingdom of God. You are stuck in a standoff: the distance of the eternal kingdom is unmovable and absolute, and the permanence of your position in this universe is unchangeable and absolute—"a great chasm has been fixed between us and you" (Luke 16:26). So how do we overcome this distance between us and God? Echoing the woman of Matthew 9:21, if I can just touch Him, I will be made well.

Kierkegaard wrote of the divine assistance that the eternal kingdom sent—about how in the two natures of Jesus's one person, we see the chasm closed, the divide mended, and disappointment appointed an end.[316] Only in Jesus's humanity and divinity dwelling together do the two absolutes break down. The infinite difference between the kingdom of God and the existence of men is reconciled. The contradiction between the kingdom of God and the world of humanity is answered. The distance between the eternal and earth closes, the outcome for us being that the believing Christian is afforded a new organ, sense, way of communicating, experiencing, and knowing "the light of the knowledge of the glory of God in the face of Christ" (2 Cor. 4:6, NET).

The reasoning of a race stuck on one planet in one galaxy and in one universe is never going to be compatible with the ways of a kingdom inhabited by an eternal species. This is where Kierkegaard's second form of religion comes in (Category B). Kierkegaard calls it religion B for ease of argument, but he is not talking about a manmade religion; he is talking about the activity of the Spirit of Jesus—the Holy Spirit. For Kierkegaard, the way to see the powerlessness end is through knowing that you can't end it. While you are filled with the

Spirit, you are not the Spirit. Jesus has two natures that are all His: a human and divine nature. You only have one nature that is yours: your human nature. The divine spirit you have is a gift of Jesus's resurrection and it is, as Martin Luther said, alien to you.[317]

The Christian life is a process of understanding that you are to live by the Holy Spirit, who is the Spirit of Jesus come from the infinitely distinct kingdom of heaven. For Kierkegaard this happens through the New Testament idea of *metanoia* (repentance). The Holy Spirit fills us in our minds and turns on a bunch of dormant perception and communication "systems." These allow us to perceive and receive power from the eternal kingdom in this life. In this we join Jesus, in the sense that we have two natures operating in us, one oriented toward earth and one toward heaven (Rom. 7:15–25). As Augustine said, we live out our lives in this world through the provision that comes from the eternal world.

If Jesus is "the door" of the sheep it seems fitting to ask where this door leads and what it is? 1650 years ago, Cyril from Jerusalem reflected on this, "He is called the Door; but take not the name literally for a thing of wood, but a spiritual, a living Door." Jesus is the living door who opens on earth the way to the primary reality. He suffers from much religionizing and mythologizing. But still He stands, over creation and within our communities, offering to "open" the way "to the Father in heaven."[318]

In Jesus's body two distinct worlds intersect, and through His salvation the same happens in us.[319] When we know the situation we are in, the need we have, and the way the power flows, we experience the radical transformation that only Jesus, through His Spirit, can materialize.[320] In Jesus a unique framework is given for comprehending existence. The contradicting realties of eternity and earth that no religion can reconcile become complementary in Christ, "For there is one God and one mediator between God and humanity, Christ Jesus" (1 Tim. 2:5, Eph. 2:13-18).

The idea that two worlds are reconciled in Jesus is a bedrock principle of theology. When approaching it there is a danger: getting lost in endless conversations with big words and long trains of complicated thought. There is a place for this, but the reality is that a lot of the time the reason theologians get lost in such practices is that they have educated themselves out of faith.[321] They have lost the ability to accept God's word and its teaching by faith and they embark on long, complicated workarounds, trying to find another path to cross this infinitely distinct divide that Jesus bridged.[322] This can be a real problem for the everyday Christian, as you can get compelled by big words, clever reasoning and long answers. But these must be wrestled to the feet of faith. If they support faith then fine, but if not they must be dismissed no matter how clever. I was once lost in this ontological, epistemological, methodological, illogical maze and the words of Dr. Graham shone like a light in the night:

> Is there a lack of power in your life? Perhaps you have neglected the preparation of your life with neglected prayer. We've neglected God's Word and the feeding of our own souls. Whatever it is, confess it, forsake it, repent of it and then walk in the power of the Holy Spirit and gain victory over it.
>
> And may God, today, lift our vision, and may the power of the Gospel break upon our world with fresh force, as we are obedient to Christ's call to repent and believe the Gospel. Repent and believe the Gospel. Hallelujah![323]

Passive Righteousness

> So I warn you, especially those of you who will become teachers and guides of consciences, to . . . bring them from the law to grace, *from active and working righteousness to passive and received righteousness*, from Moses to Christ.
>
> Martin Luther, *Commentary on Galatians*,
> c. 1535 (emphasis added)[324]

In a previous section I introduced the scriptural idea of invocation that both John Calvin and Karl Barth emphasized. When we say we must understand invocation, we mean we must understand that the inner dynamic of prayer involves us asking God's goodness to give. This dynamic is the opposite to religious prayer that operates off the principle of trying to convince God to act. Religious prayer actively begs God; true prayer actively believes God. Religion offers "help" to God; invocation receives help from God. Religion frequently takes; God freely gives. This religious prayer has no understanding of the goodness of God; it tries to prove worthiness to activate a divine transaction.

We are certain that we have understood invocation when we have grasped that God's answers to prayer are not arbitrary; they are based in His Fatherly goodness. When we understand prayer as God's goodness willing us to ask and then freely giving that which is asked in His name, we have grasped invocation.[325] Essential to invocation is the idea that God's Fatherly goodness is what we are invoking, and secondly that this Fatherly goodness gives. It does not need to be convinced or begged to act; it freely gives. We are to see the Christian life as invocation, as asking our good Father to give all we need as we ask in His name.[326]

In Romans 4 Paul presents Abraham as an example of someone who was accepted by God before he learned to meet the physical requirements that religion looks to as evidence for salvation. Abraham was uncircumcised, which under Jewish law meant he was in an unfit physical state for salvation. Abraham was declared acceptable before God before he met the human physical requirements (circumcision). Ritualistic prayer says we must be worthy for God's intervention or answer. Prayer centered in receiving from God says that even if we are immersed in unworthiness, we can call to Jesus's worthiness and receive God's unmerited response to our request.

Soteriology is a fancy theological word that means salvation–system. Soteriology is the process, system, or method that a religion uses to produce or explain redemption. It is this soteriological system that speaks of the quality and credibility of a spiritual faith. Christianity is the only faith in the world today that has a salvation-system based on a free gift of God—that is, in fact, God Himself. Every other faith requires a form of payment; you need to prove your worthiness to a higher power to activate a divine transaction.

We need to step away from the red-hot tone of modern culture wars and look at spiritual matters in the way previous generations did, with thoughtful well-reasoned dialogue. When we do this, we understand that a spiritual faith stands or falls on the quality of its soteriology, its salvation system, not its followers' actions. Followers can and do misrepresent the core truth of any ideology, whether religious or secular. The worth of any faith is in its ability to redeem and then bring someone to the next stage of life, eternity.

The crown jewel of Christianity is Jesus—specifically the exchange of death for life, hopelessness for hope, and despondency for peace. That this is all given along with assurance of eternal life is the beauty of the Christian faith. It is the thing that, respectfully, cements it at the top of the shelf in the cluttered marketplace of world religions. A good coach will tell you to play to your strengths and put aces in their places. As the church, our strength is this salvation centered around the unmerited gift of God in Jesus. No other faith can offer this.

The last living connection to the Apostles was a man by the name of Polycarp. Polycarp was a disciple of the apostle John and appointed bishop of Smyrna by John. According to Irenaeus, who was Polycarp's student, Polycarp lived to a very late age. Polycarp was burned at the stake in Rome for his beliefs, and when asked to recant to save his mortal life, Polycarp uttered these memorable words: "It is unthinkable for me to repent from what is good to turn to what is evil."[327]

The enemy offers so much distraction: religion, nationalism, traditionalism, doctrinal liberalism, doctrinal conservatism, moralism, social programs that do not focus on the Gospel, lusts, worldly wealth, fame, doubt, busyness, and "our rights." Friends, we must join Polycarp and be unmovable in how centered we are on the core Christian message: "That is, in Christ, God was reconciling the world to Himself, not counting their trespasses against them, and He has committed the message of reconciliation to us" (2 Cor. 5:19).

Charles Wesley, John Wesley, and John Bunyan all had a revelation of the grace of Christ while reading Martin Luther's commentaries on Romans and Galatians.[328] On the back of these thoughts the entire Protestant church was born. Can I encourage you to meditate on the following excerpt and ask God to reveal, through His Word, His truth?

> When Paul discusses the biblical doctrine of justification by faith he explains that there are several kinds of "righteousness." First, there is political or civil righteousness—the nation's public laws—which magistrates and lawyers may defend and teach. Second, there is cultural righteousness—the standards of our family and social grouping or class—which parents and schools may teach. Third, there is ethical righteousness—the Ten Commandments and law of God—which the church may teach but only in light of Christian righteousness. *So all these may be received without danger, as long as we attribute to them no power to satisfy for sin, to please God, or to deserve grace. . . .*
>
> Yet there is another righteousness, far above the others, which Paul calls "the righteousness of faith"—Christian righteousness. God [credits] it to us apart from our works—in other words, *it is passive righteousness, as the others are active. For we do nothing for it, and we give nothing for it. We only receive it.* This "passive" righteousness is a mystery that the world cannot understand. Indeed, Christians never completely understand it themselves, and thus do not take advantage of it when they are troubled and tempted. So we have to constantly teach it, repeat it, and work it out in practice. Anyone who does not

understand this righteousness or cherish it in the heart and conscience will continually be buffeted by fears and depression. Nothing gives peace like this passive righteousness.[329]

Never before in the history of humanity have the lives of so many depended on the actions of so few. These few are the uncommon Christians, those who understand the Christian life is not a matter of being competent but of invoking the competence of Christ. May the light of the knowledge of the glory of Christ shine in our hearts (2 Cor. 3:4-6; 4:6). May a generation rise that understands invocation and gives themselves to it.

The night Charles Wesley understood the transition from earned righteousness to passive righteousness, from works to grace, from invoking 'Charles's will' as the change agent to invoking 'Christ's will' as the change agent, he penned these words:

Long my imprisoned spirit lay,
Fast bound in sin and nature's night;
Thine eye diffused a quickening ray,
I woke, the dungeon flamed with light;
My chains fell off, my heart was free,
I rose, went forth, and followed Thee.

No condemnation now I dread;
Jesus, and all in Him, is mine;
Alive in Him, my living Head,
And clothed in righteousness divine,
Bold I approach the eternal throne,
And claim the crown, through Christ my own.

Charles Wesley,
"And Can It Be That I Should Gain," 1738[330]

14

THERE IS NO CONDEMNATION IN CHRIST JESUS . . . BECAUSE OF CHRIST JESUS

Only when the one who condemns us forgive us are we liberated from fear into perfect love.

Thomas Torrance[331]

I opened this book with a small section in the prologue on truth, specifically our modern world's perception of truth. The prevailing idea in the world today is that truth is relative; something is true if you personally believe it to be true. This seems innocent enough, and it does have some value in the sense that we must accept Jesus's teaching so that this external truth which we call the Gospel becomes our personal conviction.

However, when you add in the idea that there is no external absolute truth to believe, you end up in a place that is not so innocent. You end up in a place where your perception, feelings, and mindset is the absolute truth. Each individual person determines his or her own truth, as in values, morals, and actions. This idea rubs with great tension against the remaining civil laws in our modern western societies—laws largely written from the Bible. I mention this here as I want to cover the area of condemnation, and more specifically the unmovable truth that Jesus as God is wrathful (Matt. 13:42; Rev. 20:14). Our modern mindset of self-determined morality and truth doesn't like this at all. In fact, I feel most would agree that this is the single greatest deterrent to walking into a local church.

The primary issue here is that God is loving and is love itself. True pure love is not focused on keeping another in a constant state of pleasure; it is centered on being good. Parents will seek the best for their child even though it means disciplining them and putting up with temper tantrums. Parents have a standard of behavior (an external truth) that they want their child to grow into, and they will guide them toward it, no matter how hard it gets.

The same is true of God—the Bible is actually the origin of this parental mindset. With this in mind we need to come to understand that God's discipline (condemnation, wrath, fear, etc.) is wrapped up in this line of reasoning. God does not randomly "smite" people. He acts to see individuals, community groups, nations, and generations grow into His loving, kind, and healthy way of living.

The word "condemnation" suffers from much sensationalism in our modern world. The biblical word is not personal; it is a simple judicial judgment. If I break the law and speed on my way to church tonight, the police officer is not giving me a ticket out of personal vendetta; it is an automatic response to my breaking of the law. Karl Barth wrote that our sin must be "recognized" so that it can be forgiven.[332] Forgiveness only works when we are assured that someone (God) has looked at the full package of our misconduct and decided to forgive knowing all. Only recognized sin, condemned sin, can become forgotten sin. My point here is that condemnation has a clear purpose. It is not random, and it is not personal; it is parental.

One of the biggest problems with people's understanding of God's condemnation and wrath is that it is devoid of Christ. Earlier on I discussed how Karl Barth centered his doctrine of election and predestination in Jesus Christ. I want to do the same here when it comes to our understanding of condemnation.

In the Bible, the same voice that condemns forgives, Paul discusses this in Romans 8:3: "by sending His own Son in the likeness of sinful man, as an offering for sin. He thus condemned sin in the flesh" (BSB). Jesus is both the God who condemns and the Savior of the condemned. At Calvary the triune God condemns (judges) humanity, absolutely. He pours out all His Old Testament style wrath and condemnation onto Jesus's humanity, and in doing so annuls condemnation. It is not healthy here to say that God's condemnation is less powerful than God's love, because God's condemnation is an element of His love. God's condemnation is the boundary, or enforcement of His healthy, kind, and loving standards.

Any parent who limits the amount of sugar in the face of a mega-meltdown understands this principle. A good parent does not take such action from a place of cruelty, but rather one of experience. God is the same. He knows the universe He created inside and out. He knows what is best for humanity, and when we stray out of what is healthy He enforces a boundary.

Thomas Torrance reminds us that the same God who condemned at Mount Sinai comes and not only forgives but takes His own condemnation upon Himself in order that He can forget.[333] This leads us to the immense truth that the object of God's condemnation is Himself.[334] This is nowhere better seen than in Hebrews 10:26–31:

> For if we deliberately sin after receiving the knowledge of the truth, there no longer remains a sacrifice for sins, but a terrifying expectation of judgment and the fury of a fire about to consume the adversaries. If anyone disregards Moses' law, he dies without mercy, based on the testimony of two or three witnesses. How much worse punishment do you think one will deserve who has trampled on the Son of God, regarded as profane the blood of the covenant by which he was sanctified,

and insulted the Spirit of grace? For we know the One who has said, Vengeance belongs to Me, I will repay, and again, The Lord will judge His people. It is a terrifying thing to fall into the hands of the living God!

This passage reminds us not to turn away from Jesus's sacrifice—specifically back toward the observance of the law, but also to religion, traditions, and any and all idols.[335] Jesus's sacrifice shields humanity from the "terrifying expectation of judgment and the fury of fire." If you refuse to come behind this shield through faith, you face something God never intended you to face. You face that which Christ took, and through your personal choice to refuse Christ's protection you are consumed.

Condemnation only concerns us if we choose to not concern ourselves with Christ. We must take refuge from God in God, hiding our unholiness in the wounds of Christ (Rom. 5:9; 1 Thess. 1:10).[336] Sinai's fury is directed at the divine humanity that hung on the cross. Yahweh condemns Yeshua for you (Isa. 53:6, 10; John 3:16). The New Testament is light on highlighting God's condemnation because it is the story of how God made Himself the object of His own condemnation. Without Christ Christianity is open to the criticism of a God with a confused nature, but at Calvary we see the Lord double down on love.

Hebrews 10:31 reminds us that it is a terrible thing to fall into the hands of the living God. Verse 26 reminds us that Jesus willingly placed Himself into the hands of the living God for us, taking the fury of fire that was destined to consume us as adversaries of God (v. 27). You can see why Jesus asked if the cup of suffering could be taken from Him in Gethsemane; He knew the terrible fury that awaited Him. As you meditate on this truth, it is striking that condemnation does not concern us because God willed that it would concern Himself (Rom. 5:9).[337]

It is interesting to note Paul's words that "no condemnation now exists for those in Christ Jesus" (Rom. 8:1). These words should be taken literally as they exemplify the victory of Jesus Christ. No condemnation exists for those who, through faith, have joined themselves with Jesus's victorious annulment of condemnation. Condemnation is nonexistent because God has met the requirement of openly living outside of His boundaries. If God were to drop the boundary altogether, anarchy would follow; instead, He comes, dies, and in this death kills condemnation itself—"Thanks be to God through Jesus Christ my Lord" indeed (Rom. 7:25)!

God does have wrath and He does condemn, but He makes Himself the object of His own condemnation, and in this turns condemnation from a negative into a positive.[338] What is left and in view in scriptures like Colossians 1:24 is not punishment but coaching. God is looking to coach you into the full inheritance He has for you through Jesus. Like any good-hearted coach, He believes in you and believes in your ability to walk in all His Son has purchased for you. As your eternity-coach He will give you a plan to follow that builds you up through training you in righteousness. This is constructive coaching, never destructive condemning. The Holy Spirit convicts to construct.

That God would come to extinguish the outcome of my rebellion commands me to stand at attention before this universal wonder. In this, the most difficult objection to Christianity becomes its greatest asset.[339]

> He made the One who did not know sin to be sin for us,
> so that we might become the righteousness of God in Him.
> (2 Cor. 5:21)

Why Jesus Had to Die

I remember in my master's program learning about a "theory" outlining how the cross is child abuse. This kind of thinking bypasses any engagement with the actual rationale behind Jesus's dying and simply says that Father God sent His Son to die and that this is wrong—child abuse. While this is an isolated view, it does speak to the level of illiteracy people have with the Bible. It gives us a window into how people have formed judgments on Christianity without engaging its truths.

A large part of this is due to people approaching Christianity with prejudices that they seek to validate in any way possible. That said, another reason for this is the complicated way in which Christian thought is presented to the world at large. There are so many streams of theology: reformed, hyper reformed, orthodox, neo-orthodox, conservative, liberal, denominational, classical, modern, expository, philosophical, theology from above and theology from below . . . the list is almost endless. In this maze, thinkers like Karl Barth emerge somewhat dominant simply because they place Jesus at the center of all their thought, and in doing so give a baseline for understanding Christianity: Jesus Himself.

With this in mind, I want to surface an honest question I have been asked many times, specifically from younger people: Why did Jesus have to die? Why couldn't God just forgive like we are commanded to do and just move on? Why all the blood and violence? As some would say, what's with all the drama? To answer this, I want to look at the end goal and work backward. In this book I have presented the truth that the Christian life is a matter of a loving and reconciling God acting in us through prayer. The idea that God will supernaturally act in us to live His life through us is an astonishing claim. We should ask in a healthy way: How can this be allowed? How is this possible?

In Romans 8:1–13 Paul makes the following statements (emphases added):

> [God] condemned sin in the flesh by sending His own Son in flesh like ours under sin's domain, and as a sin offering, in order that the law's *requirement would be accomplished in us.* (vv. 4–5)

> For the mind-set of the flesh is hostile to God because it does not submit itself to God's law, for it is *unable to do so.* (v. 7)

But if *by the Spirit* you put to death the deeds of the body, you will live (v. 13).

The reason Jesus had to die is seen in Leviticus 17:11: "For the life of a creature is in the blood." Blood carries nutrients around the body; it is the carrier of life. Into Jesus's blood, into His very life, all the consequences for our rebelling was poured (Isa. 53:5). Each drop of His pure divine blood contained countless life molecules, every one taking a sin, every one conquering a sin. Jesus's blood had to be shed because it had to be opened up. It had to become available to take our sin into itself and conquer it completely (1 Pet. 2:24). Without the "law's requirement" being fulfilled in Jesus's blood we would be unable to have His life infused with our life. If this remained the status quo, then there would be no way God could, "by the Spirit," act in us, because God could not enter us.

My wife comes from a medical background and tells me that you can only mix blood types together that match. Jesus is a universal blood donor, but our blood (and the life within) is sin-stained and incompatible with divine eternal blood. To fix this, Jesus gives His blood not only as a transfusion but as a dialysis of sorts. The toxins of our sin are removed, and the life of His love transfused.

In Jesus's death, the impossible requirement needed for God to be able to act in us is fulfilled. Jesus's humanity is the only clean humanity. It is the only humanity capable of conquering the consequence of us breaking God's healthy life boundaries. Father God is able to act in and through Jesus because they are of the same nature. Through the Gospel God can act in us because our humanity and Jesus's humanity are of the same nature (2 Cor 5:21).[340] Paul describes this in Romans 8:16–17: "The Spirit Himself testifies together with our spirit that we are God's children, and if children, also heirs—heirs of God and coheirs with Christ." Through believing in the Gospel we are made one with God through Jesus. Through this oneness God is able to act in Jesus's humanity which is in us (John 14:20; 15:4; 17:22–23).

First John 5:4 (NET) says, "everyone who has been fathered by God conquers the world." The Greek word behind the English "fathered by" is *gennaō*. The NET assigns the phrase "fathered by," and in doing so captures the original meaning. The idea of this fathering in the Greek is that of procreation. No child has any say in their creation; it is something that happens by the will of their parents. We are not the instigators of our relationship with God; we have been fathered by the Father (John 1:13; 3:3). If the genesis of our faith is God's activity in us, it stands to reason that the continual growth of our faith is God's activity in us.

We do not achieve spiritual progress by willpower or self-determination. The Holy Spirit is the way to victory, the truth of how we change, and the life that makes transformation possible.[341] We change "by the Spirit" and we apprehend the Spirit's power through prayer that acknowledges our need and asks God to act in us. Employing any other change mechanism is an exercise in futility.

It is simple faith in the Bible's command to believe in Jesus's sacrifice for you that turns all this on. We must join with Paul in asking God to act in us "by the Spirit." It is God's action in us that saves us initially and saves us daily. To move off this is to cease to be Christian.

> Not by might nor by power, but by my Spirit, says the Lord Almighty. (Zech. 4:6, NIV)

It is appointed to the church of Jesus Christ to rise at this hour, and with it a truth comes forth to the forefront of humanity's consciousness: in Christ, God is reconciling humanity to Himself and has committed to His people this message of reconciling—to stand in it and stand for it, only.

15

····◆◆◆····

AN OPEN ENDING

Living Grace

> Did the Law ever love me? Did the Law ever sacrifice itself
> for me? Did the Law ever die for me? On the contrary, it
> accuses me, it frightens me, it drives me crazy. Somebody else
> saved me from the Law, from sin and death unto eternal life.
> That Somebody is the Son of God, to whom be praise and
> glory forever.
>
> Martin Luther, *Commentary on Galatians*, ca. 1535[342]

The Spirit of Jesus opens our minds, enabling us to see that our lives
and this world is sinful. From this beachhead the Spirit initiates
the questions to which human reason has no answer. The inability of
humanity to quench the thirst of this curiosity orients us upward. This
person, oriented to God and seeing human sinfulness, immediately asks:
How can I be free? The person asking this question has asked one too
many questions for religion. Religion can show you sin, and tell you to
be free, but it cannot tell you how to be free.

In Romans 7:8 (NLT) Paul highlights this: "sin used this command to arouse all kinds of covetous desires within me!" The law (or religion/works) is used by God in the Old Testament to enable mankind to understand sin and its effects, laying the foundation for Jesus Christ to come and abolish sin. The present pastoral issue is that most Christians are trying to gain victory over sin through the means of the law—through keeping regulations, through being better or more moral. The Christian stuck in this place has a problem with the change mechanism they are employing; it is salvation 1.0. They need a software update to come over to salvation 2.0, to graceware, to Jesus.

There is wonderful symbolism for this truth in the life of John Wesley. Wesley was famous for the Holy Club that he started in college. This Holy Club was centered around a desire to obtain complete and lasting holiness. It revolved around a list of twenty-two questions which the attendees asked each other in an effort to reach their goal. This club produced some effective Christian leaders, but what many people forget is that in the eyes of John Wesley, the club's founder, the primary goal of the club was not reached through the twenty-two questions or the club itself. The club became for Wesley what Paul talked about in Romans 7: it became the law which highlights sin but could not conquer it. In fact, Wesley's life and ministry after the Holy Club was hallmarked by defeat, confusion, and depression.

It was later on in life, after returning to England fresh from a failure in the American Colonies, that Wesley met and dialogued with Moravian Christians. Through a series of events Wesley came to a true understanding of salvation by faith through grace, that God can "only be appeased by putting faith in his grace, not by attempts at holiness."[343] In the turmoil leading up to this breakthrough Wesley famously declared, "I went to America, to convert the Indians; but oh! Who shall convert me?"[344] Wesley's experience accurately hits at the heart of modern-day unbelief. He believed "intellectually, but still hoped to become righteous by virtue of his own deeds, lacking the true faith that comes in an instant, bringing rebirth and an utter certainty of salvation."[345]

For Paul and Wesley, the law and our efforts to keep it is the beginning of salvation, in the sense that it highlights sin and creates the question: How can I be saved? However, both Paul and Wesley affirmed that faith in Jesus's grace is the only way to obtain salvation and that, most importantly, it is a free gift of God. The question now is: How is that gift obtained? Wesley gives two points on this—notably less than the twenty-two from the days of the Holy Club:

1. Absolutely renouncing all dependence, in whole or in part, upon my own works or righteousness
2. Continual prayer for this very thing, for the gift of living faith[346]

The nature of this gift is described by Martin Luther in the preface to his commentary on Romans. In it Luther comments, "Faith is a living, unshakable confidence in God's grace; it is so certain, that someone would die a thousand times for it."[347] Faith calls us to share (mirror or mimic) the death and resurrection of Christ so that we can "be completely clean from sin and then to rise bodily with Christ and live forever."[348] Luther then summaries the elements of law, faith, and freedom:

This freedom is, therefore, a spiritual freedom which does not suspend the law, but which supplies what the law demands, namely eagerness and love. These silence the law so that it has no further cause to drive people on and make demands of them. It's as though you owed something to a moneylender and couldn't pay him. You could be rid of him in one of two ways: either he would take nothing from you and would tear up his account book, or a pious man would pay for you and give you what you needed to satisfy your debt. That's exactly how Christ freed us from the law. Therefore, our freedom is not a wild, fleshy freedom that has no obligation to do anything. On the contrary, it is a freedom that does a great deal, indeed everything, yet is free of the law's demands and debts.[349]

Before I conclude this section, I want to make sure I am not misunderstood here. I am not denigrating the Holy Club, its aims, or its structure; I am seeking to put it in its proper place. It is not an end through which we apprehend the fullness of Christ and see His life fully formed in us (Gal. 4:19; Eph. 3:19; 4:13; Jas. 1:4). It is the precursor; it's the "law" element that enables us to see our sin, our need—and critically, that we as humans cannot meet this need. It is essential to reiterate that it is actually the Holy Spirit who brings about this realization through the law. He uses the law (or a holiness club) to elevate our minds and very being to the understanding that we are diseased. Without Him doing this we would carry on terminally ill and never seek treatment. Law and religion can only bring us so far. This is the thrust behind the apostle's words: "What a wretched man I am! Who will rescue me from this dying body? I thank God through Jesus Christ our Lord!" (Rom. 7:24–25).[350]

In this process we become aware that a strange but yet familiar gaze has been fixed upon us, one coming forth form a "totally other" reality.[351] The eternal realm which sits on the frontier of our time comes to us in Jesus Christ and calls us home. The Spirit of Jesus comes to us in the Holy Spirit and carries with Him the fulness of Yahweh. The Triune God illuminates us to understand that we are sick. The Holy Spirit joins us with Paul in Romans 7:24 and initiates a disdain for our current condition. The Spirit then leads us to Himself—to the truth that He is the eternal frontier brought near, that He is the reality that lies beyond our time brought into our mind. Through this knowledge we are linked with our primal origin and are confronted by the absolute: an absolute truth that Jesus is God, and that through Him we experience the firstfruits of our true eternal home.[352] Through the ministry of the Holy Spirit we become aware of the roaring of heaven, a rushing mighty wind which fills all the house (Acts 2:2). We see the Holy City, the New Jerusalem, coming down from God out of heaven (Rev. 21:2) and know that we are in Christ[353]—in His reality, in His being, observing creation, life, and existence from His perspective.

We do not grasp this through our intellect, but through what the Bible calls our *kardia*: the center of our being, which houses our core identity (translated as "mind" or "heart" in the English Bible). Friend, never fall into the trap that John Wesley, Sean Nolan, and many others have fallen into: the trap of trying to see the eternal God through the eyes of human reason. Human reasoning is not capable of comprehending something that operates so far beyond our level of understanding. It is not through reason, intellect, academia, religion, or obligatory service that we see. It is through a request to God in prayer, one based on the merit of His Son Jesus Christ, that we ask Him to make us see—see, in the center of our being, that we are in Christ. Faith is living union, and it is this union that enables us to see the living grace flowing from the redemption of 2 Corinthians 5:19. This redemption grasps and holds all the knowledge in this vast universe, making it subservient to the love of God reconciling us in Christ.[354] The fulness of the universe is quantified in this union.[355] Those who commune with the eternal Spirit of God look behind the curtain of creation and touch eternity.

The Cross of Christ Held

In every devastation in all the ages of humanity Christians have cried out in prayer and the cross of Christ has held. Through the Confessing Church in the concentration camps and the chaplains of the great wars, the cross of Christ held. Through the youth leaders who walked into the aftermath of school atrocities and the pastors who walked people through divorce, disease, and every type of ruin, the cross of Christ held. In the hearts of local Christians who met the devastation of natural disasters in their communities head-on, and the faithful efforts of missionaries who have traversed faraway shores in a sojourning effort to mend broken lives, the cross of Christ held. Through the diligence of believing business and political leaders and the studious care of mothers to children they choose to make their own, the cross of Christ held. In every situation, no matter what the enemy has thrown at the children of Jesus's life and light, the cross of Christ has held.

Many ideologies come and go, and many movements sweep across the world, but there is only one truth that has stood knee-deep in the hardship of every situation in human existence and held true. Religion is too often complicit in inflicting pain on mankind, but the truth of Jesus living in and through us—this way, this truth, this life—has never fallen short and never failed to bind the wounds of humanity. The life of Jesus that comes from the cross of Christ has met every hardship, every pain-inflicting ideology, and held.

My friend, whatever you are personally passing through, your family is walking through, and your community and culture is experiencing, whatever it is that troubles you, know that you have the only power in the chronicles of human history that has confronted every situation of suffering that has ever materialized on this Earth and prevailed. The cross of Christ held true in the personal lives of those mentioned above, transforming their families and communities from places ravaged by pain into places that grew His glory.[356] The life of Jesus in the lives of believers matched and overcame the destructive power of genocides, wars, and untold hardships. The darkest hours of humanity have never overwhelmed the cross and have not succeed to beat back the life of Jesus in the lives of believers. The cross of Christ held, and it still holds today; it stands as a radiant beacon of light, broadcasting the offer of life in Jesus to all and into all.

Remember, my friend, you do not stand alone. The Christian faith that we have today is a cumulative one. It is the product of generations of faithfulness from millions of believers. Long before we were born, believers were standing on the truth of Jesus, developing humanity's understanding of the message of life in and through Christ. Hundreds of millions of believers have explored the life of Jesus and experienced the provision of heaven on earth. It is emboldening to remember that when you draw on God's promises, you are not the first to do so; the very promise you grasp and hope in has been proven true by millions who have gone before. We live only in our time, but the message of Christ does not. It preceded us, and it will tarry long after we enter the Celestial City.

Heaven looks and asks if there is still faith on earth. Heaven is not concerned with the ways of the world or the flurry of religion. You may be unknown in the earth, but you are playing out your life before a far bigger theatre. All of heaven looks with fixed gaze at those who would take up the life of Jesus, and through faith build it into their generation. You are the object of heaven's gaze. Take courage that the truth you hold to has held countless others and never faltered.

The Way

Christianity is not a religion. It was known by its first followers simply as The Way. In John 14:6 Jesus says "I am the way, the truth, and the life. No one comes to the Father except through Me." The Greek word translated as "way" means, road, journey, a travelled way or path. A road or path directs us through the maze of a city and enables transportation. Jesus is the path who directs us through the maze of this life and transports us into the eternal kingdom.

I will borrow a cultural reference from my childhood and say that Jesus is the yellow brick road—one that leads from the far country, through the desolate places, and delivers us to the Celestial City. The Bible uses the language of walking in the Spirit and walking with God; this all points not toward rules to be obeyed but a path to be followed. Remember that the Holy Spirit and the Word of God are our guides; they are the Glindas in this story, directing us to ensure we are delivered correctly to our destination.

It is interesting to remember the wider context in which we live and serve God, that being the war between good and evil, between God's sacrificial heart and Satan's self-promotion. Satan's is identified with the number 666; this is as close as possible to God's number of 7. [357] Satan's greatest tool is deception; he deceives by presenting something extremely close to the truth. One with an untrained or inexperienced eye could even say it is identical, but as you look closer you realize small, subtle deficiencies that equate to a complete counterfeit. Satan's goal is not necessarily to get you to worship him; it is to get you to not worship Jesus. I imagine he would like us to worship him—we see this in his exchange with Jesus in the wilderness—but he will very happily settle for us just not worshiping Jesus.

In this way, you can frame the entire Christian journey in the context of a battle for the worship of humanity. We either give our attention to The Way, the world's way, or religion. Remember that religion comes from unwillingness to accept that we cannot do anything to save ourselves. When we won't accept this, we create religion in order to fulfil our prideful desire to save ourselves. Apart from the world's way and religion is the way to truth and life, through following the Holy Spirit and the Word of God along the pathway of Jesus's life—a path that leads to the cross, out of the tomb, through Pentecost, and then toward the place of final ascension into the eternal kingdom.

I hesitate to say this, as it is a very bold statement, but I am concerned that Satan is the architect of religion (while mankind is the architect of the rebellious life). It is his close counterfeit for the way to truth and life through Jesus—this is seen in Matthew and Luke 4 where Satan uses Scripture to produce a counterfeit version of the message of God, which is what religion does.[358] Religion presents another vehicle other than faith in Jesus and in this achieves Satan's goal of sidelining the Son of God. Religion doesn't require faith in Jesus, as it has the works and rituals of the human hand that provide a tangible and practical way of "salvation." Satan scoffs at faith in Jesus for two reasons: 1) he doesn't see its object, Jesus, as being worthy of worship; 2) he knows it is effective at exposing his counterfeit and delivering us completely home.

Romans 12:1–2 teaches us that sacrifice is the proof of genuine worship. Satan's prideful desire to be worshiped made him unwilling to sacrifice and unable to worship God with authenticity. From this pride came the deceiver who is the architect of deception (Rev. 12:9; 20:3). And to my mind, the greatest deception attacking life in Jesus is not rebellious living; it is religion—rebellion is indifferent. Under this model religion has pride as its foundation and is hallmarked by unwillingness to sacrifice and inauthentic worship.

Again, I say this reservedly, but this sounds very close to the way some in the western church choose to engage with the culture. There is a loud movement of people who are very willing to exert their rights but unwilling to sacrifice. The Bible talks more about taking personal sacrificial responsibility than exerting prideful religious rights.[359] Pride-motivated religious actions are the antithesis to our sacrificial Savior.

I pray that as you have read through this book you have grasped the Bible's view of how valuable and amazingly unique you are. Calling out religion is not about devaluing or attacking anyone; it is about placing Jesus in the proper place as Savior and us as the objects of His saving love. We must stand on the same truth that all who have fought their generation's manifestation of this issue looked to: the sacrificial message of life in and through Jesus, the truth of loving reconciliation at Calvary. If the enemy can get you to believe that you need to help Jesus along by religious effort, he has won in two ways. He has diminished Jesus's Lordship, and He has positioned you in a powerless spiral of self-salvation.

The Exchanged Life

In John 5:39–40 Jesus said, "You pore over the Scriptures because you think you have eternal life in them, yet they testify about Me. And you are not willing to come to Me so that you may have life." If you have read a book like this, I am assuming you already know to come out of the world. The time has now come to opt out of saving yourself and to come to the Way of life in and through Jesus.

In 1961 Raymond Edman, then president of Wheaton College and mentor to Billy Graham, published *They Found the Secret,* a collection of short stories of Christian men and women, pastors, laymen, and missionaries alike who had experienced the "exchanged life." Edman talks about this as a secret, which can give the idea that it is some sort of secondary knowledge over and above salvation. This has led to some teaching about a second blessing after conversion, and others shunning any mention of an exchanged life out of fear of undermining the sufficiency of Jesus's sacrifice at the cross.

The secret of Edman's book is not a secret due to secrecy. The "secret" that these twenty lives in the book point to is none other than Jesus Himself. Just like in our generation, in all the generations covered in this book Christianity had lost Jesus Himself. People had Jesus as a religious figurehead, Jesus the moral policeman, Jesus the social engineer, and Jesus the institutional patriarch, but had lost Jesus Himself. In this Jesus became a secret to those who knew Him. The people chronicled in the book were often marginalized as they bypassed religion, traditions, and culture to present the pure risen-in-their-hearts Jesus. In his introduction Edman made the following comment: "What is the exchanged life? Really, it is not something; it is some One. It is the indwelling of the Lord Jesus Christ made real and rewarding by the Holy Spirit."[360]

Earlier on in this book I quoted Karl Barth, who said, "[Jesus'] own are required only to abide in His love."[361] Second John 6 says, "this is love: that we walk according to His commands. This is the command as you have heard it from the beginning: you must walk in love." We must not get turned around here. We are told that we abide when we obey Jesus's commands. The call to abide through obeying is not a call to regulation Christianity; it is a call to relational Christianity. The highest command is to walk in love through walking with Him—for He is love. This walk is best described as a relationship, and the substance of this relationship is a conversation centered on asking Him to build His life in us. We abide through the mechanism God has put in place, which is Jesus's exchange for us. The beginning of abiding is not obeying a moral standard; it is obeying a prayer process.

This prayer process is best seen as asking the Father to ensure that the new spiritual will implanted at conversion conquers the old will of fallen flesh. Our active part is not accomplishing the act of obedience itself but obediently drawing on God through prayer to act in us. Through this prayer process Christ who is planted in us blooms in us and we realize the substance of the apostle Paul's declaration, "Thanks be to God through Jesus Christ our Lord!" (Rom. 7:25, ESV). We are to take responsibility for our lives by availing ourselves of loving reconciliation through prayer.[362] When we come to meet Jesus something unexplainable happens, all of life's values are changed.[363]

The enemy's strategy is to paralyze us with a fear that God's exchanging grace is a falsified claim. We must harness this fear and anxiety, turning it from an enemy to an ally. We do this by allowing it to drive us to this exchange with God, so that we can be shocked but not surprised by the validity of His promise.

Tabgha

> I will place My Spirit within you *and cause you* to follow My statutes…But the Lord is faithful; *He will* strengthen and guard you from the evil one…Now *to Him who is able* to protect you from stumbling and to make you stand in the presence of His glory, blameless and with great joy…Who gave Himself for our sins *to rescue us* from this present evil age, according to *the will of our God* and Father. (Eze. 36:27, 2 Thess. 3:3, Jude 1:24, Gal. 1:4, emphasis added)

The Bible records the apostle Peter sitting before two charcoal fires in the New Testament. The first is a fire of failure in John 18:18, where Peter denied Jesus. Peter had made big religious promises, but when the moment came, he had no power to fulfill them, resulting in denial and failure. The second, in John 21, is the fire of reconciliation or exchange at the beach of Tabgha on the sea of Galilee.[364] Peter comes in humility, driven to the redemption of the second fire by his failure at the first. Through the exchange of John 21:15–19 and the events of Pentecost, Peter realizes that it is not His religious efforts that produce holiness and effective missional living, it is Jesus alive in Him. Peter realizes that living in constant awareness of Jesus's presence in his very being is the way to truth and life (1 Peter 2:4–5). From this foundation the Christian faith begins, in Peter's heart and the hearts of his company (John 15:4).

Jesus's response to failure is to use the experience to get us to enter into the fullness of His finished work. In Ephesians 3:19 (NIV) Paul prays that we would know the "love that surpasses knowledge—that you may be filled to the measure of all the fullness of God." Paul reiterates this in Ephesians 4:13 (NIV), saying we are to "become mature attaining to the whole measure of the fullness of Christ." We find this again in Galatians 4:19 (NIV), where Paul says, "I am again in the pains of childbirth until Christ is formed in you." The exchange Jesus offered Peter at Tabgha was to enter into the fullness of His finished work. At Tabgha God offers all an exchange. From this beach Jesus, through His Holy Spirit, cries out: come to Tabgha, all you who are weary and heavy laden, and I will give you rest.

Peter is the first to exchange his religion for life in Jesus's name. Peter experiences the truth that it is the gift which is Jesus Himself which saves and keeps us buoyant in the Christian life (Gal. 5:5). To obtain Jesus by faith and then remain perpetually aware of His presence with you is Christianity. To have Christ fully formed in you is to attain the full measure of God's love and to know complete salvation.

It is essential here that we describe this process correctly. It is not a secondary blessing that Jesus offers Peter, and it is not an experience possible without the Holy Spirit. It is a Spirit-empowered full blooming of the seed of Jesus's life that was planted at conversion. Through faith-fueled submission the Holy Spirit can fully occupy us, eradicate all desire for sin, and form a desire for kingdom-oriented living.

Tabgha tarries. From this place each and every morning Jesus offers an exchange to all who would bend their will and pride to the truth of Him living in and through them. I mention pride because Jesus's view of humanity is that we simply cannot partake in the "divine nature" (2 Pet. 1:4). We cannot live the Christian life, nor be moral and righteous, on our own. The only way to do these things is to let Jesus do it through us. Each day, each moment, Tabgha tarries and offers you and me an instant exchange. This exchange begins with prayer that draw's God's power into our powerless situation. We are to join the defeated David when he says:

> Create for me a pure heart, O God!
> Renew a resolute spirit within me!
> Do not reject me!
> Do not take your Holy Spirit away from me!
> Let me again experience the joy of your deliverance!
> Sustain me by giving me the desire to obey. (Ps. 51:10–12, NET)

Here the heart is seen as the seat of the psalmist's motives and moral character. The resolute spirit is a request for God to take his corrupted heart and replace it with a reliable spirit in his inner being, in the seat of his moral character. The request for a desire to obey is David acknowledging that he cannot obey via the mechanism of his human will; he needs God to transplant a new will into his heart, one that willingly obeys the divine way.[365]

Little did David know how seriously God would take this prayer. In sending Jesus into our hearts God the Father implants a new will into the inner being of humanity. Jesus comes with a "superior" way of ministering to us, which is "legally enacted on better promises" (Heb. 8:6). The glory of the old covenant is surpassed by a "much greater" way; a "better covenant" that "brings righteousness" internally through the Spirit, not externally on stone (2 Cor. 3:6–11, NIV).[366]

The book of Hebrews calls this the "new covenant" and describes it, saying: "By this will of God, we have been sanctified through the offering of the body of Jesus Christ once and for all. . . . This is the covenant I will make with them after those days, says the Lord: *I will put* My laws on their hearts and write them on their minds" (Heb. 9:15; 10:10, 16, emphasis added).[367] We as His children are not to live the Christian life by the power of our will.[368] We are to give back the very thing humanity took possession of in Eden. We are to surrender our will in the pattern of our Savior, saying "not my will but yours be done."[369] We surrender our will through repentance, and we ask (invoke) God to make the will of Christ the rule of our lives, trusting Jesus for current power to subdue all inward corruption.[370] Through this God's utterly alien righteousness breaks down our sin and enables us to will what He wills (Phil. 2:13).[371] The prayer of those who have comprehended grace is not, "Lord, I make your will my desire," but "Lord, make your will my desire."[372]

I have entitled this chapter "An Open Ending," as I do not wish to neatly wrap up everything I have written into a new systemized way of approaching the Christian life. My desire is to present Jesus Himself. I pray that all would make their way to Tabgha—to sit with Jesus and have breakfast, daily. My goal is to get you to that beach, to sit with Him, before Him, letting His love consume you and compel you out of darkness, fear, failure, and unbelief. If Christ is lifted up, He will draw all mankind to Himself (John 12:35). May Jesus be lifted up in the morning watch, and may you experience hope as it should be, never thirsting again. My friend Tabgha truly tarries: "Come and have breakfast" (John 21:12).[373]

I see a great coming and then a great bringing. Come to Him. Just come.[374]

AFTERWORD

Christ, apprehended by faith and dwelling in the heart, constitutes Christian righteousness, for which God gives eternal life.

> Martin Luther, *Commentary on Galatians*, c. 1535[375]

Kardia

But everything that was a gain to me, I have considered to be a loss because of Christ. More than that, I also consider everything to be a loss in view of the surpassing value of knowing Christ Jesus my Lord. Because of him I have suffered the loss of all things and consider them as dung, so that I may gain Christ and be found in him, *not having a righteousness of my own from the law, but one that is through faith in Christ*—the righteousness from God based on faith. My goal is to know him and the power of his resurrection and the fellowship of his sufferings, being conformed to his death, assuming that I will somehow reach the resurrection from among the dead.

Not that I have already obtained all this, or have already arrived at my goal, but I press on to *take hold of that for which Christ Jesus took hold of me*. Brothers and sisters, I do not consider myself yet to have *taken hold* of it. But one thing I do: Forgetting what is behind and straining toward what is ahead, I press on toward the goal to win the prize for which God has called me heavenward in Christ Jesus. All of us, then, *who are mature should take such a view of things.* And if on some point you think differently, that too God will make clear to you. (Philippians 3:7–15, CSB, emphasis added)

As previously mentioned, I do not want to wrap up everything I have written into a new system through which to live the Christian life. That said, I do not want to swing too far the other way and not give summary to my thoughts. Instead of presenting a list of bullet points, I want to outline what I would call the *kardia* of my thoughts—*kardia* being the New Testament word for the heart or inner part.

Salvation is a work of God in us, which we respond to.[376] In his commentary on the book of Romans Martin Luther discussed how God saves us through His righteousness, which Luther called external and foreign, utterly alien to us.[377] For Luther "the righteousness of God is the cause of salvation"—we are not capable of saving ourselves; rather, "we are made righteous by Him."[378] Luther quotes Augustine, who says that God imparts His righteousness in order to make men righteous.[379] In another of his works Luther comments, "faith is a work of God in us."[380]

The Gospel and faith can be presented as a one-off event, and I believe that this is the source of much defeat. We do not transition from receiving salvation through faith to then living the Christian life through another means. The entire Christian life is lived in the same power as our initial salvation. The Christian life for Luther is one lived in the Gospel by faith. The problem for modern Christians is that we have come to see the Gospel as a one-off event. Luther did not see it this way.

It is true that the initial salvation the Gospel achieves is a one-off event, in the sense that we are saved for eternity at the moment of conversion; the common way of understanding this is the saying "once saved, always saved." The Gospel begins with our eternal salvation at the moment of conversion but it does not end there. The Gospel saves us eternally and then works backward until our daily "now" life is changed.[381] At the heart of you finding peace with God is you understanding that this peace comes through the Gospel.

Christian salvation is not achieved through daily effort in the form of Bible reading, prayer, and church attendance. Salvation, rest, and inner peace come about through the Gospel, through the good news of God's activity in us. As Paul says in Ephesians 2:8, "you are saved by grace through faith, and this is not from yourselves; it is God's gift."

The Bible also makes it clear that we are not to be passive in our spiritual life. The balance between God doing all the work and us not being passive has been the source of much confusion and many books over the two-thousand-year history of the church. Karl Barth, like many others, stood with fixed gaze at this doctrinal tussle. The Catholic Church answered it by developing salvation by faith and works, but in this they swung too far one way. Others have solved it by developing a form of salvation that is devoid of personal responsibility, and in this they swung too far the other way.

I previously covered Barth's writing on the concept of invocation, and it is this concept that solves this critical problem and does so in a balanced, biblical, way. Barth highlights that John Calvin, in his work *Institutes of the Christian Religion*, begins his section on prayer by calling invocation the "chief exercise of faith by which we daily receive God's benefits,"[382] and that "our only safety is in calling upon his name."[383] Barth himself stated, "prayer is the most intimate and effective form of human action. . . . When the Christian wishes to act obediently, what else can he do but that which he does in prayer."[384] Prayer is "the renewing and inward empowering of the Christian . . . the true and proper work of the Christian."[385]

We understand that the one thing among the many that the God who has reconciled the world to Himself in Christ requires is for man to call upon Him, through praise and petition, which is the lifeblood of invocation.[386] "God commands this action, and in performing it man does what is right and good before God."[387] God's grace empowers man for it and obligates man to it. In this it is not solely our action but of God's design, from His power and at His initiation. It is a fully set table, the call to come and the gift of a choice to choose to eat (Luke 14:23).

It is through invocation that we receive salvation, peace, and rest through prayer. Invocation is not work; it is the tool by which we receive the work already performed for us. It is not a battle to be won but a victory to experience. Obedience is obeying God's command to focus exclusively on the one action of invocation.[388] Romans 8:13 says, "But if by the Spirit you put to death the deeds of the body, you will live." Understanding that invocation is the tool Jesus gave us to receive, I am comfortable interpreting Romans 8:13 to say: if by the Spirit's tool of invocation you put to death the deeds of the body, you will live.

Many years ago, Hudson Taylor, the founder of the China Inland Mission, asked in honest frustration: How do we get the vine to give us its sap, its life, and its goodness?[389] Hudson verbalized the tussle between the promise of peace, rest, and freedom and the actual experience of it. For God's promise of peace and rest to be valid it must be experienced. The reason so many people don't experience complete peace and rest is not the promise itself—it is the way in which we seek to partake of it.

Paul laments this problem in Galatians 3:1 where he asks who has bewitched the Galatian church. The word translated "bewitched" in the English Bible means to exercise evil power over someone. If Satan can dislodge you off prayer into works or wandering, he has won. If he can convince you invocation doesn't work, he will shift you to religion—your own efforts. In the great wars the generals would seek out intelligence; if they could know where the enemy was going to attack, they would concentrate their forces and obliterate their rival.

Satan is not going to attack Calvary—that is futility for him. He knows he has lost. Instead, he attacks our capacity to partake in Calvary's bounty. He attacks our prayer life—the way of invoking the direct personal presence of God into our lives. The enemy's endgame is to get us to move off invocation, to distract you from receiving provision through prayer by convincing you it doesn't work. If you believe this, the enemy has you fixed on religion and fixed away from provision. There is much I could say here, but I feel I have said enough in this book. So I will simply say that our daily activity is to ask God to work in us.

I recently had some building work done at my house. I did not do the work or arrange the work; I didn't even design it. But I did have to greet the builders, hand them the key, and get out of the way. Invocation is opening the door daily for God to build His Son's life in us. Through invocational prayer the external, foreign, and utterly alien righteousness of God comes into us and becomes internal, native, and utterly indigenous. Invocational prayer is prayer centered around receiving our daily bread—the bread we need for our existence.

I am not wanting to give a format for this prayer. The only structure I will give is that this prayer needs to be centered around asking God to act in us or, as Paul said, asking God to "take hold."[390] Did you notice that in Philippians 3:12 God is the one who takes hold—that He is the one holding you? You cannot hold yourself in an alien righteousness, so stop trying. Only through Scripture-based prayer requesting the Father to "take hold" can you be stable and certain in the utterly alien righteousness of God—a righteousness not found in you but obtained through faith in Jesus Christ.

We obtain the promise of the Gospel through invocation. Forget what is behind, forget the law, the religion, the obligatory service, the ritualistic prayer, and the self-chastisement. Forget all these things and come, once and then forever daily, to God through the resource of prayer, and experience the truth of the Christian claim.[391] Remembering that when the Lord pulled much out of the temple, the one thing He wanted in was prayer: "My house will be called a house of prayer" (Matt. 21:13).

Paul says in 2 Corinthians 5:14 (NLT) that "Christ's love controls us." Commenting on this verse Oswald Chambers wrote: "Paul says he is overruled, overmastered, held as in a vice, by the love of Christ."[392] By basing your daily Christian life on asking God to act in you, you are basing your Christian life on God's power and not your own. You are asking God to control, compel, overrule, and overmaster you—to hold you in a vice of His will. We are not to live each day of the Christian life in vain struggle to be better and try more. We are to live each day through acknowledging that we can't live the perfect life of God and asking God to live it through us (Gal. 2:20).

When you begin to comprehend the magnitude of what is offered here you begin to see grace. You do not have to live the Christian life; you have to be dedicated to asking each day for Christ to live it through you. When this realization takes hold and you experience the power and closeness of Christ acting in you—when this happens—you begin to comprehend the offer that God has made humanity. The words of Paul in Romans 7:25 then make perfect sense: "Thanks be to God, who delivers me through Jesus Christ our Lord!"

The Greek philosopher Socrates asked a question that has echoed through the ages of civilization: "What does it mean to be a human being?" The Danish theologian Soren Kierkegaard used this statement to ask, "What does it mean to be a Christian?" To be a human is to be created in the image of God; to be a Christian is to be one who recognizes the mighty claim God has upon your whole life and daily give yourself to it (Gen. 1:27).[393]

"Simply approach to Him."[394]

APPENDICES

APPENDIX 1

MY HOUSE SHALL BE CALLED A HOUSE OF PRAYER

Both Matthew and Luke record Jesus specifically teaching us how to pray, intriguingly, Jesus never pauses to explicitly teach us how to preach. I wonder what this means. Could it be that all preaching and teaching (2 Tim. 3:36) sits under the category of invocational prayer? Is it possible that all liturgy (church service structure) is meant to build towards prayer?

To understand this better, we can observe that Jesus said 'this is how you should' about prayer alone, He also continually withdrew to pray privately, moreover, the Apostle Paul included several early church prayers in his writings. Working off this scriptural emphasis, John Calvin and Karl Barth both made statements that prayer is: 'the chief exercise of faith' or 'the one thing above all the other things', the 'general key' for the Christian life. I would add to this a pastoral reflection that Christians regularly say 'Satan attacks our prayer life'. We discover this principle, that when we read the Bible things can be calm, but the moment we begin praying the Bible's truths, the enemy attacks with many distractions. Another point to consider here is that no matter how humble the preacher, the focus of the listener is, at least partly, on the human agent in preaching. In contrast, there is a purity in prayer, where our attention is solely on God and Him alone. Prayer takes the focus off oneself and other believers and places it solely on God. Lastly, it is interesting to note that when Christians seek revival, they instinctively go to prayer. So, what does all this mean?

Before progressing any further, a clear statement that scripture upholds preaching and teaching must be made, in fact these are qualifications for church leaders and Jesus's missional command (1 Tim 3:2, 2 Tim 2:24, Titus 1:9, Mark 16:15). So, any devaluing or deconstructing of preaching and teaching should not be entertained, rather, what we arrive at is a question, which is: what is the goal of preaching and teaching the Bible? The answer to this is to be formed into the image of Christ and to glorify the Father through bearing much fruit (Eph. 3:19, 4:13, Gal. 4:19, John 15:8). However, this leads into a second question, one that this book has laboured to answer, which is: how do we attain the power to be like Christ? Is it from human spiritual works? No. Is it from preaching, teaching and reading? The answer here is both yes and no. Yes, in the sense that it is *exclusively* in scripture that we can gain this power (John 5:39-40). No, in the sense that merely hearing how to gain power and not implementing this knowledge does little (Matt. 7:24, James 1:22 ESV). So, how do we attain the power to be like Christ? The answer is: by hearing the word through preaching and reading, and then by doing the word as we obediently pray into our lives what we have heard and read. We learnt from Calvin, Luther and Barth that salvation comes by faith and not human works, the prayer of faith is not a human work, it is activating Jesus's works on our behalf.

Maybe an area of reform is surfacing here, one that encourages discipleship and church services to not only preach the Word, but also pray the Word, activating it—"Pray at all times in the Spirit. Devote yourselves to prayer. Pray constantly. Call to Me and I will answer you." (Eph. 6:18, Col. 4:2, 1 Thess. 5:17, Jer. 33:3, James 5:16). As with any area of reform, it should only be considered if Jesus calls for it, to this end we recall that He said: "My house will be called a house of prayer" (Matt. 21:13, Acts 12:5, Eph. 5:20, Rev. 5:8; 8:4). I wonder, should Christian music and preaching generate worship in the form of God glorifying prayer?

APPENDIX 2

THE CREATIVE POTENTIAL
OF CHAOS

In Genesis 1:2 we see the Spirit of God hovering over the waters. The Hebrew word "hovering" only occurs three times in the Old Testament and is difficult to precisely translate. It has the idea of a bird hovering over its young. The activity of the Spirit in Genesis 1:2 is to energize and give life. He is a favorable Spirit one bringing life and order to the formless matter of early creation.[395] It is unmistakable that God watches over the birthing of creation, and then in Jesus God comes again to parent His children who have orphaned themselves through choosing the disease of sin over the life of God. Isaiah 45:18 tells us that God created the earth to be inhabited with life. The pastoral application is immense here. God's stance toward emptiness and formlessness is one of favor. He desires anything that is not life to be life, anything that is empty to be full, anything formless to be formed into His image.

Isaiah 45:18 talks about How God did not want creation to be "empty chaos." Chaos in Genesis is not a negative thing, as in sinful; chaos in this context means unordered created material with the potential to produce life.[396] Remember Jesus's words in John 15 that the reconciled person is "clean." It is possible to be clean but unformed.

God's creation was "clean" but devoid of life; it was unformed. The Spirit brought form and life. God cleanses and redeems us, but then He seeks to fully unravel this redemption through ordering our past chaos and releasing a new potential, one focused on building His life in us and His kingdom through us. He molds us as a potter does the clay, taking our ordinary and making it extraordinary.

He took the chaos of Saul's insecurity and caused it to crown a king. He took the failure of Moses and used it to free a nation. He took the impatience of Abraham and used it to birth two peoples. He took the brokenness of Ruth and used it to set up salvation. He took the dungeon of Joseph and used it as a doorway into destiny. He took the ability of Rahab to hide men for her trade and used it to save a generation. He took the calculated murderous mind of the New Testament Saul and used it to strategize mass salvation. When you know you are saved but feel like you are lost, remember that God uses the redeemed chaos of our past to construct our future. God utilizes our redeemed earthly chaos to create the characteristics of the eternal kingdom in us. The chaos of life is not exterior to God's plan; the entrance to one's personal promised land is not through gaining status or position. The divine dream materializes when the characteristics needed to manage it are fully formed.

Remember the great cloud of witness that has gone before you. Remember the pastors who pioneered through patience perseverance: Peter, Paul, James, and John. Remember the activists who waged war with the weapon of a kingdom pen: Wycliffe, Tyndale, Luther, Beecher-Stowe, and Bonhoeffer. Remember the missionaries who pressed the darkness with the light of sacrifice: Taylor, Carmichael, Trotter, and Brainerd. Remember the evangelists who moved generations with the power of prayer: Wesley, Booth, Moody, and Graham. Remember the royalty who were crowned while lost: David, Esther, Josiah, and Hezekiah. Remember that all who entered the wilderness found riches in the wilderness.

The serious Christian belongs in being lost, for in this place the purpose and plan of God comes alive, the flesh strips away and "entry into the eternal kingdom of our Lord and Savior Jesus Christ will be richly supplied to you" (2 Pet. 1:11).

APPENDIX 3

·············· ···◆◆··· ··············

AN ESCHATOLOGY OF WORSHIP

...and some things that should not have been forgotten were
lost. History became legend. Legend became myth.

Lady Galadriel, *The Fellowship of the Ring*[397]

Before the beginning there was the One. He was mighty in love,
supreme in power and kindness. His overflowing love poured out
into all space and time, and from this overflow of love all we know and
all we have was born. Heaven was abounding in all good gifts. Peace
was the portion of the people; they wanted for nothing and wanted
after nothing.

To the people of heaven, it was not heaven; it just was home. It was
all they wanted and all they needed. Their home was known for its
great houses. The most glorious of these was the House of the Supreme
Prince of Heaven, the Archangel Lucifer. Lucifer was a being of spar-
kling magnificence; he was high in height and stature, the first morning
star of the One. Lucifer was the High Prince of the Adoration Army;
his job was to keep heaven and all creation focused on the adoration
of the One. Adoring the One was the love and duty of all: love, as it
was a thing of desire; and duty—focusing on the One keeps creation

centered, stable, and safe. The One is not a Lord of wanton need, desiring adoration for His own gain. He is the source of everything and as the source He knows that those who stray die, and that with death comes something far worse than the termination of consciousness. With death comes existence. Existence is the opposite of life; it is living without the One, living without the source. Existence is marked by fear, anxiety, strain, and turmoil. Adoration is protection, it is security. To adore is to receive life, and to live is to be free.

Lucifer had two kin: the archangel Gabriel and the archangel Michael. Both beings of nobility and stature they, with Lucifer, oversaw the great houses of heaven. Gabriel and his house are the proclaimers of life; they give and share the truth, a truth that sets all free. Michael is the warrior of heaven, His role largely ceremonial, as there is no need for courage when there is nothing to fear.

When the proclaimers are fulfilling their task, the adoration of creation is thundering in to the One. This means that the Adoration Army can perform their role of focusing the adoration of creation toward the One (Heb. 1:14). The result of this process is a centered, stable, and safe universe.

The Worship War

On a day that is beyond the ability of the human mind to imagine or comprehend, the One gathered all that was, is, and will be to Himself. On this day of all-time, all that was, is, and will be gathered in the court of heaven to hear the heart of the One.

This gathering was the center moment of all life and creation. It was and is the moment that the One chose, in the reasoning of His own mind—a reasoning that is not comprehensible to a member of His creation—to reveal the hidden inner truth of His essence, being, and nature: His Oneness abides in three.

At once the gathering erupted and something was that had never been: war. The war started in the heart of the Supreme Prince of Heaven the Archangel Lucifer, for this revelation meant that He must focus the adoration of creation toward the Son, and the Son would then pass this adoration onto the One Supreme. The One Son was the focal point of all adoration. The Archangel Lucifer was enraged. He had gained a friend and a loving Lord, but in his heart Lucifer did not see it this way. He saw that he was no longer second to the One Supreme; in his self-understanding he was now the second morning star.

The Supreme Prince the Archangel Lucifer possessed the ability to initiate expression, a gift of unparalleled splendor bestowed on him as the Supreme Prince of Heaven's Adoration Army—a gift given to help him fulfill his role as heaven's head worshiper. Lucifer, in an act of incomprehensible betrayal, chose to use this gift to initiate self-promotion—sin.[398]

The command to adore the One Son and the self-willed refusal of the Supreme Prince to do so saw the fracturing of all. Lucifer deceptively told his house that they would and could adore the One Supreme, but never the One Son, as doing this would see him become subservient to the One Son. The Archangel Michael led the most valiant of battles. Michael and His legions flung the house of adoration through the heavens, battling from galactic cluster to cluster, dimension to dimension. For generations they fought, in a battle that moved beyond time and space. The battle became their portion and the war their world.

The One Son went to earth to sacrifice His right of connection to the One Supreme and His right of receiving adoration. The One Son sacrificed this right on a temporal human cross; and in this act of sacrifice the One Son brought forth a movement of adoration within the hearts of Earth's occupants called humanity. These humans saw and knew the One Son, and for thousands of years they adored Him; they worshiped the One heaven's adoration army would not. This unleashed a torrent, the One Supreme ordained these adoring humans the renewed Adoration Army. Led by the One Son, this renewed adoration army stood with the Archangel Michael and they, together, overthrew the fallen house of heaven's darkened ones. Through the blood of the

Lamb, it was made possible for humanity to utter the word of testimony that previously only the adoration army could speak—unleashing the power of the One Supreme.

The enlisting of humanity to adore was not from need of the One Son to be empowered; rather, it was of the design of the One Supreme and the Archangel Gabriel. Gabriel assumed the mantle of the Supreme Prince and desired to proclaim against the self-initiated self-promotion of his forerunner. Gabriel waged his own war not with a sword but with the weapon of proclamation. He desired above all else to confound the pride of Lucifer with the adoration of single-solar-system beings. The humble adoration of tiny humans heaped burning coals on the head of Lucifer and his darkened adoration army—adoration through faith, confounding those who saw, touched, and still would not kneel.

Lucifer defeated, Michael empowered, Gabriel entrusted, and the One Son enthroned—the one thing left was to permanently restore the Adoration Army of heaven. The One Supreme, the One Son, and the One Spirit saw this as an opportunity: an opportunity to engross more life in their love. Humanity's destiny was sealed, stamped with the mandate to adore the One Supreme through the One Son, by the One Spirit. Adoration of Jesus Christ, commonly known as worship, being the central tenet of all creation. Humanity was born to worship the One heaven's adoration army would not.

We will struggle and give ourselves to see more and more of humanity adoring the glorious Son of God. This is not about religion; it is about a noble duty to see humanity fulfill its purpose, to worship the one rejected by Lucifer but cherished by the legions of humans who call Him friend, Savior and Lord. God is refilling the choir stalls of heaven.[399] The greatest benchmark of the return of Christ is the fervent worship of His church.

In 1402 Jan Hus became the preacher at one of the very few chapels in Europe that conducted its service in the local language, as opposed to the full Latin service of the Roman Catholic Church. Hus did something in that small chapel that still powerfully influences the church today: he reintroduced the early church practice of congregational worship. This was continued throughout the ensuing ages, with a particular focus being found in the activities of the Wesley brothers, who championed singing and congregational worship. The Wesley brothers gave rise to Methodism; Methodism gave rise to the holiness movement, which in turn gave rise to Pentecostalism. Pentecostalism, in turn, has given rise to the modern-day worship movement. I would put forward that God is building the worship of His people, a worship that is the benchmark of the return of Christ. Eschatology is not defined by political maneuvering; it is defined by God's will. God's will responds to worship above all else.

The Bible is clear that we will not know the day or hour, but Jesus did say we will know the season (Matt, 24:36; Luke 21:31). This area of theology is clear in the reality that Jesus will return, but speculative in the means of this return, so we must be careful of creating overly assured statements. But it is interesting to note the little word "hasten" in 2 Peter 3:12, which follows the instruction to be holy and godly.[400] If we combine this with Jesus's statement, "This good news of the kingdom will be proclaimed in all the world as a testimony to all nations. And then the end will come" (Matt 24:14), there is a clear element where humanity plays a role in the timing of Christ's return. I would say that all our actions sit under the timing of God. But still, our proper and true spiritual worship, defined as being "living sacrifices," can be used to *hasten* Christ's return. Nothing else is given this responsibility and power. As already said, this must be wrapped in God's sovereignty, but it is still there, a listed element in the equation of Christ's return.

Maybe, just maybe, there is a lot more stirring under the surface when it comes to the modern-day worship movement?[401] True worship occurs when sacrifice is the cemented norm.

The pilgrimage to the city of the Great King is the binding reality of all generations. Do not be afraid to migrate your humanity into His and to give yourself to that which will abide (1 Cor. 3:14).[402]

And there's another country, I've heard of long ago,
Most dear to them that love her, most great to them that know;
We may not count her armies, we may not see her King;
Her fortress is a faithful heart, her pride is suffering;
And soul by soul and silently her shining bounds increase,
And her ways are ways of gentleness, and all her paths are peace.

"I Vow to Thee, My Country," Cecil Spring Rice

ACKNOWLEDGMENTS

The personal searching for God that gave rise to this book began in the oncology ward of Westmead Hospital, the chemotherapy lounge of Blacktown Hospital, and found courage and form in the palliative care wards of Western Sydney.

The search for spiritual power that gave rise to this book took place with the toughest and truest people you could ever meet. The kind-hearted and no-nonsense people of Western Sydney who I pastored for two decades, the longsuffering people of the Christian camping community, and the resilient people of the deep Australian outback that I served alongside. It found form as my studies immersed me in the experiences of the great missionaries and theologians of the Christian faith.

The unwanted experiences that made me search for *God in Christianity* began in a childhood hallmarked by a toxic combination of spiritual disobedience, chronic illness, intense frustration, and faithful local Christians who 'snatched me from the fire'. Finding form as I watched my cancer–ridden mother push back generations of darkness and despair through scripture–based prayer.

Whilst I have many friends that I could draw upon to endorse this book, I have chosen not to. Instead, I dedicate this book to the countless Christians I served alongside, talked with about the way of holiness and power, and failed upwards with. I dedicate this book to the people who made me into what I am today: missionary–lecturers, scripture teachers, 'ordinary' local Christians, and faithful biblical preachers. I dedicate this book to my wife who taught me through marriage what I could never have learnt in my childhood: that love is sacrifice. Lastly, I dedicate this book to my mum, for modelling prayer and proving its power.

Sean A. Nolan ThD (Cand.),
Sydney, Australia, 2023

BIBLIOGRAPHY

92nd Street Y. "Bill Cunningham Recalls the Greatest Fashion Show He's Ever Seen: Fashion Icons with Fern Mallis." Sept. 12, 2014, YouTube video, 12:12. https://www.youtube.com/watch?v=aISNOtt1zk0.

Anton, Edward. *Repentance: A Cosmic Shift of Heart and Mind.* Spring, TX: Illumination Publishers, 2016.

Aquinas, Thomas. *The Summa Theologica.* Volume 1. Cincinnati: Benziger Brothers, 1947.

Augustine. *City of God.* London: Penguin Classics, 2003.

Augustine. *Confessions.* London: Penguin Classics, 1961.

Augustine. *On The Trinity.* Limovia.net, 2013.

Augustine. *Nicene and Post-Nicene Fathers: First Series Volume V—St. Augustine: Anti-Pelagian Writings, On The Spirit and The Letter.* Ed. Philip Schaff. New York: Cosimo, 2007.

Arnold, Thomas. *Christian Life, Its Hopes, Its Fears, and Its Close,* 6th edition. London: T. Fellowes, 1859.

Barth, Karl. *Anselm: Fides Quaerens Intellectum.* London: SCM Press, 1960.

Barth, Karl. "The Barmen Declaration." Barmen: German Confessing Church, 1934.

Barth, Karl. *Church Dogmatics.* 14 vols. Edinburgh: T and T Clark, 2004.

Barth, Karl. *Learning Jesus through the Heidelberg Catechism.* Eugene, OR: Wipf and Stock, 1982.

Barth, Karl. *The Christian Life*. Grand Rapids, MI: Eerdmans, 1981.

Barth, Karl. *The Epistle to the Romans*. London: Oxford University Press, 1976.

Barth, Karl. *From Rousseau to Ritschl*. London: SCM Press, 1959.

Barth, Karl. *The Göttingen Dogmatics*. Instruction in the Christian Religion, Volume 1. Grand Rapids, MI: Eerdmans, 1991.

Barth, Karl. *The Holy Spirit and the Christian Life*. Louisville: Westminster John Knox Press, 1993.

Barth, Karl. *The Resurrection of the Dead*. Eugene, OR: Wipf and Stock, 2003.

St Bernard of Clairvaux. Sermons on the Song of Songs. Sermon 8, https://www.pathsoflove.com/bernard/songofsongs/sermon08.html.

Billy Graham Evangelistic Association, "Billy Graham's 99th Birthday: Notable Reflections," YouTube video, November 7, 2017, 5:41, https://www.youtube.com/watch?v=pz4pFVVMzLw.

Billy Graham Evangelistic Association, Charlotte USA. Excuse Me, Please: Billy Graham Classics. September 15, 2020, https://www.youtube.com/watch?v=If0-mZQ1RW8&list=PL79D3613A193294B6&index=12.

Bird, Michael, and Preston Sprinkle. *The Faith of Jesus Christ, The Pistis Christou Debate*. Peabody, MA: Hendrickson Publishers, 2009.

Bloesch, Donald. "The Sword of the Spirit: The Meaning of Inspiration." *Themelios* 5.3 (May 1980): 14–19.

Bonhoeffer, Dietrich. *Creation and Fall*. New York, NY: Touchstone Edition, 1997.

Booth, Mary Warburton. *These Things I Have Seen*. London: Pickering and Inglis, 1946.

Brayley, Eli. *The Great Meaning of* Metanoia. Woodstock, GA: Timothy Ministry, 2012.

Bromiley, Geoffrey W. *Introduction to the Theology of Karl Barth*. Grand Rapids, MI: Wm. B. Eerdmans Publishing Company, 1979.

Brunner, Emil. *The Mediator*. London: Lutterworth Press, 1934

Burnett, Richard. *The Westminster Handbook to Karl Barth*. Louisville: Westminster John Knox Press, 2013.

Cable, Mildred, and Francesca French. *Something Happened*. London: Hodder and Stoughton, 1938.

Calvin, John. *Commentaries on the Four Last Books of Moses: Arranged in the Form of a Harmony*, Volume 1. Translated by Rev. C. W. Bingham. Edinburgh: Calvin Translations Society, 1850.

Calvin, John. *Institutes of the Christian Religion*. Library of Christian Classics. Ed. J. T. McNeill. Louisville: Westminster Press, 2006; Peabody, MA: Hendrickson, 2008.

Chambers, Oswald. *My Utmost for His Highest*. Uhrichsville, OH: Barbour, 1963.

Chambers, Oswald. *The Love of God*. London: Oswald Chambers Publications Association, 1938.

Clarke, Arthur C. *Profiles of the Future*. New York: Harper and Row: 1973.

Colyer, Elmer. *The Promise of Trinitarian Theology: Theologians in Dialogue with T. F. Torrance*. Lanham, MD: Rowman and Littlefield, 2001.

Comfort, Phillip. *Encountering the Manuscripts*. Nashville: Broadman and Holman, 2005.

Comfort, Phillip. *The Quest for the Original Text of the New Testament*. Ada, MI: Baker Book House, 1992.

Conselice Christopher J., Wilkinson Aaron, Duncan Kenneth, and Mortlock Alice. "The Evolution of Galaxy Number Density at $z < 8$ and its Implications". *The Astrophysical Journal* 830:83 (2016).

Cowman, C. *Streams in the Desert*. London: Oliphants, 1966.

Cunningham, Bill. *Fashion Rising*. London: Vintage, 2018.

Dean, Christopher. *Religion As It Should Be, or, The Remarkable Experience and Triumphant Death of Ann Thane Peck*. Boston: Massachusetts Sabbath School Society, 1851.

Dods, Marcus. *The Change of Joshua's Name*. https://biblehub.com/sermons/auth/dods/the_change_of_joshua%27s_name.htm. Easton, Matthew George. *Easton's Bible Dictionary*. London: Thomas Nelson, 1897.

Edman, Raymond. *They Found the Secret*. Grand Rapids: Zondervan, 1962.

Ferrara, Dennis Michael. "Hypostatized in The Logos." *Louvain Studies* 22.4: 1997.

Finney, Charles. *Finney's Systematic Theology*. Minneapolis: Bethany Fellowship Inc, 1964.

Frost, Henry S. *Uncommon Christians*. Philadelphia: China Inland Mission, 1914.

Gouwens, David, Hunsinger George, Johnson Keith L, ed, *The Wiley Blackwell Companion To Karl Barth, Volume 2*. Hoboken, NJ: John Wiley & Sons, 2020.

Graves, Dan, ed. *The Martyrdom of Polycarp*. Translated by J. B. Lightfoot. Abridged and modernized by Stephen Tomkins. Worcester, PA: Christian History Institute, 2020.

Hamilton, Victor. *The Book of Genesis, Chapters 1–17*. New International Commentary on the Old Testament. Grand Rapids, MI: Eerdmans, 1990.

Hawking, Stephen. *A Brief History of Time*. Scotts Valley, CA: CreateSpace, 2015.

Henry, Carl. *Frontiers in Modern Theology*. Chicago: Moody Press, 1972.

Hong, Howard, and Edna Hong. *The Essential Kierkegaard*. Princeton, NJ: Princeton University Press, 2000.

Hunsinger. D.v.D. The Master Key: unlocking the relationship of theology and psychology. Princeton Theological Seminary, 2001, Inspire 5 (2): 22.

Hunsinger, George. *Disruptive Grace: Studies in the Theology of Karl Barth*. Grand Rapids: Eerdmans, 2000.

Hunsinger, George. *Karl Barth's Christology, in Cambridge Companion to Karl Barth*. eds., John Webster. Cambridge, UK: Cambridge University Press, 2007.

Justin Martyr. *Dialogue with Trypho*, Chapter Eight, http://www.logoslibrary. org/justin/trypho/008.html.

KjaerHansen Kai, A*n Introduction to the Names Yehoshua/Joshua, Yeshua, Jesus and Yeshu*, March 23, 1992, Jews for Jesus, https://jewsforjesus.org/answers/ an–introduction–to–the–names–yehoshua–joshua–yeshua–jesus–and–yeshu/.

Karkkainen, Veli-Matti. *Trinity and Revelation*. Grand Rapids: Eerdmans, 2014.

Keller, Timothy. "Justice in the Bible". *Gospel in Life,* 2020, https://quarterly. gospelinlife.com/justice-in-the-bible/

Kierkegaard, Søren. *Edifying Discourses*. London: Fontana Books, 1958.

Kierkegaard, Søren. *Either/Or*. London: Penguin Classics. 1992.

Kierkegaard, Søren. *Fear and Trembling*. London: Penguin Classics, 2014.

Kierkegaard, Søren. *Kierkegaard's Journals and Notebooks, Volume 5*. Princeton, NJ: Princeton University Press, 2012.

Kierkegaard, Søren. *Journals and Papers, Volume 6*. Bloomington: Indiana University Press, 1967.

King, Martin Luther. "Letter from Birmingham Jail." *The Atlantic Monthly*. Vol. 212, No. 2 (1963): 78–88.

Kinghorn, Kenneth Cain. *Wesley: A Heart Transformed Can Change the World Study Guide*. Nashville: Abingdon Press, 2011.

Lactantius, Lucius Caecilius Firmianus. *The Divine Institutes. XXIV: Of Repentance, of Pardon, and the Commands of God*. http://www.intratext.com/IXT/ENG0292/_P48.HTM.

Lewis, C. S. *Mere Christianity*. London: Fontana Books, 1969.

Lewis, C. S. *The Screwtape Letters*. London: Fontana Books, 1955.

Lewis, C. S. *Undeceptions*. London: Geoffrey Bles, 1971

Luther, Martin. *Commentary on Galatians*, Preface. Tim Keller abridgment and paraphrase. New York: Redeemer Presbyterian Church, 2003.

Luther, Martin. *Commentary on the Epistle to the Galatians*. Luther Classic Commentary. Ed. T. Graebner. Scripture Press, New York City: 2015.

Luther, Martin. *The Career of the Reformer: Explanations of the Ninety-five Theses*. Luther Works, Volume 31. Philadelphia: Fortress Press, 1957.

Luther, Martin. *The Career of the Reformer: The Ninety-five Theses*. Luther Works, Volume 31. Philadelphia: Fortress Press, 1957.

Luther, Martin. *The Career of the Reformer: Two Kinds of Righteousness*. Luther Works, Volume 31. Philadelphia: Fortress Press, 1957.

Luther, Martin. *Devotional Writings*. Luther's Works, Volume 42. St. Louis: Concordia Publishing House, 1986.

Luther, Martin. *Preface to Romans*. Nashville: Discipleship Resources, 1977.

Luther, Martin. *Preface to Romans*. Saint Anselm Abbey, 1983.

Luther, Martin. *Galatians*. The Crossway Classic Commentaries. Eds. Alister McGrath and J. I. Packer. Wheaton, IL: Crossway Books, 1998.

Luther, Martin. *Lectures on the Epistle to the Hebrews, 1517–18*. Library of Christian Classics. Ed. James Atkinson. Louisville: Westminster John Knox Press, 2006.

Luther, Martin. *Lectures on Romans*. Library of Christian Classics. Ed. Wilhelm Pauck. Louisville: Louisville: Westminster John Knox Press, 2006.

Luther, Martin. *The Small Catechism*. Trans. Robert E. Smith. Scotts Valley, CA: CreateSpace, 1994.

Maclaurin, E.C.B. *YHWH The Origin of the Tetragrammaton*. *Vetus Testamentum*, *12* (4),439-463. http://search.ebscohost.com/login.aspx?direct=true&AuthType=ip,sso&db=lsdar&AN=ATLA0000685164&site=eds-live&scope=site.

Madman VOD (Australia). "Bill Cunningham New York." YouTube video, posted May 9, 2012. 1:24:14, https://www.youtube.com/watch?v=f0ohqOazJKo.

Manning, Brennan. *The Ragamuffin Gospel*. Colorado Springs: Multnomah, 2005.

McCrindle, Mark. "Australia's Changing Spiritual Climate" (Norwest: McCrindle Research. 2021), https://mccrindle.com.au/app/uploads/reports/Australias-Changing-Spiritual-Landscape-Report-2021.pdf.

McCrindle, Mark. *Faith and Belief in Australia*. Norwest, NSW: McCrindle Research. 2017. https://mccrindle.com.au/wp-content/uploads/2018/04/Faith-and-Belief-in-Australia-Report_McCrindle_2017.pdf.

McNair, Bruce. "Martin Luther and Lucas Cranach Teaching the Lord's Prayer." *Religions*, MDPI. Basel: 2017. https://www.mdpi.com/2077-1444/8/4/63.

Meyer, F. B. *The Life of Moses: Servant of God*. Lynnwood, WA: Emerald Books, 1996.

Migne, Jacques-Paul, ed. "Athanasius." *Patrologia Graeca*. Paris: Imprimeria Catholique, 1857.

Miller, Keith. *The Taste of New Wine*. London: Word Books, 1965.

Molnar, Paul D. *The Wiley Companion to Karl Barth*. Hoboken, NJ: John Wiley and Sons, 2020.

Molnar, Paul D. *Trinitarian Theology after Barth*. Eugene, OR: Wipf and Stock, 2011.

Morgan, Campbell. *The Morning Message*. Carter Lane: James Clarke & Co., LTD.

Morgan, Campbell. *The Practice of Prayer*. London: Hodder and Stoughton, 1907.

Mosby's Dictionary of Medicine, Nursing & Health Professions. 9th Edition. St. Louis: Elsevier Mosby, 2013.

Nicoll, Robertson. *The Expositor's Greek Testament*. Volume 5. Grand Rapids, MI: Eerdmans, 1956.

Oh, Peter S. "Complementary Dialectics of Kierkegaard and Barth: Barth's Use of Kierkegaardian Diastasis Reassessed." *Neue Zeitschrift Für Systematische Theologie und Religionsphilosophie 48, no. 4 (2006): 497–512.*

Page, Jesse. *David Brainerd*. London: S. W. Partridge and Co., 1891.

Pannenberg, Wolfhart. *Systematic Theology*. 3 vols. Grand Rapids, MI: Wm. B. Eerdmans, 1998.

Phillips, Gordon Lewis. *Flame in the Mind*. London: Longmans, 1957.

Pollock, J. C. *Hudson Taylor and Maria: Pioneers in China*. Grand Rapids, MI: Zondervan, 1976.

Powell, Ruth, and Kathy Jacka. "Australians Attending Church," (NCLS Research, 2021), http://www.ncls.org.au/articles/australians-attending-church/.

Powell, Ruth, and Miriam Pepper. "Local Churches in Australia: Research Findings from NCLS Research." NCLS Church Life Pack Seminar Presentation. Sydney: NCLS Research, 2016.

Queen Elizabeth II. "The Christmas Broadcast 2020," December 24, 2020. https://www.royal.uk/christmas-broadcast-2020.

Ramsay, William Mitchell. *A Historical Commentary on St. Paul's Epistle to the Galatians*. New York: G. P. Putnam's Sons, 1900.

Redford, Donald, Egypt, Canaan, and Israel in Ancient Times, (Princeton, NJ: Princeton University Press, 1993).

Robertson, A. T. *Word Pictures in the New Testament*. 6 vols. New York, Harper and Brothers, 1930.

Rockness, Miriam. *Turn Your Eyes Upon Jesus, A Story and a Song*. Naples, FL: Oxvision Books, 2018.

Sanders, Fred. *Jesus in Trinitarian Perspective: An Introductory Christology*. Nashville: B&H Academic, 2007.

Schaff, Phillip, ed. *Ante-Nicene Fathers*. 10 vols. Peabody, MA: Hendrickson Publishers, 1994.

Schaff, Phillip. *The Creeds of Christendom*. New York: Harper, 1877.

Schaff, Phillip, ed. *Nicene and Post-Nicene Fathers*. 8 vols. Peabody, MA: Hendrickson Publishers, 2012.

Silva, *Moisés. New International Dictionary of New Testament Theology and Exegesis*. 5 vols. Grand Rapids, MI: Zondervan, 2014.

Sinclair, Lisa. "The Legacy of Isabella Lilias Trotter," *International Bulletin of Missionary Research,* January 2002. http://www.internationalbulletin.org/issues/2002-01/2002-01-032-sinclair.pdf

Stanley, Charles. "From the Pastor's Heart." September 2020. Atlanta: In Touch Ministries, Inc., 2020.

Stanley, Charles. "30 Life Principles." Penrith, NSW: In Touch Ministries, Inc, 2015. www.intouchaustralia.org/read/30-life-principles.

Stott, John. *Basic Christianity*. Downers Grove: IVP, 1995.

Strong, James. *Strong's Exhaustive Concordance of the Bible*. Nashville: Abingdon Press, 1890.

Taylor, Hudson James. *The Growth of a Work of God*. London: China Inland Mission. 1921.

Temple, William. *Nature, Man and God*. London: Macmillan and Co, 1949.

Tillich, Paul. *Systematic Theology*. 3 vols. London: SCM Press, 1978.

Tolkien, J. R. R. *The Fellowship of the Ring*. The Lord of the Rings, Book 1. London: HarperCollins Publishers, 2009.

Tomkins, Stephen. *John Wesley: A Biography*. Oxford: Lion Publishing, 2003.

Torrance, A. B. *Kierkegaard's Paradoxical Christology.* St, Andrews, UK: University of St Andrews, 2019.

Torrance, Thomas. *Atonement: The Person and Work of Christ.* Wheaton, IL: IVP Academic, 2009.

Torrance, Thomas. *Incarnation: The Person and Life of Christ.* Wheaton, IL: IVP Academic, 2008.

Torrance, Thomas. *Karl Barth: Introduction to Early Theology.* London: T & T Clark International, 2004.

Torrance, Thomas. *The Christian Doctrine of God: One Being, Three Persons.* 2nd Edition. London: Bloomsbury T&T Clark, 2016.

Torrance, Thomas. *When Christ Comes and Comes Again.* London: Hodder and Stoughton, 1957.

Tozer, A. W. *The Knowledge of the Holy.* Carlisle, UK: OM Publishing, 1994.

Tozer, A. W. *The Pursuit of God.* India. Akola, Maharashtra: Alliance Publications, 1968.

Trotter, Lilias. *Focussed: A Story and a Song.* https://ililiastrotter.wordpress.com/out-of-print-manuscripts/

Upham, Thomas. *The Life of Madame Guyon.* London: Allenson and Co, 1940.

Webster, John. *The Cambridge Companion to Karl Barth.* Cambridge: Cambridge University Press, 2000.

Wiersma, Hans. "Martin Luther's Lectures on Romans (1515–1516): Their Rediscovery and Legacy." *Word and World,* Volume 39, Number 3: 2019.

Wesley, John. *The Journal of the Rev. John Wesley, A. M.* Ed. Nehemiah Curnock. London: Robert Culley, 1909.

Willard, Dallas. *The Spirit of The Disciplines.* New York: Harper Collins Publishers, 1991.

Wilson, Walter L. *A Dictionary of Bible Types.* Grand Rapids, MI: Baker Books, 2013.

Woodruff, Joel. "Profile in Faith: V. Raymond Edman." *Knowing and Doing,* C. S. Lewis Institute. Winter 2011.

Wright, N. T. *Paul and The Faithfulness of God, Parts III and IV*. London: Society for Promoting Christian Knowledge, 2013.

Yong, Amos. *The Dialogical Spirit*. Eugene, OR: Cascade Books, 2014.

Zellweger-Barth, Max. *My Father-In-Law*. Eugene, OR: Pickwick Publications, 1986.

Zimmermann, Jens. *Incarnational Humanism: A Philosophy of Culture for the Church in the World*. Wheaton, IL: IVP Academic, 2012.

ENDNOTES

Epigraph

1. Quoted in Jesse Page, *David Brainerd* (London: S.W. Partridge and Co., 1891), 78.

Preface

2. In AD 64 Emperor Nero commenced severe persecution of the Christian population, which would have begun Paul's time in the horrific Mamertine Prison; it is possible the apostle Peter also spent time there. You can understand why Onesiphorus struggled to find Paul (2 Tim 1:16–17) in this jail-sewer and why Paul values that his friend wasn't ashamed of his chains. You can also understand why no one came to his defense (2 Tim. 4:16) and why he wanted his cloak (2 Tim. 4:13), as it was deathly cold in the sewer-dungeon. The Roman historian Sallust describes the prison in *The War with Catiline*, 55:3–4.

Introduction

3. "Bill Cunningham Recalls the Greatest Fashion Show He's Ever Seen: Fashion Icons with Fern Mallis," 92nd Street Y, Sept. 12, 2014, YouTube video, 12:12, https://www.youtube.com/watch?v=aISNOtt1zk0.

4. "Bill Cunningham New York," Madman VOD (Australia), 2011; posted May 9, 2012. You Tube video, 1:24:14, https://www.youtube.com/watch?v=f0ohqOazJKo.

5. "Bill Cunningham New York."

Part One intro

6. A. W. Tozer, *The Pursuit of God* (Akola, Maharashtra, India: Alliance Publications, 1968), 17.

7. Augustine, *The City of God*, Book XXII, Chapter 30.

1. Who Do You Say I Am?

8. See Exodus 25:22, 30:6; Leviticus 16:2; Numbers 7:89; 2 Samuel 6:2; 2 Kings 19:15; 1 Chronicles 13:6; Psalm 80:1, 99:1; Isaiah 37:16.

9. This definition comes from the Chalcedon Council in AD 451. Philip Schaff, ed., *Nicene and Post-Nicene Fathers: The Seven Ecumenical Councils* (Peabody, MA: Hendrickson Publishers, 2012), 264–265. Also note George Hunsinger: "Jesus Christ is understood as one person in two natures. The two natures— his deity and his humanity—are seen as internal to his person." George Hunsinger, *Disruptive Grace: Studies in the Theology of Karl Barth* (Grand Rapids, MI: Eerdmans, 2000), 132.

10. Barth gives the following formula "very God, very man, very God-man." Karl Barth, *Church Dogmatics* (hereafter *CD*)*: The Doctrine of Reconciliation,* IV/1 (Edinburgh: T and T Clark, 1961), 126. Also see Barth, *Church Dogmatics: The Doctrine of the Word of God,* I/2 (Edinburgh: T and T Clark, 1998), 132); Barth*, Church Dogmatics: The Doctrine of Reconciliation,* IV/2 (Edinburgh: T and T Clark, 1958), 84, 115; and Emil Brunner, *The Mediator* (London: Lutterworth Press, 1934). Note the quotes from Irenaeus and Luther on the cover page for a quick intake of Brunner's intent.

11. Stephen Hawking wrote, "Even if there is only one possible unified theory, it is just a set of rules and equations. What is it that breathes fire into the equations and makes a universe for them to describe? The usual approach of science of constructing a mathematical model cannot answer the questions of why there should be a universe for the model to describe. Why does the universe go to all the bother of existing?" I must state that while Professor Hawking posited that something "breathes fire into the universe," he did not affirm Christian beliefs. Stephen Hawking, *A Brief History of Time* (Scotts Valley, CA: CreateSpace, 2015), 77.

12. The idea of a God of love coexisting with science has been in a hostile standoff recently. Thinkers like Thomas Torrance and Amos Yong have worked to bridge this divide. The scientific world developing new theories, such as emergence theory, has bolstered the hopefully growing reconciliation. I use the word "reconciliation," as Christianity from the Middle Ages to the seventeenth century helped launch modern science. The recent split between Christianity and science that began in the eighteenth century is far younger than its preceding friendship. Recent developments in quantum theory have unearthed underlying scientific realties that are intriguingly close to Christian teaching. For example, the discovery of superposition can be seen as a proof for the trinity, the three-in-oneness of God. Before the discovery of

superposition this was untenable to science; now we can say that the triune God is simply in superposition, or even the origin of superposition – *vestigium trinitas?* Further, light is both particle and wave. The idea of quantum entanglement is also an excellent proof for prayer.

13. Barth, *CD, II/1,* 272–296.

14. Paul Tillich, *Systematic Theology,* Volume 1 (London: SCM Press, 1978), 205; Barth, *CD* II/1, 257.

15. By taking a human form God entered into the limited existence of our created universe. Barth, *CD* IV/1, 157–210.

16. Karl Barth wrote: "Even in Himself God is God only as One who loves," *CD* IV/2, 755. Barth expands this concept in the section "The Basis of Love," *CD* IV/2, 751–783. See also Augustine, *On the Trinity,* Book XV, 17.29, 19.37.

17. Karl Barth wrote that we must define God's being of love through His activity, specifically "the completed act of divine loving in sending Jesus Christ," *CD* II/1, 275. This ensures that God's being of love cannot be corrupted for any cause other than reconciliation through Christ (2 Cor. 5:19). Further, Barth highlighted that God's being of love is not active because of our need; it is just who He is, and from this eternal identity He rescues us. Our needs do not define God's being of love. This is a subtle but important point; on it Barth wrote, "God loves because He loves; because this act is His being, essence and His nature" *CD* II/1, 279. Barth discuss this in detail in his section "The Being of God as the One who Loves in Freedom," *CD* II/1, 28.

18. Karl Barth wrote, "And this loving is God's being in time and eternity. "God is" means "God loves." *CD* II/1, 283.

19. Barth, *CD* IV/2, 755.

20. Barth wrote: "The statements 'God is' and 'God loves' are synonymous. They explain and confirm one another." For Barth, to say this is only a prediction and not "a genuine equation" is an "ill considered judgment." *CD* IV/2, 755–756.

21. "The life and rule of love is the most inward and proper life and rule of God." Barth, *CD* IV/2, 757.

22. Augustine, in his homilies (published sermons) on 1 John, comments in the prologue that "He has spoken many words, and nearly all are about love." *The Expositor's Greek Testament* notes that for Jesus, John, and Augustine, 1 John is key noted by love. Robertson Nicoll, *The Expositor's Greek Testament,* Volume 5 (Grand Rapids: Eerdmans, 1956), 157.

23. Barth, *CD* II/I, 275.

24. Barth, *CD* II/I, 283.

25. Barth wrote that God has no satisfaction in His self-satisfaction. What this means is that God does not act in love because He needs to; rather, because He chooses to from a place of self-satisfaction. *CD* II/I, 280. Digging too deep in this area is not helpful; this is a truth accepted by faith.

26. "God's loving is necessary, for it is the being, the essence and the nature of God.... This one man [Jesus Christ] is therefore the being of God making itself known to us as the One who loves." Barth, *CD* II/1, 280, 286.

27. Karl Barth highlighted 2 Corinthians 5:19 as the central statement of Christianity and theology. Theology "has no more exalted or profound word— essentially, indeed it has no other word—than this: that God was in Christ reconciling the world unto Himself (2 Cor. 5:19)." *CD* II/2, 88.

2. Hope Has a Name

28. Augustine, *On the Trinity*, Book XV, 19.37. I have reorganized Augustine's original sentence to make it read more easily. In this section Augustine develops his argument to define Jesus and the Holy Spirt as love, just like the Father, "hence the Son of His love [Col 1:13], is none other than He who is born of His substance"; "what follows more naturally than that He [The Holy Spirit] is Himself love."

29. *Cyril, Catechetical Lecture X. 12.*, in Phillip Schaff, ed., *Nicene and Post-Nicene Fathers, Volume 7* (Peabody, MA: Hendrickson Publishers, 2012), 60.

30. Moisés Silva, *New International Dictionary of New Testament Theology and Exegesis*, Volume 2 (Grand Rapids, MI: Zondervan, 2014), 527. See endnotes in section Glory Known for more.

31. Not to be confused with LORD in the OT. When the word LORD is translated with all caps, it means the Hebrew proper name for God: *YHWH,* Yahweh, or Jehovah.

32. Augustine, *On the Trinity.* Book XV, 17.29, 19.37.

33. *CD* II/I. 272. Barth outlines this in a section of *his Church Dogmatics*: "The Being of God as The One Who Loves"; note the four points on 276–280.

34. Barth wrote: [in] "Loving us, God does not give us something, but Himself; and giving us Himself, giving us His only Son, He gives us everything. The love of God, has only to be His [Jesus'] love to be everything for us." *CD* II/I, 276.

35. "Reconciliation" is from a Greek word that means to change or exchange. My reasoning for using "reconciliation" over "salvation" is based out of 2 Corinthians 5:18–19. "Reconciliation" is the word used in this critical passage to describe God's saving activity amongst us, that takes place in His very being—"in Christ." Barth looked to this verse as the central thought of the New Testament; Barth, *CD* II/2, 88. See also Silva, *New International Dictionary of New Testament Theology and Exegesis, Volume 1*, 243, 245.

36. "There is no higher place at which our thinking and or speaking rightly about God can begin than this name." Barth, *CD, II/2*, 99.

37. Phillip Comfort, *Encountering the Manuscripts* (Nashville: Broadman and Holman, 2005), 206.

38. "We are not guilty of arbitrary speculation when we begin our description of the basis of Christian love in the being and nature of God Himself. The equation of the statements 'God is' and 'God loves' [put together by John as 'God is love'] is merely the most succinct formula to describe the reality in and as which God declares Himself," to us through the Scriptures. Barth, *CD* IV/2, 756–757.

39. "Lord" here is Yahweh. Yahweh is interchangeable with YHWH and Jehovah. Out of reverence the Jewish people will not say YHWH; they use Yahweh, Adonai, and other variants.

40. For those wondering about Joseph, most scholars feel Joseph died while Jesus was young. Matthew tells us that Joseph was a good, righteous man. If the scholars are correct, we can come to the idea that Joseph's life was one that embodied the message of "He must increase, but I must decrease" (John 3:30). Joseph's life could well have been an inspiring factor behind these famous words; after all, he was John's adopted uncle—it's not too much of a stretch in my mind. Joseph's premature death served an important function in Jesus's ministry. It would have been very confusing if Jesus was saying His Father was God with Joseph walking right behind him; thus Joseph decreased so that the Lord could increase. But I'll let you decide on this one.

41. This theme is covered in Amos Yong, *The Dialogical Spirit* (Eugene, OR: Cascade Books, 2014), 102; and, Jens Zimmermann, *Incarnational Humanism* (Downers Grove: IL, 2012), 266. I would imagine that this theme arises from Anselm and then Barth's more modern-day discussion of Anslem's thought in his book: Anselm: *fides quaerens intellectum*, 17 (faith seeking understanding).

42. Page. *David Brainerd*, 138.

43. Barth, *CD* IV, I, 650–651.

44. C. S. Lewis wrote, "Once you have made the World an end, and faith a means, you have almost won your man." C. S. Lewis, *The Screwtape Letters* (London: Fontana Books, 1955), 42.

45. The group they were meant to be influencing has influenced them, as Bill Cunningham remarked: "The designers got caught wearing the customers' coats too often . . . [they] climbed too fast themselves and were soon sitting at the best tables for lunch and dinner, thus putting them in the firing line of the invaders." Bill Cunningham, *Fashion Rising* (London: Vintage, 2018), 225.

46. Campbell Morgan, "Nov 3" *The Morning Message* (Carter Lane: James Clarke & Co., LTD), 162.

47. The words of Soren Kierkegaard are of interest here: "Christendom has done away with Christianity, without being quite aware of it . . . one must try again to introduce Christianity into Christendom." Soren Kierkegaard, *Training in Christianity,* trans. Walter Lowrie (Princeton, NJ: Princeton University Press, 1944), 38–39.

48. Brunner, *The Mediator,* 13.

49. Modern western Christianity seems to be held in tension between two cultural and political ideologies, left and right. It is interesting to note that this is nothing new. Throughout its original existence Israel continually lived between the two political powers of north and south: Babylon, Persia and Egypt, Seleucida and the Ptolemaic empires. They also lived with the political occupation of the Greek, Roman, Byzantine, and Ottoman empires. Throughout all these ages many came forward seeking revolutionary action, but God's message was always the same: return to Me and I will act for you, "If only My people would listen to Me and Israel would follow My ways, I would quickly subdue their enemies and turn My hand against their foes" (Ps.81:13). It is interesting to note that the reforms of Josiah are ignored by the prophet Jeremiah. While Josiah was a godly king (Jer 22:15–16), it seems legislative reforms mean little without the hearts of the people (Jer 7:4–11). Revival comes from the Gospel in the hearts of the people.

50. While these thoughts apply to politics, I am not referring exclusively to the political sphere. These thoughts also encompass manmade philosophies that seek cultural change through ideas that align to the morals of the church, but don't embrace the Christ of the church. This noted, a distinction does need to be brought here. We have no problem and actively champion Christians in public life, the issue is not this. The problem is when the church at large fails to win hearts by faith and then resorts to politics to establish Christianity in society. The Christians of the church can be salt and light in politics, but politics cannot

become the means for establishing the Gospel in society. Our Lord is Jesus and our message the Gospel of eternal redemption.

It is essential to note that we approach this issue not in the negative but in the positive, the positive being that we cannot move off the one and only vehicle for salvation—Jesus Christ—to politics or social engineering. To do this is to raise up another salvation "idol" next to Christ. That said, the idea of the separation of church and state, while a rather necessary principle, is not a biblical doctrine; it is a manmade ideology crafted and used for various reasons. We look to save the individual and culture at large through Jesus only because this is Christianity; we do not do this because we are pushed into it by the separation of church and state. While affirming this separation, we remember that it is a manmade principle and unlike salvation through Jesus alone, it can be pushed against, although done so with much caution and even peril.

51. Howard and Edna Hong, *The Essential Kierkegaard* (Princeton, NJ: Princeton University Press, 2000), 446.

52. Note the events surrounding Karl Barth's personal and professional rejection of the letter signed by ninety-three of his colleagues supporting Kaiser Wilhelm's war policy in 1914. See Nigel Biggar, *The Cambridge Companion to Karl Barth* (Edinburgh: Cambridge University Press, 2007), 213.

53. The comments in this section are direct and I have included them with genuine reservation. I do not desire to offend anyone, but rather to raise awareness of this issue and drive us all to our knees in prayer.

54. It is worth noting that Jesus proved that the Old Testament transitioned into this new covenant easily. It was not the Old Testament that Jesus was contradicting, rather the additional moralistic and nationalistic regulations and rituals that people added to the Old Testament law.

55. Thomas Torrance, *When Christ Comes and Comes Again* (London: Hodder and Stoughton, 1957), 27.

3. Let the Word Become Flesh in Us

56. Augustine, *On the Trinity*, Book XV, 17.31,18.32. Language adapted from various translations.

57. There are two Nicene Creeds. The first was in 325 AD, the second in 381 AD, also called the Niceno-Constantinopolitan Creed. I am referring to the second creed here. There was also a church council held in 362 AD by Athanasius.

58. For additional thoughts, see Thomas Torrance, *The Christian Doctrine of God: One Being, Three Persons*, 2nd edition (London: Bloomsbury T&T Clark, 2016), xviii–xix.

59. Thomas Torrance, *Incarnation: The Person and Life of Chris* (Wheaton, IL: IVP Academic, 2008), xxxvii.

60. At the incarnation, God enters humanity. At Pentecost, humanity is placed into God. Pentecost is not a second incarnation; it is Jesus's humanity being offered as a new dwelling place for those who believe.

61. "He is no other than the presence and action of Jesus Christ Himself; His stretched out arm . . . Thus the Spirit who makes Christians Christians is the power of this revelation of Jesus Christ Himself-His Spirit. . . .Thus according to the New Testament the Holy Spirit is holy in the fact that He is the self-expression of the man Jesus." Barth, *CD* IV/2, 322–323, 331. Also Calvin, "we must remember, that the Spirit is called the Spirit of Christ." John Calvin, *Institutes of the Christian Religion* (Peabody, MA: Hendrickson, 2008), *350.*

62. Philip Comfort has a section in *Encountering the Manuscripts* that gives an introductory overview of this topic; see 232–234.

63. See comments in Thomas Torrance*, Atonement: The Person and Work of Christ* (Wheaton, IL: IVP Academic, 2009), lxviii.

64. "He does not place us merely in an external and casual fellowship with Himself, but in an internal and essential fellowship in which our existence cannot continue to be alien to His but may become and be analogous." Barth, *CD* IV/2, 757.

65. Augustine, *On the Trinity*, Book XV, 18.32. Augustine develops this to affirm that Father and Son are of the same substance and are love.

66. Augustine, *On the Trinity,* Book XV, 19.37.

67. Barth, *CD* I/1, 466. Barth wrote that the equation "God is love" is synonymous with another of John's statements that "God is Spirit," the two statements explain each other. For the apostle John, to say "love" was to say "Spirit." Barth, *CD* IV/2, 757.

68. Augustine, *On the Trinity*, Book XV, 19.37.

69. Augustine, *On the Trinity*, Book XV, 17.32. Also, Calvin wrote "he is . . . inflaming our hearts with the love of God." Calvin, *Institutes,* 350.

70. Phillip Comfort, *Essential Guide to the Bible Versions* (Wheaton, IL: Tyndale House, 2000), 209. The applications of this are almost endless; for example, this is the origin of Christian community. In Christian teaching love is impossible alone; you need to have another to be love to and receive love from. Church attendance flows from the very triune nature of God; fellowship is an eternal truth.

I have not had the time to survey the rabbinical literature on the following, so I include it in the category of speculative theology. In John 1:1-2 we see the idea of Father and Son, Yahweh and Jesus face-to-face, this is repeated in 1 John 1:1-2; 2:1 where the Apostle writes: the eternal life, which was face-to-face with the Father and has appeared to us NIV, TPT. Here we see a model of the trinity emerging. Instead of a traditional circular depiction of the triune God, or the old egg, gas-water-ice examples, John and then Augustine give us another. What we have here is two beings, facing each other with (metaphorical) arms outstretched in warm embrace. Proceeding forth from them both is their being, their eternal life, their substance of love (John 14:26). This love, which is the Holy Spirit, eternally connects, making them one while retaining their individuality. It is stunning to note that this is the exact image we see in the Mercy Seat: two divine beings outstretched, facing one another, made of "one piece" and the Shekinah Glory in the middle (Exo 25:18-20; Lev 16:2; 2 Sam 6:1-2). This Mercy Seat sat in the Tabernacle where "The LORD spoke with Moses face to face" (Exo 33:11; Num 12:8; Deut 34:10). This same Lord "became flesh and took up residence among us [literally tabernacled among us]." The disciples "observed His glory" the glory of the "One and Only Son" who has "seen [looked upon] God" "at the Father's side [in the arms of the Father, NASB]" and "has revealed Him" (John 1:14;18): We observed His glory, the glory of the One and Only Son who has looked upon God and who is in the arms of the Father—revealing Him fully to us.

The reason Jesus would not claim to be Yahweh directly when questioned is that He is, strictly speaking, not Yahweh, He is the second being of the trinitarian Mercy Seat in Human form—which is depicted by a Cherub (A Type; Exo 23:20-21; John 3:14. Note: Isaiah 63:9, "the Angel of His Presence [literally face, faces] saved them." Also, Ezekiel 10:4 "Then the glory of the LORD rose from above the Cherub."). You can feel Jesus's controlled frustration in John 18:23, Jesus, to me, is thinking "You unbelieving and rebellious generation" you can't even have a conversation without igniting. How am I meant to convey to you that I am Jesus the Son—the cloud-riding King of Daniel, not Yahweh the Father? It is not that Jesus does not directly claim divinity in the New Testament, rather, He uniquely claims it as He is revealing the trinitarian nature of God. Segal Alan, *Two Powers in Heaven*, (Waco, Tx: Baylor University Press, 2012). Heiser Michael, *The Unseen Realm* (Bellingham, WA: Lexham Press, 2015). Walter L. Wilson, *A Dictionary of Bible Types* (Grand Rapids, MI: Baker Books, 2013), entry for Ark. Typology can be overused.

71. Augustine wrote that "the Spirit of both is a kind of consubstantial communion of Father and Son." Augustine, *On the Trinity*, 27.50.

72. Barth, *CD* 1/1, 469. Augustine gives some further comments in this area: "The Holy Spirit is neither the Father nor the Son, but only the Spirit of the Father and of the Son." Augustine, *On the Trinity*, Book 1, Chapter 4.2; "The Father is not the Son nor the Holy Spirit; the Son is not the Father nor the Holy Spirit; the Holy Spirit is not the Father nor the Son: but the Father is only Father, the Son is only Son, and the Holy Spirit is only Holy Spirit." Augustine, *On Christian Doctrine*, trans. J.F Shaw (Mineola, NY: Dover Publications, 2009), Book 1, Chapter 5.

73. Barth, *CD* I/1, 359–361, 366. Barth, along with every other theologian, is working off the idea Basil of Caesarea began in the fourth century: three persons (*hypostases*) in one substance (*ousia*). Phillip Schaff, ed., *Nicene and Post-Nicene Fathers, Basil Letters and Selected Works* (Peabody, MA: Hendrickson, 2012), 278 (6); 254 (4). This is a somewhat heavy but essential point for Christian salvation. Father God is freely in union with His only begotten Son, who while of the same substance is eternally different from Him. From this eternal union of the different, God has the freedom to enter into another eternal union of the different: the union of His Trinity with redeemed humanity. A critical point here is that God does not throw together a triune structure in order to make Himself understandable to humanity; this Trinity is who He is eternally, and it is from this place that He saves. Just like a rib was taken from Adam's side to create women, a relational structure is taken from the Trinity, creating a bridge, allowing the return of sin-stranded humanity. At the cross God makes Himself available for a saving union with a species completely different to Himself; this saving-relational-mechanism is grounded eternally within God Himself. In the Gospel we are made aware of a prior self-differentiation in God from which His freedom to rescue us arises. See Trevor Hart, *The Cambridge Companion to Karl Barth* (Edinburgh: Cambridge University Press, 2007), 50.

74. The Holy Spirit is not begotten, but breathed, "the result of their common breathing." Barth, *CD* I/I, 470.

75. Barth, *CD* II/I. Page 297.

76. Augustine wrote: "Therefore the Holy Spirit is a certain unutterable communion of the Father and the Son." Augustine, *On the Trinity*, Book 5, Chapter 12; Barth, *CD* I/I, 470.

77. Note Karkkainen: "Augustine focused much of his attention on love as the proper biblical category for developing the idea of the triune God." V.

Karkkainen, *Trinity and Revelation* (Grand Rapids, MI: Eerdmans, 2014), 252–253.

78. Here I am working primarily off Barth and Augustine's writings. Barth, *CD* I/I, 470; Augustine, *On the Trinity*, Book XV, 27.50.

79. As a point of clarity, "basic to this structure is the derivation of the trinity of persons from the concept of the unity of substance." Wolfhart Pannenberg, *Systematic Theology*, Volume 1 (Grand Rapids: Wm. B. Eerdmans, 1998), 288, citing Aquinas. This basic structure cannot be moved away from; it is a theological absolute. Remembering that this structure arose from the Nicene Creed (325 and 381), Athanasius, the Cappadocian Fathers, and many others. See Philip Schaff, ed., *Nicene and Post-Nicene Fathers: The Seven Ecumenical Councils* (Peabody, MA: Hendrickson, 2012), 264–265.

80. Barth, *CD* I/1, 470.

81. Dallas Willard defined "spirit" as unbodily (or unembodied) personal power. Dallas Willard, *The Spirit of The Disciplines* (New York: Harper Collins, 1991), 64–65.

82. "If, as is properly understood, the Father is he who kisses, the Son he who is kissed, then it cannot be wrong to see in the kiss the Holy Spirit." St. Bernard of Clairvaux, Sermon 8, "Sermons on the Song of Songs."

83. John Calvin is comfortable applying the word "Person" to the Father and the Holy Spirit by transferring it across from the Son in Hebrews 1:3. Calvin notes that the Greeks use *hypostasis*, the Latin "Person," while his favored word is "subsistence." Calvin, *Institutes*, 67.

84. "The Church doctrine distinguishes in the Holy Trinity three persons (though not in the ordinary human sense of the word)." Schaff, *History of the Christian Church*, Volume 3. 142. Thomas Torrance discusses the meaning of Person when employed for description of the Trinity. Torrance draws a contrast between the individualization of Person in western thought and the understanding of Person, "derived from the Communion of Being in Love in God himself." Torrance highlights that the definition of Person in the Trinity is crafted through the "understanding of the three Persons in the one God as onto-relational realties in God." This is a new concept of Person for humanity and it is an example of the type of person we become once saved. We are no longer fully individual; we are persons in union with God (1 Cor. 6:19). Thomas Torrance, *The Ground and Grammar of Theology: Consonance between Theology and Science* (Edinburgh: T&T Clark, 1980), 173–174.

85. This area of theology is complex and highly nuanced. There are varying ways of describing the same basic Trinitarian formula: three persons (*hypostases*) in one substance (*ousia*). The Nicaean-era thinkers—Athanasius, Basil, and Augustine—all have their variants. John Calvin, who some say was working from thinkers like John Duns Scotus, has his. In more modern times Karl Barth and Thomas Torrance have presented similar but differing solutions. These thinkers angled the basic Trinitarian structure to meet the needs of their generations—some successfully, some questionably. Errors do come in the form of brazen heresies; however, errors often arise from slow drifts in language and cultural understanding. Christianity is old; thus terminology, like Person, is old. Our modern cultures are not; they are young and highly changing. I have put a lot in the footnotes in this section in an attempt to resource you well, but I don't want this to muddy my intention. I am not trying to remove Person from the Trinitarian structure. I am wanting to halt any incorporation of the modern understanding of the word, that if accepted dramatically changes the theological meaning, pastoral application, and personal perception.

86. Paul D. Molnar, *The Wiley Companion to Karl Barth* (Hoboken, NJ: John Wiley and Sons, 2020), 31.

87. Barth, *CD* II/1, 296–297. Barth affirms the uniqueness of the Holy Spirit through extrapolating His uniqueness from His place in the Trinity. The full quote: "Thus, even if the Father and the Son might be called 'person' (in the modern sense of the term), the Holy Spirit could not possibly be regarded as the third person. In a particularly clear way the Holy Spirit is what the Father and the Son also are. He is not a third spiritual Subject, a third I, a third Lord side by side with two others. He is a third mode of being of the one divine Subject or Lord." Barth, *CD* I/1, 469. Also note Augustine: "He comes forth, you see, not as being born but as being given, and so he is not called son, because he was not born like the only begotten Son, nor made and born adoptively by grace like us." Augustine, *On the Trinity*, Book V, Chapter 14. Remember that these are technical theological definitions; the point for everyday pastoral ministry is that the Holy Spirit is deeply personal—not an "it" or force, but the loving personal God Himself.

88. The idea that the Father, Son, and Spirit are three individual Gods is a heresy called Tritheism. Due to the modern-day understanding of the term "person," adjusting our language for the Spirit helps avoid this idea resurfacing.

89. Barth's adjustment of Person for the Holy Spirit is centered around the Greek neuter in the Nicene Creed. Barth's adjustment works off this neuter to affirm

that the Holy Spirit's distinctiveness exists paradoxically in His commonness with the Father and Son. While I find general agreement with Barth, my book is not the forum for such a thick conversation. Barth, *CD* I/I, 469.

90. When Thomas Torrance came to Karl Barth as a student wanting to do his doctoral dissertation in this area, Barth said he was too young and steered him in another direction. We must remember that this is the heart of the mystery and all conclusions, such as mine, should be open to critique and development. Elmer Colyer, *The Promise of Trinitarian Theology: Theologians in Dialogue with T. F. Torrance* (Lanham, MD: Rowman and Littlefield, 2001), 308.

91. I cannot leave this topic without commenting on the issue of modalism. Barth discusses how the German *Seinsweise*, which is translated into English as "modes of being," could be rendered as "way of being" to avoid any contamination of his doctrine by Modalism. Barth, *CD* I/1, viii, 359. Barth's idea of three divine modes of being of the one divine Lord is not modalism. Modalism is the idea that the Trinity is one God who just appears in three different modes. Barth is not affirming this. For Barth, all members of the Trinity are one and they are also fully unique. Barth extrapolates the Holy Spirit's distinctiveness, paradoxically from His commonness. I am employing Barth's thought here as I am wanting to avoid the modern existential idea that "person" equals "fully separate and self-conscious," leaving modern people with the mindset that they have a God of sorts in the Holy Spirit but are orphaned from Jesus. See *CD* II/I, 287–288, for a discussion on how incorrect usage of the term Person in the Trinity resulted in God being replaced by reason. The Father, Son, and Spirit are fully unique, but they are also fully one. "Person" in our culture equals "individuality"; the Holy Spirit is unique from the Father and Son, but he is not individual from them. He is completely one with them. Barth, *CD* I/1, 357–358; II/1, 297. This all said, let us know it is a revealed mystery. What we see is Jesus. We see Him through the Spirit and we trust, by faith, that Jesus is the Father revealed. What we know without doubt and can see free of questioning is that God consummated reconciliation by sending the Spirit of His Son into our hearts, promoting us to call to our Father as His Spirit gives us sight. We see you Lord Jesus, yesterday, today, and forevermore—oh, how we see you.

92. Augustine wrote that perhaps the reason the Holy Spirit is named the Holy Spirit is that holiness and spirit is what the Father and Son have in common. The very name Holy Spirit is meant to remind the believer of the holiness of the Father and Son, and the fact that both Father and Son (*logos*) are Spirit. Augustine, *On The Trinity*, Book 5, Chapter 12.

93. Barth, *CD* IV/2, 322–323, 331.

94. Barth, *CD* II/2, 780.

95. See John 1:12–13; Romans 8:15; 2 Corinthians 6:18; Galatians 4:5; Ephesians 2:19; 3:6.

96. The Jewish community did not have orphans like Roman society did or our society does. Jewish law gave strict guidelines for how the community was to care for parentless children. Basically, the extended family took the children in; hence the concept of an orphan was almost unheard of in Jewish society. A similar example is seen in the book of Ruth, with the family dealing with her as an abandoned widow. In contrast to this, Roman society openly practiced infanticide, which meant there were lots of orphans. Rescuing children who were the victims of infanticide, and or, disfigured from failed abortions was one of the first social welfare acts of the early Christian church, AD 50 onwards. See, Didache, circa AD 50-70, Chapter 2.

97. William Mitchell Ramsay, *A Historical Commentary on St. Paul's Epistle to the Galatians* (New York: G. P. Putnam's Sons, 1900), 352–353.

98. This parallels, or foreruns, the events of Acts 10. See also, Luke 15:25-32. Again, using this concept to devalue life, and or Israel, is not textually supported.

99. Barth, *CD* IV/2, 758.

100. Brennan Manning, *The Ragamuffin Gospel* (Colorado Springs: Multnomah Books, 2005), 195–197.

4. Ultimate Concern

101. Tillich, *Systematic Theology*, Volume 1, 12.

102. Keith Miller, *The Taste of New Wine* (London: Word Books, 1965), 40.

5. The Lazarus Discourse

103. Queen Elizabeth II, "The Christmas Broadcast 2020," December 24, 2020, https://www.royal.uk/christmas-broadcast-2020.

104. This statement is attributed to Dietrich Bonhoeffer.

105. William Temple, *Nature, Man and God* (London: Macmillan and Co, 1949), 54.

106. It is interesting to note that if light, air and gravity were visible everything else would be blocked out and unseen, likewise, if God was tangibly visible free–will would be impossible.

107. William Temple, *Nature, Man and God* (London: Macmillan and Co, 1949), 54.

108. Christopher J. Conselice, Aaron Wilkinson, Kenneth Duncan, and Alice Mortlock, "The Evolution of Galaxy Number Density at z < 8 and its Implications", *The Astrophysical Journal* 830:83 (2016): 12–13.

6. Hope as It Should Be (Part One)

109. Note that the KJV translates *hypostasis* as "person" in Hebrews 1:3.

110. Through God becoming man the Word of God becomes hearable and the primary thing faith hears is that the Man Jesus is God. Barth, *CD* I/2, 167–168.

111. In the hypostatic union of Jesus Christ "human existence has been redefined and transformed forever. The paradoxical twofold nature of Jesus Christ is the one and only nexus for the eternal relationship with the triune God. . . . Christians cannot think of themselves apart from Jesus Christ but in Him and in Him alone. The members of the Church through God's Spirit must unite with God-man Jesus in faith because He is the cornerstone providing the principle of unity of the Church from here to eternity." Peter S. Oh, "Complementary Dialectics of Kierkegaard and Barth: Barth's Use of Kierkegaardian Diastasis Reassessed," *Neue Zeitschrift Für Systematische Theologie Und Religionsphilosophie* 48, no. 4 (2006): 511.

112. Torrance, *Incarnation*, xxxiii.

113. Torrance, *Incarnation*, xxxiv, Barth, *CD* I/2, 163. A synodical letter written from bishops in Constantinople to those in Rome from 382 contains an early use of "person" as a translation for *hypostasis*. It is also worth noting that Athanasius, who was secretary/deacon to the leader of the resistance against the Arians at the Council of Nicaea (325), defined *hypostasis* as "being"—which is aligned with "person," as opposed to the modern English translations of "reality," "confidence," and "assurance." Jacques-Paul Migne, ed., *Patrologia Graeca*, Athanasius, 1857, PG 26:1036. Also see Calvin, *Institutes*, 67; and Philip Schaff, ed., *The Creeds of Christendom* (New York: Harper, 1877), 9. Phillip Schaff, ed., *Nicene and Post-Nicene Fathers, Volume 2* (Peabody, MA: Hendrickson Publishers, 2012), 9.

114. Torrance discusses this in *The Christian Doctrine of God*. In 553 the Second Council of Constantinople explained this process through the *anhypostasis* and *enhypostasis*. Sometimes heavy theological words can be unnecessary and serve to only complicate matters. However, in an instance such as this, using technical words to finely describe a very important point is essential. *Anhypostasis* and *enhypostasis* give the idea that Jesus is one person with two natures. *An* is a negator, used to halt the idea that Jesus as the divine *logos* entered into a

human embryo in Mary's womb and married with the identity of the person present in that embryo. This stops Jesus from having two persons: His eternally divine person (*logos*), and the person who would have been in Mary's embryo. *En* is the equivalent of the English word "in" and gives the idea that Jesus human nature is personal, but with a personhood that comes from the divine *logos*. *Anhypostasis* and *enhypostasis* teach us that Jesus does not get His personhood from His human nature, as in from Mary; rather, His human nature gets its personhood from the eternal Son of God. Jesus is not the composite of the divine *logos* mixing in with a person present in Mary. Instead, Jesus's eternally divine person entered into a (impersonal) human nature present in Mary, resulting in one person with two natures, not two natures with two persons. We tend to see ourselves as a body containing a person or a consciousness. Jesus is an eternal divine person (*logos*) who has had a human nature placed in His eternal person, so that He can redeem us. Barth, *CD* I/2; 163; Fred Sanders, *Jesus in Trinitarian Perspective: An Introductory Christology* (Nashville: B&H Academic, 2007), 29–31, note footnote on page 30 for historical overview. For some additional terminology clarification see Torrance, *Incarnation*, 84, 228. From *anhypostasis* and *enhypostasis* you get the idea that humanity's identity is restored by it being placed in divinity—in Christ. This is the throbbing heart of redemption.

The Bible says that we are made in the image of God, formed in the womb by Him and through Him. *Anhypostasis* and *enhypostasis* teach us who Jesus is, but they also remind us of how special we are. We are handcrafted by God in our mother's womb, the zygote and embryo being elevated from the status of mere flesh to a being filled with personhood by the very hand of God. In the incarnation the curtain is pulled back and we are given a vantage point of what it means to be created in the image of God. The mother's womb is a personalised Eden, where God forms a being in temporality that is capable, through faith, of touching eternity. What a precious task our mothers have, let us be diligent in praying for them. "God's ways are as mysterious as the pathway of the wind and as the manner in which a human spirit is infused into the little body of a baby while it is yet in its mother's womb" (Eccl. 11:5, TLB).

115. See comments in Torrance. *Atonement*, lii, lxviii.

116. Augustine, *On the Trinity*, Book XV, 18.32.

117. Note Emil Brunner's definition of faith, "For faith is the entrance into the movement of God in Christ." Brunner, *The Mediator*, 619.

118. For me, it is not logical for something unseen to be the proof of what is not seen. Therefore, faith must be seen, touchable and tangible. It must be a seen "thing" that has come from the unseen place so that it can testify in the real world. I cannot think of anything, anyone, any substance other than Jesus of Nazareth that fits this requirement—Jesus Himself, His very person and being: "That which was from the beginning, which we have heard, which we have seen with our eyes, which we have looked at and our hands have touched-this we proclaim concerning the Word of life" (1 John 1:1, NIV).

119. In Hebrews 11:1 *hypostasis* is translated as substance, reality, assurance, or confidence in English Bibles. Who or what is the substance, reality, assurance, or confidence of our faith if not the person of Jesus? Faith is the person that we hoped for, the person who is the evidence of the unseen eternal Kingdom dwelling with us.

120. Martin Luther, *Commentary on the Epistle to the Galatians*, ed T. Graebner (New York: Scripture Press, 2015), 43.

121. Barth's idea of what faith is, is a truly brilliant and truly complex piece of Christian thought. Barth sees faith as the determination of human action by Jesus Christ. Faith is not something we create; it is God's activity in us which we respond to. See Barth, *CD* I/I, 17; III/III, 264.

122. Luther wrote: "Faith is a work of God in us, which changes us and brings us to birth anew from God (John 1). It kills the old Adam, makes us completely different people in heart, mind, senses, and all our powers, and brings the Holy Spirit with it. What a living, creative, active powerful thing is faith!" Luther, *Preface to the Letter of St Paul to the Romans*. John Calvin translated Acts 26:18 as "I send thee—that they may receive forgiveness of sins, and inheritance among them which are sanctified through faith which is in me." Calvin, *Institutes,* 355. Also, Pannenberg wrote, "Faith is directly in God and his Word." Pannenberg highlights Thomas Aquinas who links faith with God Himself and also to love—which is God's substance. Pannenberg, *Systematic Theology*, Volume 3, 14; Thomas Aquinas, *The Summa Theologica*, Volume 2 (Cincinnati: Benziger Brothers, 194),. 2, q. 4, a. 3. See also Karl Barth, *Anselm:* Fides Quaerens Intellectum (London: SCM Press, 1960), 17.

123. Barth, *CD* I/1. Page 121.

124. We must be careful here to remember that it is three different forms of the Word of God, not three different Words of God. Barth, *CD* I/1, 121.

125. "Proclamation" is a term referring to the witness of the Church. It is not just preaching; it is the sharing, or proclaiming, of the Bible's message to the world through all means: preaching, acts of love, conversations in coffee shops, Instagram updates—proclaiming truth in all spheres.

126. Scripture, the Bible, is God's very Word. Carl Henry's critique of Barth is necessary reading for those delving deep into Barth's thought in this area. Carl Henry, *Frontiers in Modern Theology* (Chicago: Moody Press, 1972), 66.

127. We see this outworked in the story of the prodigal son. Barth, *CD* I/1, 244–247.

128. See Kierkegaard, *Training in Christianity*, 68, What we "live contemporaneous with is reality—for thee."

129. Augustine, *Confessions* (London: Penguin Classics, 1961), books 11, 18.

130. The inner workings of this process are a true mystery. We do not know how it worked, but we do know that it happened, that this is true hell, and it was taken for us by the Son of God. See Philippians 2:7.

131. I know that some will not like the idea that Christ suffered emotionally, but remember Jesus wept. He also "cried out" loudly on the cross (Greek: vehement cry that is emotionally charged). Further, the main Greek words used in the New Testament to describe Jesus's suffering have, at their core, the idea "to feel heavy emotion, especially suffering." See James Strong, *Strong's Exhaustive Concordance of the Bible* (Nashville: Abingdon Press, 1890), #3958.

132. It is a hard thing for our human minds to intake, but the events of Calvary take place both in time and beyond time—beyond time in the sense that the events of the cross travel throughout the human timeline, both backward and forward, offering the free gift of redemption to all people in all ages. Or perhaps you could say the human timeline circles the cross. The redemption of Calvary is so weighty and impacting, that like gravity, it affects time. His mercies are new every morning because each day circles back to the cross. Humanly speaking, tomorrow is a new day, salvation-wise, it is nonlinear time, it is day returning—thus the Bible's claim that "today is the day of salvation," i.e., the day of the Lord's salvation returning over and over again. No matter the failure His mercies are new every morning, great is His faithfulness. Each day sets before the cross and each day rises before the potential of the empty tomb and power of Pentecost.

It is interesting to note that science has now advanced human understanding to the level where we can offer an explanation of the Bible's statement that "a day is like a thousand years." Scientists have realized that time can be slowed down. It is possible that God has placed humanity (our universe) in a time dilation bubble, with time slowed to the point where a day outside the bubble equals one thousand inside. Under this theoretical but workable model, the events of the Gospels happened two days ago, David's kingdom three days ago and the garden of Eden around eight days ago. He is closer than we know, an ever-present help in time of need: "But beloved, do not let this one thing be hidden from you, that with the Lord one day is like a thousand years, and a thousand years like one day" (2 Pet. 3:8, BLB).

133. Ben Myers says the following in this area: "If the resurrection is the universalization of Jesus's particular history, then the work of the Spirit is the making present of this history to specific human persons. It is the Spirit's work to manifest the history of Jesus to each specific person, and to open each person to the reality of Jesus's history." Michael Bird and Preston Sprinkle, *The Faith of Jesus Christ: The Pistis Christou Debate* (Peabody, MA: Hendrickson, 2009), 306.

134. Tozer, *The Pursuit of God*, 23–24.

135. Zimmermann, *Incarnational Humanism*, 266. Full quote: "Christianity is not to offer culture another religion but the gift of life, true humanity. Truly, in Christ life—life in all its totality—was returned to man."

136. Torrance, *When Christ Comes and Comes Again*, 26.

7. Hope as It Should Be (Part Two)

137. Some scholars have noted that the kingdom of God is less prevalent in the letters of the disciples as opposed to the four Gospels. The Gospels are centered in Jesus's life and ministry; they are focused on communicating this core message. The letters of the New Testament have another purpose; they are pastoral letters dealing with the formation of local churches. This means that the disciples have to cover a myriad of pastoral issues. This for me is the answer to the smaller mention of the kingdom of God. From the start of the church, the leaders had to deal with the same thing local pastors are dealing with all over the globe today: people and their pasts being woven together with the divine message of heaven. The Gospel is a simple message, but not a simple process. The New Testament writers spent a lot of time penning words that allow people to enter the kingdom of God.

138. This is in the present tense, indicative mood, and active voice. This means that Jesus Himself is the one who has made the kingdom "at hand."

139. "In His human person He [Jesus] is the kingdom of God come down from heaven to earth." Barth, *CD* IV/1, 208.

140. "If you want to know the kingdom of God, do not go far afield in search of it. If you wish to have it, you will find it close to you. Yes, it is not only close to you, it is in you." Martin Luther, *Devotional Writings,* Luther's Works, Volume 42 (St. Louis: Concordia Publishing House, 1986), 41.

141. Barth, *CD* IV/2, 760.

142. Schaff, *Nicene and Post-Nicene Fathers, Volume 2,* 2. See also, Phillip Schaff, ed., *Nicene and Post-Nicene Fathers, Volume 1* (Peabody, MA: Hendrickson Publishers, 2012), 491.

143. Treadwell Walden, *The Great Meaning of* Metanoia (New York: Thomas, 1896), 7–8.

144. A similar comparison would be how the English language only has one word for "love," while the Greek New Testament has several, all describing varying types of love.

145. See A. T. Robertson, *Word Pictures of the New Testament,* specifically the entry for Matthew 3:2 for a potential Greek origin of the word repent. Robertson's father in-law, John Albert Broadus, who Spurgeon called the "greatest of living preachers," famously said the word "repent" was the worst translation in the New Testament.

146. Walden, *Great Meaning of* Metanoia, 14.

147. "Repentance," *International Standard Bible Encyclopedia,* James Orr, gen. ed., https://www.internationalstandardbible.com/R/repentance.html.

148. Walden, *Great Meaning of* Metanoia, 14; Edward Anton, *Repentance: A Cosmic Shift of Heart and Mind* (Spring, TX: Illumination Publishers: 2016), 39.

149. The Greek word *metanoia* does not come prefilled with meaning. *Metanoia* (repentance) adopts meaning from the determining words in the sentence it is used in. For example, the Bible does say to *metanoia* because of sin (Mark 1:4; Luke 24:47; Acts 5:31; 13:24). This does not mean that the word *metanoia* itself means to repent of sin, but rather that *metanoia* has been employed by a biblical writer to give a tool for leaving sin behind. *Metanoia* needs to be used with another word to tell the reader what the writer wants them to change their mind about. In Mark 1:15 Jesus wants us to change our mind because of the good news about His kingdom. In Acts 3:19 Peter wants us to change our mind so our sins can be wiped out, bringing forth a refreshing season in our lives.

Further to this, it is important to remember that the command to *metanoia* (repent) from sinning is given by the King of heaven in light of His kingdom coming. The call to change from sin must be accompanied by a revelation of the King and His kingdom; if it isn't, there is nothing to contrast against.

If the contrast is not made, the illumination of sin becomes condemning and not constructive, as an alternate way is not presented. The Holy Spirit convicts to construct.

150. It is worth noting that some people feel this is what Tyndale was aiming for. We must be kind to William Tyndale here; he did a wonderful and courageous thing in making the adjustment that he made. "Repent" for him and his time could have meant something different in the popular understating than its etymological origin indicates. Tyndale was also looking to push reform without completely enraging his opposition. There is a great deal that can be said here and in truth it is enough for a standalone volume; for now, I just want to say that we owe a great deal to William Tyndale, one of God's great ambassadors.

151. Walden, *Great Meaning of* Metanoia, 3.

152. Walden, *Great Meaning of* Metanoia, 13.

153. Eli Brayley, *Great Meaning of* Metanoia (Woodstock, GA: Timothy Ministry, 2012).

154. Tertullian, in Phillip Schaff, *Ante-Nicene Fathers, Volume 3* (Peabody, MA: Hendrickson Publishers), 252.

155. Lucius Caecilius Firmianus Lactantius, *The Divine Institutes. XXIV: Of Repentance, of Pardon, and the Commands of God.* http://www.intratext.com/IXT/ENG0292/_P48.HTM.

156. Martin Luther, *The Career of the Reformer: Explanations of the Ninety-five Theses,* Luther Works, Volume 31, Philadelphia: Fortress Press, 1957), 83–84. Note also Luther's comments in his letter to John Staupitz accompanying the resolution to the ninety-five theses, dated 1518.

157. Charles Finney, Finney's Systematic Theology (Minneapolis: Bethany Fellowship Inc, 1964), 300-301.

158. Torrance, *Atonement*, 443.

159. The context of James 4:8–10 is essential here. James is not telling us to feel sorrow when we repent (*metanoia*), he is telling people who are unwilling to repent (*metanoia*) to feel sorrow about their stubbornness. It is a critical difference. James is not calling for a Gospel involving sorrow; James is calling for people who are unwilling to accept the Gospel to be sorrowful about this decision. For James, the Gospel produces joy (4:10), ignoring that joy should not be celebrated but mourned and then corrected through *metanoia*. Similarly, the godly grief or sorrow of 2 Corinthians 7:10 is not a form of sorrow aligned to punishment and pain.

160. This is not to be confused with confessing our sins. We can and should confess that we have sinned and fallen short of the glory of God. But this confession is a constructive one that looks forward and not back. Confession not personal chastisement is the command of the Bible (Jas. 5:16; 1 John 1:9). I strongly feel that the modern-day generations do not understand repentance as Jesus said it, when they hear "repent," they interpret it as chastisement, hence the need to adjust the word back to its original meaning, ensuring it conveys the biblical concept of constructive confession and change.

161. "If confession of sin is understood in an adequate theological context, it would lead not to lowered self-esteem, but rather quite the opposite. When one is led to confess one's sin before God, it is always in the context of the gospel, namely with a *foreknowledge* [meta] of God's mercy, grace, and forgiveness. If one's relationship with God is the context of confession, one cannot despise or scorn oneself, for God lifts one up, welcoming one with open, loving, joyful arms. To be loved and forgiven by such a Father is hardly to perpetuate low self-esteem." Deborah van Deusen Hunsinger, *The Master Key: unlocking the relationship of theology and psychology*, 2001. Inspire 5 (2): 22. Emphases added.

162. John 8:36 (NIV) says: "So if the Son sets you free, you will be free indeed." We are freed to be elevated to the status of an heir with Christ. Romans 8:17 (NIV) adds: "Now if we are children, then we are heirs—heirs of God and co-heirs with Christ, if indeed we share in his sufferings in order that we may also share in his glory." This is our identity, this is our position; we focus on the fact that we have been freed and made heirs with Christ. We are not who we were; we have been transformed by the work of the Son of God. Suffering will come, but this is not a result of God punishing our sin; Jesus took this punishment. When the Bible says we share in His suffering it not a matter of suffering to purchase salvation; it is suffering to further His kingdom, hardship as a matter of worship—as a living sacrifice.

163. A good exercise here is a Bible word search on "thankfulness." The idea of coming to God and living with Him through thankfulness is a strong consistent theme; examples include Philippians 4:6 and Colossians 2:6–7; 3:15.

164. Notice that the word "Gospel" is made up of two roots words. One of them, *aggelos*, brings the idea that the message is found in a supernatural messenger. This gives the idea that it is not a doctrine or religion; rather, it is a person who contains truth and in Jesus's case, literally is the truth, coming to us: "The truth is in Jesus" (Eph. 4:21).

165. Strong, *Strong's Exhaustive Concordance,* #3445.

166. English translations such as the NIV, ISV, and BSB have the phrase "the light of life" or an equivalent as they are following the LXX (Septuagint) and the Dead Sea Scrolls, it is present in both of these. Translations that follow the Masoretic Text do not have the phrase as it is not present there. As a note: a few translations have "He will see it", the "it" is a nondescript reference to the light of life. For those undecided in whether to follow the Septuagint and Dead Sea Scrolls or the Masoretic Text, it is interesting to note that Jesus reads from the Septuagint in Luke 4 when he recites Isaiah 61:1–2 in the Synagogue. The Septuagint is also widely quoted by the Apostles in the New Testament.

167. It is interesting to note the line in the Nicene Constantinopolitan creed, "Light from Light." I wonder if these thoughts were in the church fathers' minds when they crafted such a statement. See Barth, *CD* I.1, 427–428.

168. This mind transfiguration is not the result of self-reflection or inner meditation; this is the way of modern-day spirituality. Modern spirituality says: look inside yourself and you will find the answer. This is not what we are discussing here. The Christian Gospel is not a self-reflection. In the Christian Gospel we accept that our human nature is sinful and that looking within to gain victory will never produce. For the Christian it is not looking within, but rather looking to Christ; it is accepting the mind of Christ. God came to earth in Christ and Christ comes to us through His Holy Spirit. This is not a belief based on human temporal understanding, for we are assured as beings bound to one solar system that our reasoning is limited.

169. The New Testament word "believe" comes from the Greek word for "faith."

170. "Repentance means that you are willing to let God change your life. It means that you change your mind so much that it changes the way you live. And you are willing to give up all those things which are sinful in your life and turn over to Jesus Christ your life." The University of Life: Billy Graham Classics, September 16, 1980, Billy Graham Evangelistic Association, https://billygraham.org/audio/the-university-of-life.

171. Full quote: "It is clear that the sinner was an enemy before the reconciliation took place. Human action, incl. Even repentance and confession of sins, is not a work that initiates reconciliation and to which God reacts. Rather it is the work of God, to which we respond." Silva, *New International Dictionary of New Testament Theology and Exegesis,* Volume 1, 245. Also, Luther discusses how "faith is a work of God in us" in his preface to Romans.

172. There is a preconversion work of the Holy Spirit. He comes to us to offer a change of mind; it is only when we agree through confession that this becomes actualized. Also, Martin Luther, *The Career of the Reformer: Two Kinds of Righteousness,* Luther Works, Volume 31, 299.

173. Martin Luther, *Luther Lectures on Romans, Library of Christian Classics,* ed. Wilhelm Pauck (Louisville: Westminster John Knox Press, 2006), Rom. 1:17. Luther gave these lectures in 1515–1516 and they were unpublished at his death. His family held them for a good many years and through a series of almost incredible events they were published hundreds of years later in 1908, with the first English edition in 1961. The story of these lectures' safekeeping and eventual publishing is a worthwhile read and to my mind a brilliant example of how the Lord guards His truth (John 16:13). I feel it is necessary to print the name of Johannes Ficker, who in his own words "ransacked all of Europe to locate the original." Hans Wiersma, "Martin Luther's Lectures on Romans (1515–1516): Their Rediscovery and Legacy," *Word and World,* Volume 39, Number 3 (2019). It is also worth noting that since we have only had these documents in English since 1961, only in our modern time has so much truth been so accessible. Many generations labored and sacrificed to give us the above quoted line. Luther's original is in the Berlin State Library, with an early transcript in the Vatican. There are also surviving copies of Luther's original students' personal lectures notes in circulation.

174. Luther and Erasmus debated the idea of free will throughout the 1520s. Central to this debate was whether salvation is an action of God in us or if it is a matter of our human will partnering with God. Luther resoundingly wins the argument by using Scripture, something Erasmus struggles to do. Luther's grace-based salvation is in the background of the thoughts shared in this section.

175. Confession of Christ's lordship is twofold. It is an acknowledgment of Jesus's person and His works. Once this is seen, a constructive confession of sin is initiated. This is not about denigration; sin is a disease and acknowledging we have this disease is essential to treatment.

176. Augustine's writings helped inspire this realization. Note his comments from *On the Spirit and the Letter,* Chapter 60, "The very will by which we believe is reckoned as a gift of God . . . this will is to be ascribed to the divine gift . . . because God acts upon us by the incentives of our perceptions, to will and to believe. . . . Since God, therefore, in such ways acts upon the reasonable soul in order that it may believe in Him, it surely follows that it is God who both

works in man the willing to believe." See chapters 50, 57 and 60 for more on this topic from Augustine. Philip Schaff, ed., *Nicene and Post-Nicene Fathers: First Series Volume V—St. Augustine: Anti-Pelagian Writings, On The Spirit and The Letter* (New York: Cosimo, 2007).

177. Martin Luther, *The Career of the Reformer: The Ninety-five Theses,* Luther Works, Volume 31, 25–33.

178. John Calvin wrote, "I would fain know, from those who pretend that man meets God with some righteousness of works, whether they imagine there is any kind of righteousness save that which is acceptable to him." Calvin, *Institutes,* 506.

179. "Faith, however, is something that God effects in us. . . . Offer up your prayers to God, and ask Him to create faith in you. . . . No one can give faith to himself, nor free himself from unbelief." Martin Luther, *Preface to Romans* (Nashville: Discipleship Resources, 1977), 6–7.

180. Walden, *Great Meaning of* Metanoia, 13.

181. Kierkegaard, *Training in Christianity*, 70–72.

182. I have noticed in my time as a pastor that removing a personal acceptance of sin results in people being stuck in a cycle of validation. The modern-day version of the removal of sin seems to be the validation of sin because of past hurts. The Bible has endless compassion for people who have been hurt, but it never makes this next step and removes personal responsibility for wrongdoing because of past hurts. I was abused as a child, but this does not allow me to be free of personal responsibility if I abuse my family now as an adult man—I am responsible for my adult actions. Removing sin results in powerless Christianity and misrepresenting repentance results in condemning Christianity. We need to do exactly what Jesus said to do: acknowledge our sin in light of the offer of forgiveness and salvation from a kind Father.

183. Brunner, *The Mediator,* 13.

184. Statics:"Australias Changing Spiritual Climate" (McCrindle Research. 2021). "Australians Attending Church", (NCLS Research, 2021). "Faith and Belief in Australia" (McCrindle Research. 2017).

185. McCrindle, "Faith and Belief."

186. Max Zellweger-Barth, *My Father-In-Law* (Eugene, OR: Pickwick Publications, 1986), 4.

187. Barth attested to this phrase; see discussion in *The Word of God and The Word of Man.*

188. A good exercise here is a word study on "growth" in the New Testament; note passages like Colossians 1:9–10 and the parable of the sower in Luke 8.

189. Cyril, *Catechetical Lecture IV. 10,11,12.*, in Schaff, *Nicene and Post-Nicene Fathers, Volume 7*, 23.

190. In Exodus 25:12–15 God gives clear instructions on how to transport the ark of the covenant. Fast-forward many centuries and we see King David break this commandment and move the ark, not via the poles as commanded but by a cart. This results in one of David's subjects dying and him asking, "How can the ark of the LORD ever come to me?" (2 Sam. 6:9). It is perplexing as to why David, as king, did not know of this command or why one of his priestly advisors did not communicate this to him. David being so unaware is in violation of another command. In Deuteronomy 17:18–19 the kings were commanded to write out a copy of the law in front of the Levitical priests and keep it with them. There is no record of David obeying this instruction (David also broke the two previous commands about wives and wealth). In this vacancy David followed the lead of secular culture. In 1 Samuel 6:7 the Philistines made a cart to send the ark away from their lands. David transports the ark after this occurs, making this action of the Philistines the likely origin of his idea to transport the ark on a cart (the Bible uses the same phrase "new cart" in both accounts). David is now, without realising it, following the secular culture and not God's commands. This results in David's question, "How can the ark of the LORD ever come to me?" Meaning, how can I have God's direct presence with me—as God manifested on the mercy seat above the ark? This is the same question so many ask nowadays: How can we see revival? How can we see God's direct presence powerfully in our lives, families, churches, and communities? Let us learn from David. The answer is in knowing and then standing in the longstanding command of God.

191. The following is a good theological summary of this by C. S Lewis. But don't misunderstand Lewis's use of the word "myth" here: "Now myth transcends thought, incarnation transcends myth. The heart of Christianity is a myth which is also a fact. The old myth of the dying God, without ceasing to be myth, comes down from the heaven of legend and imagination to the earth of history. . . . To be truly Christian we must both assent to the historical fact and also receive the myth (fact though it has become). . . . We must not be ashamed of the mythical radiance resting on our theology." C. S. Lewis, *Undeceptions* (London: Geoffrey Bles, 1971), 42–43.

192. Often habitual sin in the genuine believing life is not rebellion-related; it is a coping mechanism left over from the old life (Rom. 7:15). God rarely miraculously frees us from these coping mechanisms. Rather, He removes

the underlying belonging or rejection issue that we have been medicating by offering belonging with Himself, His approval speaking louder than old voices. When we realise that, through the miracle of the cross, we have been freed from our master bondage, we are empowered through the mechanism of our redeemed will to leave the coping mechanism that has been made redundant. God does the heavy lifting and empowers us, so as to mature us, letting us experience His power in our hands.

193. Donald Bloesch, "The Sword of the Spirit: The Meaning of Inspiration," *Themelios* 5.3 (May 1980): 14–19.

194. Alexander of Lyon, in Phillip Schaff, ed., *Ante-Nicene Fathers Volume 8, Pseud-Irenaeus* (Peabody, MA: Hendrickson Publishers).

195. Quoted in N. T. Wright, *Paul and the Faithfulness of God, Parts III and IV* (London: Society for Promoting Christian Knowledge, 2013), 651. Also see Augustine. *On the Trinity,* Book VII, 5.10.

196. The academic quote from Wright on this is: "Jesus's first followers found themselves not only (as it were) permitted to use God-language for Jesus, but compelled to use Jesus-language for the one God." Wright, *Paul and the Faithfulness of God,* 655.

197. Cyril, *Catechetical Lecture X. 11.,* in Schaff, *Nicene and Post-Nicene Fathers, Volume 7,* 60.

198. John Calvin, *Commentaries on the Four Last Books of Moses: Arranged in the Form of a Harmony,* Volume 1, trans. Rev. C. W. Bingham (Edinburgh: Calvin Translations Society, 1850), 73.

199. 1700 years ago, in Israel, Eusebius wrote about the connection between the revelation of God to Moses and the name Jesus Christ. Eusebius notes two key points 1. In Numbers 13:16 Moses changes Joshua's (Hebrew) name from Hoshea to Yehoshua (or Jehoshua). As Marcus Dods observed, "originally called Hoshea, or Salvation, this name was changed, when he led the spies, to Jehoshua, or The Lord is Salvation." As Jehoshua is the origin of the name Jesus, here Eusebius provides the direct connection between the name Jesus and Moses. 2. Eusebius notes Exodus 25.40 where God says to "be careful to make them according to the pattern you have been shown on the mountain." Here Eusebius is connecting the name Jehoshua to the revelation YHWH gave Moses. Eusebius goes on to connect the title "Christ" with Moses. Cyril picks Eusebius thought up and in doing so provides a second Church Father attesting to the idea of a direct connection between the name Jesus and the revelation of YHWH to Moses. Eusebius: "Moses was the first to make known the name of Christ...the name of Jesus, which had

never been uttered among men before the time of Moses, he applied first and only to… his successor." Essentially, the names Joshua and then Jesus come from YHWH via Moses. Eusebius, *Book 1*. III, 1-6., in Schaff, *Nicene and Post-Nicene Fathers, Volume 1*, 85. Cyril, *Catechetical Lecture X. 11.*, in Schaff, *Nicene and Post-Nicene Fathers, Volume 7*, 60. Marcus Dods. *The Change of Joshua's Name*.

200. The phrase *L'Éternel* has its origin with John Calvin's cousin Pierre-Robert. This translation is found in interpretative Tanakh (Jewish Bible) translations, see Exodus 3:14; Leviticus 1:1 in *Torah Yesharah*, translated and edited by Chas. Kahane, New York, 1963; www.sefaria.org is an excellent resource in this area.

201. Barth discusses that we can reverse the statement "God is love" to explain that love is God. Barth, *CD* IV 2, 756. Barth discusses how the threefold name of Father (YHWH), Son (Jesus Christ), and Spirit is the basis of God's history and also the name of God's work and word in history. God naming Himself and revealing these names is Him turning to us and coming into our clutches. Without His name(s), God is not personable; through them He is a Lord humanity can address and also claim (Barth, *CD* IV/4, 92–93, 99). More simply put, the only way to understand the Father is through Jesus. Likewise, we understand Jesus through the Father, specifically by seeing the history of the Father in the Old Testament as Jesus's historical actions in humanity, and by the Spirit's ongoing work as Jesus's continuing activity in humanity. Father and Son are individual names, but also complementary names. They can and must be used to comprehend each other.

202. "To know Him is to know His love as that in which He is and also is God." Barth, *CD* IV/2, 756.

203. "The life and rule of love is the most inward and proper life and rule of God." Barth, *CD* IV/2, 757.

204. The French Geneva Bible rendering YHWH as The Eternal One opens lines of reasoning. If God is eternal and love, then love is eternal. Thus, Yahweh as the Eternal One is directly linked with eternal love.

205. Mark 14:62–63 gives us insight into this crucial exchange between Jesus and His own high priest and Sanhedrin: When asked, "Are You the Messiah, the Son of the Blessed One?" Jesus replies "I am." This was clearly understood by the high priest as a claim to oneness with YHWH, as "the high priest tore his robes."

206. Jesus comes to us through the Holy Spirit and through Jesus the God of the burning bush also (John 14:6–7, 18–19; Heb. 1:3). YHWH is the great I Am; in Jesus we learn that the great I Am is love. It is as if Jesus is saying "I Am YHWH" and YHWH is saying "I Am Love." Two generation defining theologians, 1,500 years apart, both affirmed this interpretation of John's writing: Augustine: "Love, therefore, which is of God and is God, is specifically the Holy Spirit." (Augustine, *On the Trinity*, Book XV, 18.32); and Barth: "God is love" (1 John 4:8;16) and "God is Spirit" (John 4:24) explain each other. For the apostle John, to say "love" is to say "Spirit"; these two explain each other. (To make this easy to intake, I have constructed this statement from a few sentences in the final paragraph of Barth, *CD* IV/2, 757).

Augustine puts all this together and presents Jesus as a God of love who comes to us as the Spirit of Love—the Holy Spirit: "the Holy Spirit, of whom He hath given us, makes us to abide in God, and Him in us . . . through Him the whole Trinity dwells in us. . . . [He] is distinctively to be understood as being the charity [love] which brings us through to God" (Augustine, *On the Trinity*, Book XV,17.31, 18.32).

207. As noted, Eusebius and Cyril highlight the connection between the revelation YHWH gave Moses and the name Yehoshua, from which we get the English name Jesus. Yehoshua means "the Lord is salvation" and was given to Joshua as he was a "savior" figure, leading the nation into the promised land. Yehoshua has a prefix that is an abbreviation of the tetragrammaton as its first element, making it a theophoric name, cementing the connection between the names Jesus and YHWH—allowing them to interpret each other. Maclaurin, E.C.B. *YHWH The Origin of the Tetragrammaton. Vetus Testamentum, 12* (4), 439, 445.

The oldest accepted reference to YHWH from outside the Bible is the Soleb Inscription, from the temple of Amenhotep III, in modern day Sudan, dated to 1400 BC. Sudan was under the control of the Pharaoh and this inscription refers to his enemies, one of which is "the nomads of YHWH." Thus, this name is verified by secular scholarship to be 3400 years old–the time of Joshua. See, Donald Redford, *Egypt, Canaan, and Israel in Ancient Times,* (Princeton, NJ: Princeton University Press, 1993), 272-273.

208. Silva, *New International Dictionary of New Testament Theology and Exegesis,* Vol. 2, 527.

209. Torrance, *Atonement,* 179.

210. Adapted from Barth, *The Christian Life,* 115.

9. Citizens of Eternity

211. Billy Graham Evangelistic Association, The University of Life: Billy Graham Classics, September 16, 1980, https://billygraham.org/audio/the-university-of-life.

212. Matthew George Easton, *Easton's Bible Dictionary* (Nashville: Thomas Nelson, 1897), *kuriakon*.

213. Strong, *Strong's Exhaustive Concordance of the Bible*, #1577 *Ekklēsía*.

214. Wright, *Paul and the Faithfulness of God*, 1493.

215. Augustine, *City of God*, Book XIV, Chapter 28.

216. Augustine, *City of God*, Book XIV, Chapter 25.

217. *Either/Or* by Kierkegaard uses pseudonyms and topical content that only a nineteenth-century Danish citizen would understand. If you wish to read *Either/Or* I would suggest an abridged version (London: Penguin Classics, 1992) or the good book by Howard and Edna Hong, *The Essential Kierkegaard*. Due to the way Kierkegaard writes and the way he draws conclusion, I would refer you to his later comment on *Either/Or* in another of his works for a referenceable and clear statement on his intent: "this book . . . was a necessary deception in order, if possible, to deceive men into the religious which has been my task all along." Søren Kierkegaard, *Journals and Papers*, Volume 6 (Bloomington: Indiana University Press, 1967), 134. Kierkegaard uses the idea of deception because he is trying to "deceive" a city full of religious clergy and secular citizens into seeing beyond an ethically focused religious life and the pleasure-driven ascetical life toward the true "religious" existence put forward by the New Testament (his ethical arguments don't specifically target religious people but the state church is clearly in view). Personally, I think Kierkegaard calls this deception because the idea of the true religious life was virtually nonexistent in his city. The church was a moral-ethical system. Kierkegaard saw this and knew that the ideas of the New Testament would be so foreign that he used the writing style he did to slip the Gospel into people's minds. *Either/Or* ends with a section called "the Ultimatum," in which Kierkegaard hints that either/or is actually neither/nor. Neither the pleasure-driven life nor the ethical life is worth living for; it is only the religious life that is worth our allegiance. Kierkegaard picks this theme up in later works like *Repetition* and *Stages on Life's Way*. I feel it is worth sharing that Kierkegaard feared his life being wasted; in order to have the freedom to write he stayed out of the priesthood and bankrupted himself publishing his books. It was not in his lifetime

that he saw the fruit; his works were translated by others who came after his death, resurrecting them as they saw their immense value. His ideas became foundation stones in the movements that gave a personal (existential) relationship with Jesus back to the church. Kierkegaard died at age forty-two; he collapsed in the streets of Copenhagen after years of ridicule and scorn, his life hallmarked by a daily repetition of living in and through his Jesus. See Kierkegaard's book *Training in Christianity* (or more recently *Practice in Christianity*) for a summary of his life's work.

218. Søren Kierkegaard, *Fear and Trembling* (London: Penguin Classics, 2014), Problem 1.

219. Kierkegaard highlights a male and female example as knights of faith, Abraham and Mary. Women are equals in this area and if anything, they lead the men. The women were first at the tomb.

220. This debate has its origin with Richard Hays who ignited a worthy debate on how it should be translated. Barth also highlighted the issue in his commentary on Romans in 1919.

221. Bird and Sprinkle, *The Faith of Jesus Christ*, 1, 170. The debate centers around either an objective genitive interpretation "faith in Christ" or a subjective genitive interpretation "the faithfulness of Christ."

222. Karl Barth, *The Epistle to the Romans* (London: Oxford University Press, 1976), 35, 91.

223. Bird and Sprinkle, *The Faith of Jesus Christ*, 169.

224. The idea of one being elected for all is an idea that carries over from the Old Testament. Thomas Torrance makes the point that Israel was elected "as the instrument of divine love for the redemption of all mankind and creation. The election of one for the salvation of all characterized the whole story of God's dealings with Israel." Torrance, *Incarnation*, 52.

225. Barth, *CD* II/2, 145, 153. It is worth noting that Barth's idea of election is a reworking of Calvin's double predestination and is actually in a synergy of sorts with Calvin's concept. Barth's doctrine is in fact double predestination. It is just that, per Barth, Jesus is double predestined, to death and life, crucifixion and resurrection.

226. Barth, *CD* II/2, 117.

227. Barth, *CD* II/2, 94.

228. Barth, *CD* II/2, 167.

229. Barth, *CD* II/2, 161, 165.

230. Barth, *CD* II/2, 165.

231. Barth, *CD* II/2, 167–168.

232. The area of how Jesus's election and rejection on our behalf works with our command to choose to follow Jesus is a mystery in the Scripture. The answer to this mystery is not found in academic work; it is found in simple trust— trusting that a God who is made of love has set up a system that is fair and just. How the choice operates in the unseen background is not our concern. If it was Jesus, would have openly told us. We are called to choose to trust Him and trust in His salvation.

233. Barth, *CD* II/2, 506.

234. C. S. Lewis, *Mere Christianity* (London: Fontana Books, 1969), 55.

235. Bird and Sprinkle, *The Faith of Jesus Christ*, 306.

236. Bird and Sprinkle, *The Faith of Jesus Christ*, 291–308.

237. Barth, *CD* IV/4, 33.

238. Thomas Upham, *The Life of Madame Guyon* (London: Allenson and Co, 1940), 498.

239. John links "our faith" with believing in Jesus here. The "faith of us" is personal faith, personal in the sense that it knows the one it is putting faith in and getting faith from. I see this truth from 1 John 5:4 affirming my conclusions in this book, that Jesus's faithfulness is the origin and object of faith and that faith can be seen as union with Jesus.

240. Martin Luther recalls the following thought from Augustine in his commentary on Romans 1:17: "Saint Augustine writes in the eleventh chapter of *On the Spirit and the Letter:* 'from the faith of those who confess it by word of mouth to the faith of those who prove it by their obedience.'" Luther, *Lectures on Romans*, Rom. 1:17.

241. This as a summary statement. Around this topic I have quoted Jesus and His Word (the Bible), Augustine, Barth, Kierkegaard, Martin Luther, and others like, Torrance, Aquinas and Pannenberg. As you read all these voices you begin to see a thread of commonality between them. This statement is my summary of their collective voices.

242. "Faith is a work of God in us." Luther, *Preface to Romans*.

243. John Calvin wrote, "faith itself is produced only by the Spirit." Calvin, *Institutes,* 351. Also, Cyril, *Catechetical Lecture V. 11.,* in Schaff, *Nicene and Post-Nicene Fathers, Volume 7,* 31.

244. "Human reason has the law for its object . . . but faith in itself has no object but Jesus Christ, the Son of God, given up to death for the sins of the whole world." Luther, *Galatians,* Galatians 2:4–5.

245. Calvin, *Institutes,* 355. Calvin later defines faith as "a firm and sure knowl edge of the divine favor toward us, founded on the truth of a free promise in Christ, and revealed to our minds, and sealed on our hearts, by the Holy Spirit" (360).

246. Luther said, "I do not think that it is possible for anyone to believe by unformed faith." Luther went on to say that the only thing an objectless or unformed faith can accomplish is to give an insight of what must be believed; this mere insight leaves us "in suspense." For Luther, objectless or unformed faith is not faith at all; in fact it is so hollow and weak that it requires faith itself. This formless "faith" becomes "the object to which faith is directed," as it has no substance to assure us with. The person trying to believe through this model needs to have faith in their faith. What a mess! No wonder these poor people are so exhausted. The answer to this is Jesus's faithfulness being presented synonymously with faith. When we speak of having faith or being saved by faith, we must always speak of having faith in Jesus's faithfulness or being saved by Jesus faithfulness. Also see Pannenberg, *Systematic Theology,* Volume 3, 141; Aquinas, *Summa Theologica,* Volume 2, 2, q. 4, a. 3.

247. Barth, *CD* I/I, 4, 12, 18; I do not draw a distinction between Jesus's faith-fulness and Jesus Himself; to me they are one in the same. But if so desired you could say: Faith is not arbitrary. Jesus Himself and His faithfulness is the object of faith. Jesus Himself and His faithfulness is the thing we have faith from and in.

248. Barth was heavily influenced by Anselm's thoughts on faith; faith "is a par-ticipation in God's mode of being . . . in the matchless glory of his very self." Barth, *Anselm,* 17. See also Hans W. Frei, "The Doctrine of Revelation in The Thought of Karl Barth, 1909 to 1922: The Nature of Barth's Break with Lib-eralism" (Ph.D. dissertation, Yale University, 1956), 193–194.

The idea that faith is living union with God, a union in which we are drawn into God's being (Barth) and become our true selves in this divine-human relationship (Kierkegaard) is not new to theology. It is present in Anselm, Luther and Calvin and becomes one of a few key controlling thoughts in Kierkegaard and then Barth's break with the theological liberalism of think-ers like Schleiermacher, providing the church a doctrinal pathway into what we call modern evangelical Protestantism. See Oh, *Complementary Dialectics of Kierkegaard and Barth,* 506.

249. God uses the example of marriage in the book of Hosea, but in light of the New Testament we know that God and human relationship is different to human marriage. God regenerates our spirit and it is this regenerated spirit that comes into relationship with God. In this God orchestrates 100% of the union. God brings faith about and God brings this "thing" of faith to us. Once we are alive in it, our choices help shape its power and health.

250. Kierkegaard once said, "In our age everyone is unwilling to stop with faith but goes further. It perhaps would be rash to ask where they are going." How salvation happens is important to understand. What happens behind the veil is worth discussion, but ultimately resolved by faith, or the confidence that comes by the union of faith. Hong and Hong, *The Essential Kierkegaard*, 94; also: Augustine, *On the Trinity*, Book 1, 1.1.

251. "The relation between man and God is not part of man; it is not a capacity, a possibility, or a structure of his being but a given, set relationship." Dietrich Bonhoeffer, *Creation and Fall* (New York, NY: Touchstone Edition, 1997), 41.

252. Luther discusses this theme, particularly how "faith is a work of God in us" and that faith is "a living, creative, active powerful thing" in his *Preface to Romans*. The interested reader will find this rich additional reading.

253. I have constructed this with quotations from Barth, *CD* IV/4 Fragment, 33. Note *CD* IV/4, *The Christian Life* (1981) is a posthumously published and somewhat revised version of the earlier *CD* IV/4 Fragment (1967; English translation, 1969). Barth died before finishing *CD* IV 4; the only part he published of *CD* IV/4 was his *Thoughts on Baptism*. In 1981 *CD* IV/4 was updated; various lecture notes and loose writings were edited together into what is now known as *CD* IV/4 *The Christian Life: Lecture Fragments*. Readers with the 1981 *Christian Life* version will need to get the original 1967 (1969 English) version of *CD* IV/4 to find this quote. See editor's preface in 1981 *CD* IV/4 for more information.

10. Thought Warfare

254. Billy Graham Evangelistic Association, Charlotte USA. Excuse Me, Please: Billy Graham Classics. September 15, 2020, https://www.youtube.com/watch?v=If0-mZQ1RW8&list=PL79D3613A193294B6&index=12.

255. Strong, *Strong's Exhaustive Concordance of the Bible*. #1410, 1411.

256. Barth, The Epistle to the Romans, 284–285.

257. Arthur C. Clarke, *Profiles of the Future* (New York: Harper and Row, 1973), 21.

258. It is interesting to note that the greatest evils in the world are not the result of military force but the result of ideologies. Whenever great evil and warfare comes to mankind, it always comes on the back of an evil ideology. Likewise, the greatest beauty in the world, acts of sacrifice and valor, are not birthed in the body, but rather in the mind.

259. Justin Martyr, *Dialogue with Trypho,* Chapter Eight; also G.L. Phillips, *Flame in the Mind* (London: Longmans, 1957).

260. This is called the *imago dei,* the image of God, which is Jesus Christ. "For God, who said, 'Let light shine out of darkness,' made his light shine in our hearts to give us the light of the knowledge of God's glory displayed in the face of Christ" (2 Cor. 4:6, NIV). Thomas Torrance has an excellent section on this in his book, *When Christ Comes and Comes Again,* 24–30.

261. The idea of God acting in us through the mind is a frequent theme in John Calvin's *Institutes of the Christian Religion.* For example, see his definition of faith; faith is "a firm and sure knowledge of the divine favor toward us, founded on the truth of a free promise in Christ, and revealed to our minds, and sealed on our hearts, by the Holy Spirit. Calvin, *Institutes,* 360; see also 9.

262. Strong, *Strong's Exhaustive Concordance of the Bible*; #5424; also, *Mosby's Dictionary of Medicine, Nursing & Health Professions,* 9th Edition (St. Louis: Elsevier Mosby, 2013), 1391.

263. Luther, in his *Preface to Romans,* wrote about how the law is spiritual, as it does not speak about our outward actions but rather the inner thoughts of our mind and the desires of our hearts. Luther mentions that Christians who outwardly act righteously but privately entertain sinful and lustful thoughts are hypocrites. For Luther, the law must be obeyed in your very heart, not just in your actions. Not one to hold back, Luther took it further and said that if you outwardly obey, but inwardly (in your mind and heart) entertain sinful desires, that you in fact hate God's commands—you hate the very commands that you are outwardly forcing yourself to obey, as your inner desire is to not keep them. It is not joyful allegiance; it is not free choice; it is forced choice. Those in this situation are in conflict with themselves. They are not experiencing peace, love, and joy (salvation); they are being torn apart. They are, as Paul said of himself, wretched people, in need of deep internal rescue (Rom. 7:24).

For Luther, this law of slavery to sinful thoughts and desires must be abolished (or superseded), not just appeased through shallow irregular righteous acts (religion). For Luther, this is where the Spirit of God comes in. The Spirit, as Christ to us, conquers our hearts, fulfilling the abovementioned need. The specific thing the Spirit gives us here is the inner will to obey; He gives us a new heart that wants to keep God's laws. In the Old Testament God gives the law; in the New Testament He gives the power to not just obey, but to want to obey. It is from this activity of God in us that our hearts are changed, our minds renewed, and then and only then, our outward actions adjusted. I will cover this later on, but this activity of God in us comes about through daily prayer and takes the form of living union with Christ or faith in Christ. For Luther, Christianity rests on Christ's activity. The person looking for victory should not try harder; he or she should acknowledge that even endless effort will never produce the desired outcome—and then come to the cross, asking the crucified King to act in them. Luther, *Preface to Romans*, 3–6.

When we come to this line of thought we have approached the heart of the mystery, the Holy of Holies of New Testament salvation. The baptism of the Holy Spirit is spiritual surgery; the old clogged will is cut out (crucified) and the will of the willing suffering Servant transplanted in. Our part is not to do something, but to allow someone else to do this to us.

264. Augustine, *City of God*, Book XIV, Chapter 28.

265. Martin Luther King, "Letter from Birmingham Jail," *Atlantic Monthly*, Volume 212, No. 2 (1963): 78–88.

266. Edman, Raymond. *They Found the Secret* (Grand Rapids: Zondervan, 1962), 135.

267. Christopher Dean, *Religion as It Should Be, or, The Remarkable Experience and Triumphant Death of Ann Thane Peck* (Boston: Massachusetts Sabbath School Society, 1851), 9.

Disclaimer: Throughout this section I have referred to ideas that would align with what is called "Keswick teaching." Hudson Taylor from the China Inland Mission is, in my opinion, an excellent example of fruitful Keswick teaching. Dr John Piper, in his biography of Hudson Taylor, suggests a few qualifying points that are important to remember: 1. These ideas are not to be seen as new information; they are classic Christian truth illuminated. 2. This is not passive or lazy holiness; it is obedience to resting: the work is Mine and Mine alone, Thy work—to rest in Me. 3. These ideas do not lead to an experience to be had; they are a truth to be accepted.

11. Uncommon Christianity

268. J. C. Pollock, *Hudson Taylor and Maria: Pioneers in China* (Grand Rapids, MI: Zondervan, 1976), 125.

269. Henry Frost, *Uncommon Christians* (Philadelphia: China Inland Mission, 1914).

270. As Brainerd observed, "I must press you to ... live above the rate of *common Christians*." Page. *David Brainerd*, 136-137.

271. The Catholic Church has the Apocrypha, which touches on this time.

272. Eusebius, *Book 1*. II, 6., in Schaff, *Nicene and Post-Nicene Fathers, Volume 1*, 83.

273. Augustine, *On the Trinity*, Book XV, 27.50.

274. George Hunsinger, *Karl Barth's Christology,* eds., John Webster (Cambridge, UK: Cambridge University Press, 2007), 138.

275. Note: by taking a human form God was able to enter into the limited existence of our created universe. Tillich, *Systematic Theology*, Volume 1, 205.

276. Barth wrote that the events of Calvary did not take "place only in the past. It took place in its own time for every time, for our time." Barth, *The Christian Life*, 164.

277. Karl Barth, *The Holy Spirit and the Christian Life* (Louisville: Westminster John Knox Press, 1993), 1.

278. Wright, *Paul and the Faithfulness of God,* 1101–1102.

279. Wright, *Paul and the Faithfulness of God,* 1103.

280. Brunner, *The Mediator*, 15.

281. Keller, "Justice in the Bible," 3:6.

12. Life above the Common

282. We see this process outworked in Acts 19 in the local silversmith's revolt against the apostle Paul. Paul's mass conversions meant that people were no longer buying idols to use in ritualistic prayer.

283. Barth, *The Christian Life*, x–xi. See John Webster, ed., *The Cambridge Companion to Karl Barth* (Cambridge: Cambridge University Press: 2000), 55, 154.

284. Barth, *The Christian Life*, 49–50.

285. Barth, *The Christian Life*, 59. Note also Martin Luther's comments on "Our Father": "In this introduction, God invites us to believe that He is our real Father and we are His real children, so that we will pray with trust and complete confidence, in the same way beloved children approach their beloved Father with their requests." Martin Luther, *The Small Catechism*, trans. Robert E. Smith (Scotts Valley, CA: CreateSpace, 1994).

286. Webster, *Cambridge Companion to Karl Barth*, 54–55.

287. Barth, *The Christian Life*, 49.

288. Barth, *The Christian Life*, xi.

289. Petition in Philippians 4:6 (NIV) means to present a felt or urgent need. Petition in the modern world means a written request for change toward a faceless and unwilling authority. We do not come to God with a petition because he needs to be forced into action. We call on his willing heart and receive his good response.

290. Barth wrote that: "to give thanks is to recognize an unobligated and unmerited favour." Barth, *The Christian Life*, 279.

291. Barth, *The Christian Life*, 67.

292. Barth, *The Christian Life*, 59.

293. Barth discusses this dynamic in great length in *The Christian Life*, particularly in the section "The Children and Their Father." I would encourage a reading of the editor's preface. This helps to orientate the reader as The Christian Life is a compilation of unfinished transcripts Barth left behind. These transcripts are the only surviving remnant of Barth's outline for his final and concluding section of Church Dogmatics.

294. Luke's version of the Lord's prayer is almost unused in church practice as it is shorter and seemingly less complete. But it is important to note that only in Luke's account do we get Jesus's direct explanation of the Lord's Prayer. In Luke 11:5–13 Jesus explains the Lord's prayer through invocation, thorough asking. Those who seek will ask and those who ask will find. The NIV adds in the words "shameless audacity" (unembarrassed boldness to carry out God's plan, Strong's #335). Those who have shameless audacity in asking for God's provision in their situation will receive from the Lord. Personally, I see Luke 11:10 as Jesus's explanation of what Calvin and Barth called invocation: "For everyone who asks receives; the one who seeks finds; and to the one who knocks, the door will be opened."

295. Strong J. *Strong's Exhaustive Concordance of the Bible*, #3686.

296. Jesus and therefore His kingdom is completely other to this world, to our politics, nationalisms, and social structures (John 18:36). Jesus entered humanity; He "became flesh" so that there would be a bridge between us and His completely other reality—the kingdom of heaven. When we equate Christianity with a political persuasion, national identity, culture, or race we fall short of representing our other God and adorn ourselves with dreaded religion. We transform our reality when we transcend it (1 John 2:17; Rev. 21:1). It is time for those searching for God in Christianity to find Jesus—the wholly other One. The phrase "wholly other" (*totaliter aliter*) comes from Barth's commentary on Romans and as stated is based on Kierkegaard. Barth, *Epistle to the*

Romans, 10, 272, 291. See Richard Burnett, *The Westminster Handbook to Karl Barth* (Louisville: Westminster John Knox Press, 2013), 220–222.

297. Barth, *CD* II/2, 5.

298. Oswald Chambers, *The Love of God* (London: Oswald Chambers Publications Association, 1938), 105.

299. Barth, *Epistle to the Romans*, 29–30.

300. Barth, *The Christian Life*, 238.

301. Dr. and Mrs. Howard Taylor, *Hudson Taylor's Spiritual Secret* (Peabody, MA: Hendrickson, 2008), 1.

302. Barth, *The Christian Life*, 157.

303. Note Martin Luther's thoughts on "May Your name be holy" in his *Small Catechism*.

304. Edman, *They Found the Secret*, 18.

305. Campbell Morgan, *The Practice of Prayer* (London: Hodder and Stoughton, 1907), 91. Origen is the one who originally suggested the term.

306. Strong, *Strong's Exhaustive Concordance of the Bible*, #2588. Literally: the heart; mind, character, inner self, will, intention, center.

307. Torrance, *Incarnation*, 1 (my paraphrase).

308. Søren Kierkegaard, *Edifying Discourses* (London: Fontana Books, 1958), 34.

309. Aquinas, *Summa Theologica*, Volume 1,. I, q. 2, a. 3. Fifth way.

310. Barth, *The Holy Spirit and the Christian Life*, 1.

311. Aquinas. *Summa Theologica*, I, q. 2, a. 3. Fifth way.

312. Martin Luther wrote in his commentary on Hebrews 11:1, "If these "things hoped for" are conceived as being without substance, then faith provides them with substance. Or better still, it does not provide them with substance but is their very essence." Martin Luther, *Lectures on the Epistle to the Hebrews, 1517–18,* Library of Christian Classics, ed. James Atkinson (Louisville: Westminster John Knox Press, 2006), 203.

313. Kierkegaard, *Edifying Discourses*, 34.

13. Spiritually Competent

314. "Footy" is Australian slang, short for Australian Rugby League.

315. Thomas Torrance, *Karl Barth: Introduction to Early Theology* (London: T & T Clark International, 2004), 85–86.

316. Oh, *Complementary Dialectics of Kierkegaard and Barth*, 504.

317. Barth, *The Holy Spirit and the Christian Life*, 1; *Luther, Lectures on Romans*. Also, Martin Luther, *The Career of the Reformer: Two Kinds of Righteousness*, Luther Works, Volume 31, 297,299.

318. Cyril, *Catechetical Lecture X. 3.*, in Schaff, *Nicene and Post-Nicene Fathers, Volume 7*, 57. (John 10:9, 2 Chron. 16:9).

319. Thomas Torrance tells us that Kierkegaard and Barth emphasizing the infinite difference between God and man was not done to make God seem lofty and distant, but to emphasize the "nearness, the impact of God in all his Majesty and Godliness upon man." The significance of a God who is infinitely different in his qualities from mankind coming near had been lost in the Church. Kierkegaard and Barth employed this tool to jump start the memory of the religiously minded clergy. Thomas Torrance, *Karl Barth, An Introduction to His Early Theology 1910–1931* (Edinburgh: T&T Clark, 2000), 44. This realization is the foundation of understanding grace. When you grasp how vast the distance is between God and man, you come to realise what has taken place in Jesus's incarnation. The truth takes hold that there is "nothing whatever' that humankind can do, in and of themselves, to relate directly to God. From this we accept Kierkegaard's statement that God "gives everything, He makes us able to have faith. This is grace, this is the major premise of Christianity." Soren Kierkegaard, *Kierkegaard's Journals and Notebooks, Volume 5* (Princeton, NJ: Princeton University Press, 2012), 244; Andrew B. Torrance, *Kierkegaard's Paradoxical Christology* (St. Andrews, UK: University of St Andrews Press, 2019), 1. For more see, David Gouwens, Hunsinger George, Johnson Keith L, ed, *The Wiley Blackwell Companion To Karl Barth, Volume 2* (Hoboken, NJ: John Wiley & Sons, 2020), 553.

320. Oh, *Complementary Dialectics of Kierkegaard and Barth*, 504.

321. The words of Kierkegaard are worth repeating here: "In our age everyone is unwilling to stop with faith but goes further. It perhaps would be rash to ask where they are going"? Hong and Hong, *The Essential Kierkegaard,* 94. And Barth, "In the very places where the theology of the Reformation had said 'the Gospel' or 'the Word of God' or 'Christ' Schleiermacher, three hundred years after the Reformation, now says, religion or piety." Karl Barth, *From Rousseau to Ritschl,* (London: SCM Press, 1959), 339. It is also worth noting that in the many instances where Billy Graham came up against academic opposition from the theological community, the theologians later apologized or were kindly confounded by simple faith in Scripture and fruit that lasted.

322. Kierkegaard's thoughts on being contemporary with Christ is the master answer here from which all else flows. It is rich additional reading. Kierkegaard, *Training in Christianity*, 4, 67–68.

323. Billy Graham Evangelistic Association, "Billy Graham's 99th Birthday: Notable Reflections," YouTube video, November 7, 2017, 5:41, https://www.youtube.com/watch?v=pz4pFVVMzLw.

324. Martin Luther, *Commentary on Galatians*, xxi–xxii. I have put "circa" on the date of 1535, as there were various Latin translations, 1519 (based on lectures in 1516–1517), 1535 (based on lectures in 1531) and the first English translation in 1575.

325. Prayer is "invoking the name of the Most High." Karl Barth, *The Göttingen Dogmatics: Instruction in the Christian Religion,* Volume 1 (Grand Rapids: Eerdmans, 1991), 3. See also Calvin, *Institutes*, 578. Prayer is a dual activity which draws on God's nature of loving reconciliation through requests and simultaneously receives it by thanksgiving. God's name and nature is, as Luther and Barth said, alien to us. We must be commanded to draw upon it, as left unchecked we will never desire something not native to us. Once drawn upon in prayer, God's loving and righteous nature becomes normal to us. Prayer achieves change through making that which was once alien normal and that which was once normal alien. Barth, *CD* IV/2, 757.

326. Jeremiah 44:26 says, "Therefore, hear the word of the LORD, all you Judeans who live in the land of Egypt: 'I have sworn by My great name, says Yahweh, that My name will never again be invoked by anyone of Judah in all the land of Egypt, saying, "As the Lord GOD lives."'"This verse comes at the very end of the Israelite kingdoms; the second exile has taken place and the remaining people are lost through multiple layers of disobedience, the final one being noted in 42:6:"Whether it is pleasant or unpleasant, we will obey the voice of the LORD our God to whom we are sending you so that it may go well with us.We will certainly obey the voice of the LORD our God!"Then, 42:19:"The LORD has spoken concerning you, remnant of Judah: 'Don't go to Egypt.' Know for certain that I have warned you today!"; followed by 43:7:"and they went to the land of Egypt because they did not obey the voice of the Lord."

This is the last we hear of Jeremiah and the remaining Judean people. This is the end of the line, the last stop; the train terminates and the people disembark from a critical thing, invocation (44:26), one of the key tools that brought them into their now-forsaken promised land (Deut. 30:19 NET). It is of interest that this really is the last we hear of these people; poor besieged Jeremiah endures with them till the end (43:4–6), and it is the end in every possible way. The exiled people return from Babylonian captivity, but not these—they wander off into oblivion, becoming the subject of much rumor but not blessing. These people do the unthinkable; they return to the place their ancestors fought so hard to leave. They returned to the place their forefathers begged deliverance from (Deut. 17:16). It cannot be seen as anything other than an intentional declaration that they deem God unfaithful, unaware till the end of the origin of their problem: their own unfaithfulness, obfuscation, and self-validation overruling obedience. It is ironic: those forced into exile return, but those offered permanent protection in the land (42:7–12) are exiled permanently by their disobedience. They had already lost their temple, city, and king, but God kept the pipeline of invocation open. It is this pipeline that is the very last thing to be removed, and in this we see its preeminence and importance.

In stunning grace, God doesn't just reopen the pipeline—He brings the reservoir to them, the Name that is above every name (John 7:37–38). Amazing.

327. Dan Graves, ed., *The Martyrdom of Polycarp,* trans. J. B. Lightfoot, abridged and modernized by Stephen Tomkins (Worcester, PA: Christian History Institute, 2020), 11.1.

328. Luther, *Commentary on Galatians*, xii.

329. Luther, *Commentary on Galatians*, Preface (emphasis added); Tim Keller abridgment and paraphrase, Redeemer Presbyterian Church, 2003. Luther continues on, outlining how this passive righteousness births active godly living. I encourage you to read Martin Luther's commentary on Galatians, particularly the preface and the last few verses on chapter two.

330. Charles Wesley, "And Can It Be That I Should Gain," 1738. It is said that Charles Wesley wrote this hymn on the night the Holy Spirit revealed salvation by grace through faith to him. If this is true, then this hymn is not speaking of conversation from death to life, but rather from works to grace, from law to faith, from religion to relationship, from confusion to Christ. See Kenneth Cain Kinghorn, *Wesley: A Heart Transformed Can Change the World Study Guide* (Nashville: Abingdon Press, 2011), 33–34.

14. There Is No Condemnation in Christ Jesus . . . because of Christ Jesus

331. Torrance, *When Christ Comes and Comes Again*, 179.

332. Barth, *CD* II/2, 780.

333. Torrance, *When Christ Comes and Comes Again*, 178–179. Aaron's sons Nadab and Abihu were both consumed by fire from the mercy seat (Lev. 10:1–2)

and Uzzah was struck down by God for touching the ark (2 Sam. 6:6-7). In Hebrews 9:1–14 the fury of the mercy seat is answered by Jesus Christ's blood and redemption.

334. This truth cannot be undervalued. This truth alone makes Christianity unique from all other world religions. Only in Jesus Christ condemning Himself at the cross does God become the means of salvation; in all other world religions human effort is the means of appeasing God. In Christianity the means of appeasing God is God Himself. This to me is the single greatest proof of the validity of the Christian faith. No human would ever construct this, as it does not provide control to human religious leaders—control that they can leverage for power and profit. It is from eternity (Ps. 93:2). Silva, *New International Dictionary of New Testament Theology and Exegesis,* Vol. 1, 245.

335. This passage does not mean that if you sin after you have confessed Jesus as Lord, you are condemned. The phrase "no sacrifice for sins left" means that outside of Calvary there is nothing that can save us. Frequently in the New Testament the Apostles were targeting Jewish converts who were wanting to "go back," by mixing the Old Testament law with the Gospel. This mixing is the focus of these words, as in, "If you can't accept Jesus's sacrifice exclusively, then there is no other sacrifice to turn to." We see this by the writer sandwiching verses 26–27 in the context of faith in Jesus as the exclusive way of salvation, verses 20, 22 and then 38–39. The phrase "there no longer remains a sacrifice for sins, but a terrifying expectation of judgment and the fury of a fire about to consume the adversaries," is in reference to Leviticus 10:1–2 where Aaron's sons offered "unauthorized fire" before God and are burned up and consumed. If we come before God in heaven with any offering other than faith in Jesus Christ, we will be consumed—hell. Jesus's sacrifice is the only authorized offering (Heb. 9:11–12). Also, verse 29 is not focused toward backsliding believers. It is, again, in keeping with the writer's theme of warning those who refuse to be covered by Christ (Mark 14:61–63).

336. A. W. *Tozer, The Knowledge of the Holy* (Carlisle, UK: OM Publishing, 1994), 141–142.

337. Barth, *CD* II/2, 167–168.

338. F. B. Meyer said, "Dare to trust Him; dare to follow Him! And discover that the very forces that barred your progress and threatened your life at His bidding become the materials of which an avenue is made to liberty." Perhaps the words of Lilias Trotter capture this best: "Three of us stood there, looking at our battle-field, none of us fit to pass a doctor for any society, not knowing a soul in the place, or a sentence of Arabic or a clue for beginning work

on untouched ground; we only knew we had to come. Truly if God needed weakness, He had it!" See also Zechariah 8:11–13. Lisa Sinclair, "The Legacy of Isabella Lilias Trotter," *International Bulletin of Missionary Research,* January 2002, http://www.internationalbulletin.org/issues/2002-01/2002-01-032-sinclair.pdf. F. B. Meyer, *The Life of Moses: Servant of God* (Lynnwood, WA: Emerald Books, 1996), 86. Cited in C. Cowman, *Streams in the Desert* (London: Oliphants, 1966), 189.

339. About this Martin Luther wrote that God would say "I am that big sinner. His sin and his death are mine, because he is joined to me, and I to him." Luther, *Commentary on Galatians,* 43.

340. John Calvin wrote, "it is by prayer that we call him to reveal himself as wholly present to us." The exchange within Jesus's blood results in us simply having to call to God through prayer, with confession. It is not cheap grace, it is free grace." Calvin, *Institutes,* 851.

341. The Holy Spirit is the life or energy that makes change possible. As we are seeking to change into the image of something eternal, it stands to reason that only something eternal can change us. No temporal substance can achieve eternal transformation.

15. An Open Ending

342. Luther, *Commentary on Galatians,* 45.

343. Stephen Tomkins, *John Wesley: A Biography* (Oxford: Lion Publishing, 2003), 58.

344. Tomkins, *Wesley: A Biography,* 57.

345. Tomkins, *Wesley: A Biography,* 58.

346. John Wesley, *The Journal of the Rev. John Wesley, A. M.,* ed. Nehemiah Curnock (London: Robert Culley, 1909), 472

347. Luther, *Preface to the Epistle to the Romans.*

348. Luther, *Preface to the Epistle to the Romans.*

349. Luther, *Preface to the Epistle to the Romans.*

350. Luther's commentary on Galatians was read to William Holland, by Charles Wesley, and used by God to lead Holland to an understanding of grace. It was Holland who a few days later read from Luther's *Preface to Romans* in a sermon, which was used by God to bring John Wesley to grace. These words from Luther's commentary on Galatians are most relevant here:

O law! You would climb up into the kingdom of my conscience, and there reign and condemn me for sin, and would take from me the joy of my heart which I have by faith in Christ, and drive me to desperation, that I might be without hope. You have overstepped your bounds. Know your place! You are a guide for my behavior, but you are not Savior and Lord of my heart. For I am baptized, and through the Gospel am called to receive righteousness and eternal life...So *trouble me not!* For I will not allow you, so intolerable a tyrant and tormentor, to reign in my heart and conscience—for they are the seat and temple of Christ the Son of God, who is the king of righteousness and peace, and my most sweet Savior and mediator. He shall keep my conscience joyful and quiet in the sound and pure doctrine of the Gospel, through the knowledge of this passive and heavenly righteousness.

Luther, *Commentary on Galatians*, Preface; Tim Keller abridgment and paraphrase.

351. Barth, *Epistle to the Romans*, 271–272.

352. Barth, *Epistle to the Romans*, 271–272.

353. Barth, *Epistle to the Romans*, 271–272.

354. For the inner workings of this see Torrance, *The Ground and Grammar of Theology*, 165.

355. Eusebius called Jesus the "God Word," the "substance which lived and subsisted before the world." In prayer we are communing with the "essence of the pre-world," the substance (ouisa) that had a prior existence, the living and subsisting genesis of all – the Son is no mere creature, "but Power." Eusebius, *Book 1*. II, 14;26., in Schaff, *Nicene and Post-Nicene Fathers, Volume 1*, 83. Theodoret, *Book 1*. VII., in Phillip Schaff, ed., *Nicene and Post-Nicene Fathers, Volume 3* (Peabody, MA: Hendrickson Publishers, 2012), 45.

356. A story exemplifying this can be found in Mildred Cable and Francesca French, *Something Happened* (London: Hodder and Stoughton, 1938); also, Mary Warburton Booth, *These Things I Have Seen* (London: Pickering and Inglis, 1946), 25–30.

357. In the Bible, the number seven signifies completeness. God created the world in seven days, Joshua marched around Jericho for seven days, Naaman bathed seven times and the seventh day was set apart as holy, etc.

358. In Leviticus 10:1–2 Aaron's sons offer what the Bible records as "unauthorised fire," meaning to be a stranger, or alien before God, resulting in some translations of "strange" or "alien" fire. The idea behind this sacrifice is that if done correctly it would indicate that the priest belongs before God. The smoke from the fire of incense acted as a shield between God's direct presence and themselves, making communion safe (Lev. 16:13). This alien fire that the sons of Aaron brought positioned them as strangers before the altar of

God. Resulting in them having no shield between the presence of God and themselves. Jesus's righteousness is alien to us, but local to the Father, when we come before God in prayer and worship clothed in Jesus's righteousness God identifies us as "those who are near Me" and shows Himself (Lev. 10:3; John 10:7-9). When we come with the alien, unauthorised fire of religion, disobedience, or even a secularised Gospel, God does not have anything to recognise in our offering. Religion, in whatever form, is an unauthorised offering, alien to God.

359. From the cross comes two powerful principles for cultural change. First is sacrifice—true, lifelong, genuine sacrifice. When this is modeled it brings credibility and in effect heaps "burning coals" (Rom. 12:20) on the opposing ideology (2 Cor. 4:4). Second, is accepting responsibility for our actions (Matt. 7:5) over bypassing personal responsibility through validation (Luke 22:42). The first point of call for the Christian seeking change in society is to look inside and deeply accept responsibility for personal wrongdoing, not obfuscating responsibility. Second, is to ask what can be sacrificed, even to the point of it benefiting an enemy (Rom. 12:20). Only then comes any external articulation. Loud pronouncements feel good in the moment (John 18:10), but they change nothing—"No more of this!" (Luke 22:51). It is interesting to note that Dr. D. Martin Lloyd-Jones outlined four points for reconciliation; the first was, "learn not to speak." Cited in Charles Stanley, "In Touch Devotional," Vol 43, No 8 (Atlanta: In Touch Ministries, 2020), 38.

360. Edman, *They Found the Secret*, 6.

361. Barth, *CD* IV/2, 758.

362. Manning, *Ragamuffin Gospel*, 176.

363. Edman, *They Found the Secret*, 37-38.

364. It is interesting to note that coals in the Old Testament symbolize spiritual purification (Lev. 16:21; Isa. 6:6).

365. The Davidic covenant is foundational to the new covenant. This is seen through the writer to the Hebrews' incorporation of Psalm 40:6–8 in Hebrews 10:5–7. This Davidic lament—that David desires to do God's will but cannot as he is "afflicted and needy" (v. 17)—is foundational to the new covenant in Hebrews 10. The writer to the Hebrews wants us to see Hebrews 10:5–7 effectively as "Psalm 40:18," meaning: David is "afflicted" by his inability to do God's will through the means of his willpower. Christ comes as "deliverer" to do God's will in the flesh and offers this powerful divine will to humanity in

order to end the powerlessness that David laments. See also Augustine's comments in *On the Spirit and the Letter*, Chapter 60: "The very will by which we believe is reckoned as a gift of God." Schaff, *Nicene and Post-Nicene Fathers, On The Spirit and The Letter.*

366. The person in which Jesus Christ truly exists "does not then in any sense believe in himself...to believe means to believe in Jesus Christ" exclusively and absolutely. Barth, *CD* II.1, 159. Also, Paul Molnar, *Trinitarian Theology after Barth* (Eugene, OR: Wipf and Stock, 2011), 20.

367. In the chapter "Spiritually Competent," I noted how invocation was the final thing God turned off in Jeremiah 44:26 and that God in His grace reinstitutes invocation in the New Testament. It is essential to note that Hebrews 8:10 and 10:16 quotes from Jeremiah 31:33. God prophesies that invocation will return in 31:33 through a new covenant, before it is ended in 44:26. The writer of Hebrews including this quote as the primary statement of the new covenant is intentional. The structure here is important: 31:33, invocation and a new covenant prophesied; 44:26, invocation turned off; 31:33, restated in Hebrews 8:10 and 10:16 and explained as fulfilled through the new covenant of Jesus Christ. I previously covered that as a result of the blood of Christ being shed God can act in us. Through this, we see that invocation is established in Christ's blood (Luke 22:20; Heb. 9:12, 14; 10:19, 29), as opposed to the old way of the mercy seat. It is again interesting to note that many feel the ark of the covenant, and with it the mercy seat, was taken to Egypt by Jeremiah. After the return of the exiles there is no record of the temple having a functioning mercy seat, and therefore direct invocation. It is only when the God who appears on the mercy seat comes to calvary that this is possible again.

368. Note Luther's comments on the Lord's Prayer in his Large Catechism, specifically, in the section "Thy will be done on earth as it is in heaven." Also, Hebrews 4:10, "For the person who has entered His rest has rested from his own works" — for they have learned to invoke God's works into their restlessness.

369. Luke 22:42. Miller, *The Taste of New Wine*, 40–41.

370. Edman, *They Found the Secret*, 18.

371. Bruce McNair, "Martin Luther and Lucas Cranach Teaching the Lord's Prayer," *Religions,* MDPI, Basel (2017): 5.

372. This is a summary statement that we have walked toward slowly through the Word of God—along with Barth's writings in *Church Dogmatics* on the nature

and being of God; through Luther's writings on faith and righteousness in Romans, Galatians, and Hebrews; through Augustine's writings in *On the Spirit and the Letter, On the Trinity,* and *The City of God*; and many others like Kierkegaard, Calvin, and Torrance.

373. Do not wander around the fire waiting for it to all make sense. As Dr. Stanley says so well, "Obey God and leave all the consequences to Him." Charles Stanley, "30 Life Principles," Penrith, NSW: In Touch Ministries, Inc, 2015, http://www.intouchaustralia.org/read/30-life-principles.

374. My heart in writing this book is to stimulate discussion. To me the function of theology is to form and support the presentation of the Gospel to each and every generation. Too often theology results in a heavy spirit and introspective arguments that fail to further hope to the hopeless. I share the heart of Augustine, who at the conclusion of his writings on the Trinity said: "*Domine deus une, deus trinitas, quaecumque dixi in his libris de tuo agnoscant et tui; si qua de meo, et tu ignosce et tui. Amen.*" Translated: "O Lord the one God, God the Trinity, whatever I have said in this book that is of Yours, may they acknowledge who are Yours; if anything of my own, may it be pardoned both by You and by those who are Yours. Amen."

I like this quote; I feel it embodies a proper humble stance. We all stand in awe and wonder gazing into the mystery that is Christ revealed. I desire to contribute to the ongoing conversation within the kingdom. If I have written truth, I pray it is upheld and embraced. If any errors sit within these pages, I pray that God will raise up others who can add clarity and if need be correction. It is not a matter of being right, but rather working together to lean further into "Christ in us, the hope of glory."

Afterword

375. Martin, *Commentary on Galatians*, 2:16.

376. Silva, *New International Dictionary of New Testament Theology and Exegesis,* Vol. 1, 245.

377. Luther, *Lectures on Romans*, Rom. 1:1. Also, Luther, *The Career of the Reformer: Two Kinds of Righteousness,* Luther Works, Volume 31, 297, 299.

378. Luther, *Lectures on Romans,* Rom. 1:17.

379. Luther, *Lectures on Romans,* Rom. 1:17.

380. Luther, *Preface to Romans.* Also, "Christ daily drives out the old Adam more and more in accordance with the extent to which faith and knowledge of Christ grow. For alien righteousness is not instilled all at once, but it begins,

makes progress, and is finally perfected at the end though death." Luther, *Career of the Reformer*, 299.

381. "The righteousness of God is entirely from faith, yet growth does not make it more real but only gives it greater clarity." Luther, *Lectures on Romans*, Rom. 1:17.

382. Invocation is a master concept for Calvin used throughout his section on prayer, a section McNeill has under the heading: the way we receive the grace of Christ. This leads to the unmistakable truth that we find God in Christianity through invocation. We receive the Everlasting Father into our humble lives by calling upon Him "to reveal himself as wholly present to us." Calvin, *Institutes*, Book 3, specifically chapters 1–2, 20. McNeill gives summary in his index; see entry for Invocation/calling upon God. See also Barth, *The Christian Life*, 43.

383. Calvin, *Institutes*, 564. Here Calvin joins together the Name and identity of God, faith, invocation-prayer-calling upon God, and entering into the provision of heaven on earth. It is well worth absorbing.

384. Barth, *CD* III/III, 264.

385. Barth, *CD* III/III, 265. Also, "prayer of the Christian to God is the basic act of the obedience engendered in faith," 283.

386. It is worth noting that Barth builds this culminating truth off Calvin's *Institutes* (for example, Barth follows Calvin in expounding the Lord's prayer) and the Heidelberg Catechism, (Q116). This, along with Calvin's own writing, provides solid Reformed ground. Barth, *The Christian Life*, 43; Barth, *Learning Jesus through the Heidelberg Catechism* (Eugene, OR: Wipf and Stock, 1982), 115. See also Psalm 50:15; 2 Corinthians 5:19.

387. Barth, *The Christian Life*, 43.

388. Barth, *The Christian Life*, 49–50.

389. Taylor, *The Growth of a Work of God*, 172.

390. Reading and then praying scriptures in the context of asking God to act in us is a good starting point, some examples: Ps. 50:15; 51:10–12; 66:18; Matt. 6:9–13; Luke 11:1–13; Rom. 7:14–25, 8:1–8; 2 Cor. 3:1–11; Phil. 2:13; Heb. 8:6–13; 9:8, 15; 10:11–18. The interested reader can also read John Calvin's thoughts on invocational prayer: Calvin, *Institutes*, Book 3, 20, 35–52; and Barth, *The Christian Life*, 41–46. Both Calvin and Barth expound the Lord's Prayer in their section on invocation, I have followed this tradition. You could argue that prayer should begin with praise, then contain

petitions and then end with praise, as this is the format of the Lord's Prayer (HCSB, NASB, NKJV).

391. Both Calvin and Barth wrote that the truth of the Christian claim is known through prayer. You can find their thoughts in their sections on prayer as referenced throughout this book.

392. Oswald Chambers, *My Utmost for His Highest* (Uhrichsville, OH: Barbour, 1963), February 4. Calvin wrote, "it is his secret irrigation that makes us bud forth and produce the fruits of righteousness . . . he so breathes divine life into us, that we are no longer acted upon by ourselves, but ruled by his motion and agency." Calvin, *Institutes,* 350.

393. Karl Barth, "Barmen Declaration," German Confessing Church, Barmen, 1934.

394. Tozer, *The Pursuit of God*, 17.

Appendix 2: The Creative Potential of Chaos

395. Victor Hamilton's notes are a good resource for further study here. Victor Hamilton, *The New International Commentary on the Old Testament: The Book of Genesis, Chapters 1–17* (Grand Rapids, MI: Eerdmans, 1990), 114–115.

396. Interestingly, planetary scientists theorize that chaos is the phase that gives rise to ordered life.

Appendix 3: Eschatology of Worship

397. J. R. R. Tolkien, *The Fellowship of the Ring*, The Lord of the Rings, Book 1 (London: Harper Collins Publishers, 2005), 69.

398. Self-promotion being the opposite of worship. Augustine, *City of God*, Book XXII, Chapter 1.

399. Augustine, *City of God*, Book XXII, Chapter 1.

400. The Greek word translated as "godliness" in 2 Peter 3:11 is *eusebia*, Myk Habets makes the following observation from the ministry of Thomas Torrance: Torrance was fond to point out from his favorite theologian, Athanasius of Alexandria, that true knowledge of God—*theologia*—actually equals or is equivalent to godliness and worship—*eusebia*. From this, we come to the Athanasian understanding that the deepest theological truths are not manifested through academic undertakings, but in worship. Myk Habets, T&T Clark Handbook of Thomas F. Torrance (London: T & T Clark, 2020), 260. Also see Calvin, *Institutes,* 61.

401. Jan Hus instigated worship through congregational singing, but he modeled it as a "spiritual act of worship" by being a living sacrifice in his martyrdom. I imagine most readers understand that music becomes worship through sacrifice.

402. Edman, *They Found the Secret*, 5, 37-38.

Printed in the United States
by Baker & Taylor Publisher Services